Aaron Burr

Aaron Burr

Conspiracy to Treason

BUCKNER F. MELTON, JR.

John Wiley & Sons, Inc.

This book is printed on acid-free paper. ∞

Copyright © 2002 by Buckner F. Melton, Jr. All rights reserved

Published by John Wiley & Sons, Inc., New York
Published simultaneously in Canada

This publication is designed to provide accurate and authoritative information in regard to the subject matter covered. It is sold with the understanding that the pub-lisher is not engaged in rendering professional services. If professional advice or other expert assistance is required, the services of a competent professional person should be sought.

Library of Congress Cataloging-in-Publication Data:

Melton, Buckner F.
    Aaron Burr : conspiracy to treason / Buckner F. Melton, Jr.
      p. cm.
    Includes bibliographical references (p.) and index.
    ISBN 0-471-39209-X (cloth : alk. paper)
      1. Burr Conspiracy, 1805–1807. 2. Burr, Aaron, 1756–1836. 3. Burr, Aaron, 1756–1836—Trials, litigation, etc. I. Title.

E334 .M45 2001
973.4′8′092—dc21

Printed in the United States of America   2001024234

10 9 8 7 6 5 4 3 2 1

Contents

Maps and Illustrations

Treason against the United States, shall consist only in levying War against them, or in adhering to their Enemies, giving them Aid and Comfort. No Person shall be convicted of Treason unless on the testimony of two Witnesses to the same overt Act, or on Confession in open Court.
—United States Constitution, Article III, Section 3

Europe stretches to the Alleghenies; America lies beyond.
—Ralph Waldo Emerson

I am determined to prove a Villain . . .
—William Shakespeare, *King Richard the Third,*
Act I, Scene 1

Prologue

This is the story of the most famous criminal trial in American history, and of the strange conspiracy that spawned it.

The defendant was a former vice president, a man who had once come within a hairsbreadth of becoming the nation's chief executive. His accuser was the general in command of the United States Army. Among his defense counsel and the prosecutors were four past, present, and future federal attorneys general. Some congressmen served on his jury; others stood indicted with him. His schemes implicated not only leading foreign diplomats but American majors and colonels, captains and commodores, men pledged to defend their country from the likes of him. His judge was the Supreme Court's chief justice, the greatest that bench has ever held. His ultimate opponent, the man who caused the trial to be and directed it from afar with near obsession, was the nation's president. The formal charge against him was the most heinous in Anglo-American law, the only crime grave enough for the Constitution itself to define. The act of which he stood accused was nothing less than the destruction of the United States. The penalty he faced, if convicted, was death.

To this day, despite the mass of judicial opinions, the transcripts, the secret correspondence, the encoded messages, the endless newspaper accounts that held the country spellbound for nearly a year—despite all of these things, no one has been able to discover what this man really plotted. Too many people told too many different stories, and too many people had things to hide. The record is vast; but it is full of gaps, and rumors, and lies. All that we know for certain is that whatever Aaron Burr planned, it had something to do with the land beyond the Appalachian-Allegheny Range, the great Mississippi and Ohio River Valleys, which held in themselves the key to what America would or would not one day become. We can start with this fact, and from that point on we must imagine, and try to reconstruct, what really happened.

But before we can hope to sort out the authors and players who created and starred in the Burr Conspiracy, we first have to understand the stage on which they acted out their drama: the place that people in those days called, quite simply, the Western Country.

Part One

The Cauldron

*T*he land had been there forever. Or so it must have seemed, anyway, not only to the tribes that had lived there for thousands of years, but to the Europeans who arrived much, much later.

It stretched from the Great Lakes in the North to the Gulf of Mexico in the South, from the Appalachians to the Rockies, a million square miles and more. The rainfall was good, and after the rains watered the soil, they trickled away into the many rivers, deep, wide, and long. Through the eastern part of the valley flowed the Cumberland, the Tennessee, and above all the Ohio, whose name the French would swear translated as *La Belle Rivière*, the Beautiful River. "Its peculiarity is that it is all beautiful," a New Englander later said. "There are no points bare of beauty."[1] To the west were the Red and the Arkansas and, of course, the Missouri, the wide, flat, and muddy stream that Lewis and Clark would one day ride to fame.

Through the heart of it all flowed the river that gave the valley its name: the Mississippi. It was the core of the vast riparian network that stretched to the region's every corner. All of the other rivers flowed into it, directly or indirectly. Together these watery highways cut through dense woodlands, impassable swamps, and grassy prairies that could take days to cross on foot. The rivers were key to movement here. With the Europeans' coming, control of the rivers meant control of not only travel but commerce, defense, and projection of military force. Control of the rivers was everything.

The lands that the rivers watered were fat and productive. In some places they were giant compost heaps, fertilized by generations of lush vegetation. Nearly anything would grow there. In the South were miles of pine forests, interspersed with live oak and hickory, magnolia and cypress. Farther north the hardwoods were magnificent; centuries-old stands of hickory and sycamore grew rampant. In the Ohio country stood the great black walnuts that would go to make stocks of Kentucky long rifles. Here and there the dogwoods bloomed, and along the riverbanks the wildflowers exploded in spring and summer like silent fireworks. Fruits and nuts were so plentiful that in some places going hungry was impossible. Early travelers told of huge strawberries, masses of grapes, and storms of pecans and chestnuts that came rattling down in autumn winds.[2]

With all of this food just lying around waiting for someone to pick it up, farming seemed needless. "If an Indian were driven out into the extensive woods, with only a knife or tomahawk, or a small hatchet," wrote one latter-day traveler, "he would fatten, even where a wolf would starve."[3] Still, some of the tribes took up farming. Acres of corn, squash, pumpkins, and beans, and orchards of trees by the hundred crowded the landscape in spots. But other parts of the valley knew no cultivation. Among these places were the hunting grounds of a place called Kan-tu-kee.

Buffalo and deer here abounded. So, too, did bear, which many— European and Indian alike—considered a great delicacy, especially since bears often dined on the luscious grapes that made their meat rich and flavorful. And Kentucky held no monopoly of such riches. All over the valley, flocks of birds could be so dense as to darken the sky. In the rivers fish were huge and muscular enough to upset canoes. Meat on the wing, meat on the hoof or paw, was everywhere. All a hunter had to do was reach out and take it, without so much as a thought. In time the carnage would be horrible.

Despite the forests' vastness in the eastern side of the valley, hunters and travelers could walk them easily. The trees were very old by the time the Europeans arrived. They were great in girth, and so tall that no low limbs got in the way. The upper branches blotted out the sunlight; the weaker saplings died in the gloom of the forest floor, and humans and other animals could pass along with ease. But this wasn't always true. In some spots bushes and briars thrived, so that even clothes of leather weren't protection enough. Along the rivers grew dense bands of thick cane, or canebrakes, filling the fine bottom lands. They were good eating for cattle, and good hiding places for fugitives, but a wound from a jagged cane end could be painful and deadly, especially in a time before antisepsis.

But for all the brambles and cane, the real barrier was the mountain range, the Appalachians, named for a now-extinct Indian tribe. Only a few hundred miles at most separated the eastern coast from the first high hills. The English, when they came and settled there, would find themselves neatly hemmed in, the valley beyond inaccessible. The Spanish and French, who had arrived earlier on, exploring the continent's northern and southern reaches, approached that valley not from the east but from the flanks, up the St. Lawrence and down through the Great Lakes, and along the Mississippi. But in the South the Spanish were busily plundering and developing their holdings in Central and South America. Somehow they missed or ignored the Mississippi's mouth, leaving the river's whole length to France.[4]

Moving downward from the North, the French first found cold and barren climes, "the land God gave to Cain," as Jacques Cartier described it.[5] Farming was no option there. Instead they moved up and down the streams, seeking the thickly furred animals that abounded. Things with roots might stay in place, but beavers and foxes moved; so, too, did the hunters and trappers move, never putting down roots of their own. They reached the valley's interior quickly, but they settled lightly, never taking a strong hold on the land, so the French population there stayed small.[6]

This was odd, and in more ways than one. First, so much of the valley was so obviously rich, in soil and game, that budding empires should have been paying attention. For another thing, the region's strategic importance should have been equally plain. Some people saw it early; in the 1680s Robert Cavelier, sieur de La Salle, envisioned a string of French forts along the Mississippi stretching from Lake Ontario to the Gulf of Mexico, designed to keep both the Spanish and the English out, but nothing much came of it. In 1719 John Baptiste Lemoyne, sieur de Bienville, founded New Orleans a hundred miles from the river's mouth. Since nearly all of the western waters ultimately flowed past that point, any city there would become the region's gatekeeper, the jumping-off point between the interior and the Caribbean, the East Coast, Europe, and the rest of the world. But for the most part, explorers and early settlers, and their European masters, were so busy taking Indian gold and silver to the south, or looking for the Northwest Passage to Asia near the continent's top, that they failed to see a geopolitical fact of crucial importance.

North America's East Coast lies relatively close to Europe. Its West Coast makes up part of the Pacific Rim, opposite huge Asian markets and sources of raw materials. The first of these two vital truths brought forth the United States as an offshoot of Europe; the second truth has been of ever greater importance to it for more than a century, helping to make it an empire. But before the nation could reach out into the Pacific, before it could even gain a foothold there, it first had to take solid hold of its own landmass. The crucial fact that its leaders eventually grasped, the fact that most of Europe saw too late, was that control of the Mississippi Valley, with its resources and its network of rivers, meant control of the continent.

Europe, at first, neither knew nor cared. La Salle never got to build his forts along the Mississippi. The Spanish mostly ignored the river. Even when French Canada began to thrive, Louisiana (La Salle named the whole of the Mississippi Valley, east and west both, for Louis XIV) remained wild and desolate. Perhaps, despite the fat lands and plentiful rains, something unnerved those who came there. The forest was vast, dark, and daunting. "In the eternal woods," a traveler wrote, "it is impossible to keep off a particularly unpleasant, anxious feeling, which is excited irresistibly by the continuing shadow and the confined outlook."[7] These woods were home to armies of ticks and fleas. The marshy lands were home to clouds of mosquitoes, whose kisses brought malaria.[8] Alligators stalked the valley's southern reaches; voyagers spoke of them in fear. "Their noise is louder than the bellowing of the most furious Bull, or a Lyon," wrote one. "The deep swamps & banks of the rivers & Forest reechoing the dreadfull roar, the noise is communicated from one to another, fills the whole country with a noise like dreadfull thunders."[9] And when the alligators weren't singing, other things took up the cry. One traveler, safely out of that country, told of "the music of great gangs of wolves around our camp every night," and the hooting of countless owls echoed in the darkness.[10] On high bluffs over the Mississippi were Indian paintings of terrible monsters; now and then the river banks, eroded away by the currents, would come crashing down, trees and all. For all of its richness and strategic importance, the valley inspired disquiet and fear. And justly so. People had a habit of dying there. Pánfilo de Narváez's 1528 expedition to the Gulf Coast started with four hundred men; only five survived. Hernando de Soto found a watery grave in the lower Mississippi, and La Salle's own men, rather than following him farther inland, finally murdered their leader. The valley was a dangerous place.

Only in the mid-eighteenth century did France come to see the value of her North American lands, and by then she had slept too long. The rising tide of English settlements, hemmed in behind the mountains for more than a hundred years, was beginning by then to spill over the ranges, finding its way through gaps and passes into the Ohio Valley. By 1753 the French decided to force these invaders out. The result was the latest in a string of colonial wars between England and the Latin alliance of France and Spain. The earlier conflicts had been relatively minor things, offshoots of struggles that centered in Europe. But the fighting that started along the Ohio would spark a war, the Seven Years' War, that would spread around the world and decide North America's fate.

New France ceased to exist in that war. England's sea power, both commercial and naval, came to full flower in those seven years, and she used it masterfully to finance her military effort and to blockade her enemies, sealing off Canada and Louisiana from outside help. Montcalm's death on the Plains of Abraham in 1759 spelled the end of the long debate. England took Canada and everything to the Mississippi, with the sole exception of New Orleans. Florida she took from Spain. To compensate the Spanish for that loss, and to keep the English from taking still more, France gave everything west of the Mississippi to Spain. The lands there were still undeveloped, still lightly settled, but maybe Spain could do something with them.

England was the big winner, but she had troubles of her own. She had more than doubled her North American holdings, though for now she wanted her colonists to stay close to the coast instead of moving west in search of better land. That was the problem with the Americans. They had little wealth or means of production, but they had a seemingly endless supply of lands. If they moved into the interior, one British official noted, "planting themselves in the Heart of America, out of reach of Government," English control could not possibly follow. England wanted the colonies built up, productive, and under her watchful eye, and justifiably so, after she had spent so much to defend them. So in 1763 the Crown proclaimed that the colonists were not to settle beyond "the sources of any of the rivers which fall into the Atlantic." This was the first in the chain of events, of restrictions on the colonies, that caused the American Revolution.[11]

The colonies' war for independence slowed their westward expansion for a while. But as soon as the guns fell silent, the American trek west started in earnest, through the Appalachian passes to the banks of the Ohio and Tennessee Rivers. Within a decade the numbers had swelled; by 1795 at least 150,000 Americans lived beyond the mountains. But the frontiersmen settled in pockets, mostly along the rivers—

hence their name for themselves, the women and men of the "Western Waters." Trans-Appalachia was still in the main a wild and empty place.

From beyond the Mississippi the Spanish looked warily on. Louisiana was a place they held lightly, as the French before them had held it. All of their efforts were going toward Mexico. Even New Orleans, Louisiana's seat of government, was far more French than Spanish, with more than a dash of other flavors as well. The city, sitting on the very fringe of Western civilization, was an exotic blend of non-Teutonic cultures. Caribbean, Native American, African, and Latin worlds all met there. Sprightly and busy, muddy, messy, with human and animal filth running free in the raw dirt streets, it was a study in contrasts, where gaily dressed and beautiful quadroons walked barefoot to the elegant balls rather than ruin their fine shoes in the muck. The Spanish, as latecomers, had little control over this odd town.

But while New Orleans wasn't Spanish, at least it wasn't Anglo-American, either. Spain's greatest hope for Louisiana was that it would be a buffer zone—that its breadth and wilderness would staunch the flood of American frontiersmen that was already lapping the banks of the river. Hector, Baron de Carondelet, one of Louisiana's Spanish governors, understood the American strategy all too well. The New World's newest empire, the United States, was out to conquer its oldest, that of New Spain. But the warfare was largely one of cultures, not armies. Americans were a tough lot of individualists. First the hunters and trappers arrived, fleeing civilization, searching for something in the forest; then came the traders and squatters. After them the farmers and merchants showed up. And the first waves to arrive cared little about international boundaries, especially when those boundaries were vague or in dispute, as was the case in the West. Carondelet could see the writing on the wall.

> This prestigious and restless population [he wrote], continually forcing the Indian nations backward and upon us, is attempting to get possession of all the vast continent which these nations are occupying between the Ohio and Mississippi Rivers and the Gulf of Mexico and the Appalachian Mountains, thus becoming our neighbor; at the same time that they are demanding with threats the free navigation of the Mississippi. Their writings, public papers, and speeches, all have as their object the navigation to the Gulf by the Mississippi, Mobile, Pearl and Appalachicola Rivers which empty into the gulf; and the rich fur trade of the Missouri. And in

time they will demand the possession of the rich mines of the interior provinces of the very kingdom of Mexico. Their method of spreading themselves and their policy are so much to be feared by Spain as are their arms.... Their wandering spirit and the ease with which those people procure their sustenance and shelter quickly form new settlements. A carbine and a little maize in a sack are enough for an American to wander about in the forests alone for a whole month. With his carbine he kills the wild cattle and deer for food and defends himself from the savages. The maize dampened serves him in lieu of bread. With some tree trunks crossed one above another, in the shape of a square, he raises a house, and even a fort that is impregnable to the savages by crossing a story above the ground floor. The cold does not affright him. When a family tires of one location, it moves to another, and there settles with the same ease.... If such men succeed in occupying the shores of the Mississippi or of the Missouri, or to obtain their navigation ... nothing can prevent them from crossing those rivers and penetrating into our provinces on the other side.[12]

If the hunters and trappers were unlikely conquerors, the following wave of Americans, the squatters, were still less likely empire builders. The squatters, the first semipermanent settlers, were usually illiterate, filthy, and poor. They might farm a little, clearing a small patch of forest for corn, but they, too, were mainly hunters. Everything about them said so. Squatter families' rude cabins, each standing alone deep in the backwoods, had deerskins for doors and bear hides for roofs. Strips of drying meat hung near the huge fireplaces. A bearskin, spread before the fire, might serve as a bed, with raccoon skins for pillows. Decorations were rare and primitive. Dried bits of entrails might hang around a split-rail cabin's single room, interspersed with dried red pepper pods. Outside the cabin yelped a pack of hounds. While useful for hunting, it was also a good early-warning system, for the cabin was usually miles from any white settlement, and Indians were everywhere.

Inside the cramped cabin the squatter and his woman raised a brood of animalistic children. The adults may have learned some Bible or Shakespeare when they were back East; even today, two centuries later, Appalachian language echoes the words of the King James translation.[13] But their children rarely had any book learning at all. Some squatters dismissed books as "trash."[14] Fistfights, even stabbings of one child by another, were signs of prowess, things to be proud of. And at any rate, the children were as needed as they were unpreventable. Labor was scarce, and eking a living from the forest took all the energy and hands that a family had.

The most important energy source was powder. A rifle was essential for food and defense. Muskets were for soldiers. A mass of men, firing in unison, could make do with smoothbores that they could reload quickly in battle, since accuracy counted for little. But in the forest, on the frontier, the hunter's first shot had to count. The rifle was far more accurate than a smoothbore, and it had far greater range to boot. It even used less of the precious powder. An experienced ear could easily tell the difference between the boom of a musket, the bark of a rifle, and the still flatter crack of a rifle in Indian hands, since Indians could afford to spend even less of their scarce powder supplies with every shot.[15]

In the squatters' wake came more, and more permanent, settlers. They, too, hunted, but they were much more serious about farming. Their fields fanned out around armed stockades, called stations in the South and forts in the North. The military buildup was necessary. The various tribes—the Creek, Cherokee, and Chickasaw in the South; the Wyandot and Shawnee farther north—were just as resentful as the Spanish were of the rising tide of whites.[16] Now and then the alarm was sounded; and the settlers would make for the station. The doors would close, the marksmen would man the blockhouses, and then the shooting would start. The stations, though often formidable, were not invulnerable, and now and then they were overrun. Surrounded by miles of wilderness, a settlement was on its own.

Despite the dangers, the white inroads increased as the years went by, just as Carondelet had foreseen. And he was not alone in knowing what the change would mean to Spain's North American holdings. Others saw it even more clearly. "This federal republic is born a pygmy," a Spanish diplomat had supposedly said at the close of America's war with England. "A day will come when it will be a giant, even a colossus. . . . In a few years we shall watch with grief the tyrannical existence of this colossus."[17]

The Spanish refused to stand idly by and witness the death of their empire. In 1784, as soon as the westward flood began, they closed the Mississippi River to all United States traffic. They claimed two justifications. The first was their view that Spanish Florida stretched far to the north, to the banks of the Ohio River. That claim, if true, meant that they owned both banks of the Mississippi, and so, under international law, they could keep the Americans off it. The Americans thought Florida much smaller, of course, but the issue was debatable. What was not in debate was Spain's second point. New Orleans, which Spain clearly owned, was just as clearly on the eastern bank. So for a couple of hundred miles, at least, Spain *did* own both banks of the river, and because it owned that short stretch of the river strip it could choke off the West's access to the Gulf of Mexico, and thus to the world's oceans.[18]

The Gulf was a Spanish lake. New Orleans was the plug that stopped American tobacco, American hams and hides, from draining out of the valley into the flow of maritime commerce, to the East Coast, to Europe, to any potential buyers. Taking goods in bulk back over the mountains on nearly nonexistent roads was practically impossible. Ocean access was crucial. But as if Spain's hostility weren't enough, the frontiersmen had problems with their own countrymen. The states, all of them with coastlines and many of them with ports, were much more concerned with their own Atlantic trade than with the Westerners' troubles. On the Atlantic, England and not Spain was sovereign, and England was a valuable trading partner. New Orleans was of little concern to the East. The states couldn't even be bothered to protest the fact that England still maintained forts on American soil in the Northwest. The Eastern merchants would rather put up with those distant forts than risk their English business. The forts were the West's problem, anyway—they didn't affect the Atlantic trade.

So the American West found itself ringed around by three great enemies: the English to the northwest and north; Spain to the southwest and south; and their fellow citizens to the east. The frontiersmen had lands to settle, money to make, tribes to destroy, creatures to slaughter, worlds to conquer—but their enemies stood in the way. And New Orleans was, more than anything else, the key. So they focused on that one small stretch of the river with something close to obsession. As America's war with Britain ended and an uneasy peace fell on the valley, the big question was how far they were willing to go to get what they wanted.

❧

In the spring of 1787 a remarkable man, about thirty years old, set out in a flatboat from Kentucky. He had served, as had many frontiersmen, in the war for independence, attaining the rank of brigadier general despite his youth. He had seen a lot of action, some of the hottest being with Benedict Arnold during the invasion of Canada and the fighting around Saratoga. But the war was over, and though he would soon return to the army, for now he was just another merchant who had come west to make a fortune.

He knew a little of everything—teaching, soldiering, lawyering, even doctoring. That made him useful in the remote West, and something of a backwoods prodigy. He was a gregarious sort, a lavish entertainer who knew that the way to men's hearts was "*down their throats*," as one Kentuckian put it.[19] His proportions were not particularly elegant; one friend thought that he was a little too short. But he was still a charmer. Now, three years after the Spanish had closed the Mississippi, he began to charm his way downriver. While in the East he had learned of New Orleans's commercial importance, for the Philadelphia merchants saw the town as a market and source of supply. He asked for passports to enter New Spain; when he was refused, he did not let it stop him. He loaded a boat with Kentucky tobacco and hams and started down the Ohio. As he took to the Mississippi, he greased his way with gifts to Spanish officials, and three months after starting his voyage he arrived in New Orleans, where he asked to see the governor.

The traveler's name was James Wilkinson.

The tale that this Wilkinson had to tell was partly, but only partly, familiar to his Spanish hosts. Kentuckians were angry, he said. So were all of the other frontiersmen. They were angry not only at Spain, which kept them bottled up in the valley, but at the states to the east of the mountains. The people there, with their fine seaports and easy avenues of trade, only cared about relations with England, whose navy could lay waste to America's growing commercial fleet. As long as Eastern merchants could trade, fumed Wilkinson, they would happily ignore the West. Already Congress was talking about giving Spain its way on the river, if only it would play ball in the Atlantic (Spain, too, had a navy). This left the frontierspeople with enemies all around. The West was encircled.

Esteban Rodriguez Miró, the Spanish governor, knew much of this already. What he did not know, and what Wilkinson now told him, was what the frontiersmen were thinking of doing to open up their little world to trade and settlement.

Once, not too long before, England had taxed and controlled its North American colonies while doing little to benefit them. At least that was how the colonies had seen things, warped as that view may

James Wilkinson. *(Courtesy Independence National Historical Park)*

have been. So the colonies had revolted, seceded, withdrawn from the British Empire by force of arms and with crucial help from a foreign alliance with France. Now the West was in the same position the colonies had been in, except that the oppressor was not London, but the national capital of New York, which sacrificed Western to Eastern interests. Since the ailment was the same, folks in Kentucky were considering the same remedy, independence from the East, perhaps with foreign help.

The West was willing to sell itself. That was what Wilkinson told Miró. Kentucky wanted help from Spain. An independent West could be a great asset to Spain. It would consume Spanish goods and produce goods, too, and it would be a good buffer against the powerful Eastern states. Wilkinson spoke for a leading clique of Kentuckians. He had friends in the local assemblies. If Spain gave him and his friends its help, in the form of money and arms, then they would be in a position to scratch Spain's back when the West had won independence.

But Wilkinson also made threats. If Spain refused to play ball, he warned, Kentucky would look somewhere else for aid, north, perhaps, to Canada. The English would probably be happy to help, and once they were back on the river's eastern shore, they could take Louisiana easily. Wilkinson made no apologies. This was business. The West would go to the high bidder. If Spanish leaders were smart, he told Miró, they would help the frontiersmen and win their favor. The first, best way for them to do this would be to keep the river closed, except to Wilkinson and his friends. That would increase the pressure in Kentucky and bring things to a boil, even while funneling in money through Wilkinson and others, money that would go far to assist the revolt.

Miró listened carefully, but he was hesitant. So Wilkinson took another step. He swore a pledge of allegiance to the Spanish Crown. He even wrote it out himself, a long and elaborate oath. "Self-interest regulates the passions of nations as well as individuals," it began, "and he who imputes a different motive to human conduct either deceives himself or endeavors to deceive others."[20]

That was enough for Miró. He made Wilkinson his agent in Kentucky and put him on a retainer. The following year Wilkinson began to ship goods down the river, which remained legally closed to everyone else on the eastern bank. Wilkinson, though, was mainly just blowing smoke. He did have some support in Kentucky from men such as John Brown and Harry Innes. But most people there merely wanted statehood for Kentucky, not independence. Wilkinson might have been able to round up a small force if necessary, but he would have been hard-pressed to start a new nation in the West even with Spanish help. The fierce independence of the average settler made cooperation there, with Spain and with each other, unlikely. And help from Spain was grudging, anyway. Miró's masters in Madrid were fearful of pushing things too hard. Spain's power in North American was on the wane, while the United States's was growing. Better for Spain to wait and see for a while instead of provoking a war it might not win.

Kentucky got statehood in 1792, but the irritants didn't change. Nor did Wilkinson. He wanted martial fame, and by this time he was back in the army to get it, but he wanted fortune, too, and he saw the West as the key to both. The country was hard to control. The same things that made it an unstable region—the geographical isolation, the sparse settlements, the fierce individualists who peopled it—also made it hard for a few intriguers to manage it. But that didn't keep intriguers from trying, since success, no matter how improbable, might well have brought them the fame and fortune that Wilkinson sought for himself.

By the early 1790s the swirl of eddies and currents in the West—the frontiersmen, the Spanish, the English, the Indians—felt the tug of a powerful new force. The French Revolution, having begun in 1789, was reaching out to engulf all of Europe and lapping even at America's coast. Unlike the revolt in England's colonies, what was happening in France was a true ideological revolution, a major crisis of government in one of the greatest of Old World powers. Jacobin France, in the eyes of most of Europe, was a monster that threatened the fabric of civilization. In 1793 the disease started spreading, as France went to war with her neighbors while sending her own king and thousands of nobles to the guillotine. Even America, an ocean away from Europe, was not altogether immune.

Early in 1793, Citizen Edmund Charles Genêt arrived from France at Charleston, South Carolina. Genêt was the French Republic's new minister to the United States. France had helped America win independence, and now France wanted America's help in their own revolutionary struggle against England and Spain.[21]

The United States, Genêt's masters believed, could be a valuable base from which to revolutionize the whole New World. His instructions were clear on this point. His goal was "the emancipation of Spanish America, the opening up to the inhabitants of Kentucky of the navigation of the Mississippi, the deliverance of our ancient brothers of Louisiana from the tyrannical yoke of Spain, and the addition, possibly, of the beautiful star of Canada to the American constellation.... Take all measures comportable with [your] position," they said, "to plant the principles of liberty and independence in Louisiana and other provinces adjacent to the United States." Genêt soon got busy. Before long he sought the help of a famous, disgruntled frontier general, George Rogers Clark.[22]

Clark was one of the frontier's early heroes. He had fought the British ruthlessly from St. Louis to Vincennes and beyond in America's war for independence—vicious, wilderness fighting, a lot of it—and he had made quite a name for himself. His dominance in the Old Northwest forced the British to give up their claims there after the war. His brother William Clark would go on to cross the continent as the partner of Meriwether Lewis. But by 1793 George Rogers Clark was a bitter, drunken sloth, angry at the country that had forgotten him. Now and then he stirred up trouble, crossing into Louisiana and burning Spanish property. Because of his zeal and his hatred of Spain, Genêt decided to use him to launch an attack in the West. The plan was simple. A wave of frontiersmen, led by Clark and other important frontiersmen, would swoop down from the backwoods and capture New Orleans. A small French fleet would blockade the mouth of the Mississippi, preventing reinforcements.[23] Soon New Spain would be French.

As he set about his task, Genêt found both friends and enemies high up in the American government. One of the latter was Alexander Hamilton, President Washington's de facto prime minister. He was something of an Anglophile: as secretary of the treasury he viewed trade with England as key to American economic advance, and he dreaded the dark forces that the French Revolution had unleashed. Hamilton distrusted Genêt, and therefore so did George Washington. But Thomas Jefferson, the secretary of state, took a different view of things. Oblivious to the guillotine's horrors, the author of the Declaration of Independence was no opponent of revolution. In fact he was anxious to help enlarge what Genêt's orders called "the empire of liberty." If Genêt weakened Spain in the West, and its ally England as well, hoped Jefferson, perhaps the United States could grab Spanish Florida. Thus, behind Washington's back, Jefferson supported Genêt for a time. He even went so far as to write a letter of introduction to Kentucky's governor for one of Genêt's secret agents. As long as the French minister did not drag the United States into the struggle officially, Jefferson wrote later, "I did not care what insurrections should be excited in Louisiana."[24] But beyond this Jefferson was not willing to go.

Wilkinson watched all of this with interest. Still selling information to Spain, he sensed that with rumors of Genêt's plans echoing up and down the frontier, the time was ripe for him to shake down his Spanish employers again. By now he was a member of the "Secret Committee of Correspondence of the West," a subversive group that took its name from similar things that had sprung up in the colonies during the Revolution. This group sent the Spanish an ultimatum via a mysterious messenger, a young, restless soul named Mitchell. We know almost nothing of him. We are not even sure of his first name; perhaps it was Thomas, or Medad, or John. But whenever a frontier intrigue came to a simmer in the late eighteenth century, Mitchell was sure to be there. This time the message he brought was so secret that he dared not commit it to paper, and simple enough for him to remember: Kentucky was ready to take up arms. Spain must help it, by giving it weapons and money, and by opening the Mississippi to Kentucky trade at once. This would make Kentucky Spain's friend. If Spain refused, then Louisiana would not be the frontiersmen's ally; it would be their target.

In the end all the plans came to nothing. Washington found out what Genêt was up to and demanded his recall. Congress enacted a law, the Neutrality Act, to help stop such things from happening again. The French government decided that Genêt had gone too far and did what Washington wanted. Afraid of the guillotine, Genêt remained in America, but his power was gone. Clark had had no power to begin with, except the power of inflated words. He had no backwoods army, and no French fleet cruised the Gulf. As for the cabals of Wilkinson and his secret committee, Spain did not take the bait. Instead it began to negotiate directly with the federal government, finally agreeing to open the river to defuse the Westerners' anger. Wilkinson's threats had helped bring a Spanish defeat, but he profited little from it. New Orleans was still Spanish, though, and the idea of grabbing the city had fired backwoods imaginations. Rumors and tales of plots began to race from Georgia to Kentucky. The cauldron known as the Mississippi Valley, long at a simmer, was beginning to boil.[25]

In 1796 came the wildest intrigue yet. By then the hunters and squatters had given way to the land speculators, the large-scale gamblers who spent all that they owned and more on buying up acres, as many acres as they could get, hoping to sell to settlers and make a killing. One of the best-known was Tennessee's William Blount. He was the territorial governor of the Old Southwest, but he was happy to speculate on the side. His holdings were vast, and his profits potentially huge, but unless he could find buyers by the thousand, he stood to lose his shirt. So in 1796 Blount revived Genêt's scheme, though for financial and not ideological reasons. By now the players had changed sides; Spain was England's enemy again, and Blount sought English help. As Genêt had planned, the buckskin army would descend the Mississippi from Kentucky and take New Orleans, while a second army from Tennessee would move against Spanish Florida. This time the blockading fleet would be not French, but British. By early 1797 Blount, by now a federal senator, was trying to line things up with Sir Robert Liston, England's minister to the United States.

At the conspiracy's height, one of Blount's chief henchmen found the new senator dining with General Wilkinson and Vice President Jefferson. Not a shred of direct evidence, other than the mere fact of this dinner, suggests that either man was in on Blount's plan. All three took a strong interest in the West; two of them were clearly plotters. The dinner's timing was odd, but we have no record of what went on at the table. When Blount said too much a few months later, he implicated only himself and not his dinner companions. In April 1797 he wrote a damning letter to one of his lackeys. "When you have read this letter over three times, then burn it," he told the man in no uncertain terms. The lackey got drunk instead, and he gave the letter to Blount's political enemies. They delivered it to President John Adams, who in turn sent it to Congress. The day it arrived on the floor of the Senate, Blount strolled into the chamber just in time to hear the clerk read it aloud, and the fireworks began. This was the greatest scandal to hit the country since the coming of independence. Shouts of "Treason!" rang everywhere on the East Coast. Within a week Blount was on the run for the West with federal marshals after him, having been expelled from the Senate as well as impeached and charged with violating the Neutrality Act.[26]

Blount's conspiracy had blown apart, but the frontier was still ripe for something. New Orleans and Florida remained in Spanish hands. The frontiersmen were angry. They wanted access to the Gulf. Even uncaring Easterners knew by now what was bubbling in the West. Blount's exposure lifted the veil from the cauldron beyond the mountains, giving those who lived near the Atlantic a glimpse of the smoke and the flames.

One of those Easterners, in particular, was probably taking note. He was a very good friend of Wilkinson and a sometime business partner of Blount. He may even have been in on the Blount Conspiracy. We do not know that for certain, but we do know that he was discussing a "land scheme" with Blount at precisely that time.[27] And we also know that a few years after Blount's downfall, another conspiracy occurred, a plot strikingly similar to Blount's, even down to the cast of characters. And at the heart of it stood this friend of Blount and Wilkinson: Colonel Aaron Burr of New York.

Part Two

The Conspirator

A dangerous man, and one not to be trusted with the reins of government."

That was one of the mildest things that Alexander Hamilton had to say of his arch-rival Burr, as well as one of the last. For more than a decade Hamilton had gone after his fellow New Yorker in both word and deed. Each passing year found him slamming Burr again and again, calling him "a profligate," "a voluptuary," and "extortionate."[1] His most famous rant against Burr rang with one of the classical allusions that people used in those days. "He is as unprincipled & dangerous a man as any country can boast; as true a *Catiline** as ever met in midnight conclave."[2]

Hamilton did not let it rest there. Once, in 1804, he uttered an opinion of Burr that a listener described as "despicable." That got Burr's attention. He knew that Hamilton was after him, all right. He had known it for years. But for some reason or other, news of this latest insult was the final straw. When Hamilton would neither explain what he had said nor deny that he had said it, Burr, who was vice president at the time, called him out and shot him on a muggy July morning.

Hamilton was smart and capable. In fact he was a prodigy, one of the most gifted Americans of any generation. His judgment of others, whether friends or foes, was usually excellent. If Hamilton, whose

* Catiline, or Lucius Sergius Catilina, was an official of the early Roman Empire. In 63 B.C. he ran against Cicero for consul and lost. He then plotted an uprising to seize power by force, to plunder and burn Rome, and to destroy the Senate into the bargain. When Cicero got news of the plan, he delivered his famous Orations against Catiline, revealing the conspirator's treachery and forcing him and his backers to flee the city. Under a death sentence, Catiline tried to reach Gaul, but he died in battle in central Italy.

brains and energy made him a force to be reckoned with, thought Aaron Burr a dangerous man, then Burr must have been dangerous in the extreme.

Of course, Hamilton could not be objective where Burr was concerned. Despite Hamilton's abilities, Burr had bested him more than once in the arenas of law and war and politics, so much so that in the end Hamilton lost all perspective. But Hamilton wasn't alone. People from every part of the country, of every political ilk, had much the same things to say of Burr. George Washington apparently hated him.[3] John Adams rued the day when Burr won the vice presidency. "What a discouragement to all vigorous exertion," he lamented, "and what an encouragement to party intrigue, and corruption!"[4] Virginia senator Wilson Cary Nicholas called him a "modern Machiavel."[5] James A. Bayard, the man whose vote in the House of Representatives denied Burr the presidency, gave a simple reason. As chief executive, he said, Burr "would have been the most dangerous man in the community."[6] As for Thomas Jefferson, who became president in his place, the record is clear. No one, perhaps not even Hamilton, tried harder than Jefferson did to destroy Aaron Burr.

We know why Hamilton felt as he did. He and Burr were too much alike for comfort. Each was a soldier, a first-rate lawyer, a denizen of up-and-coming New York in the post-Revolutionary years. Each had a taste for politics; each had a liking for women, and an attraction for them as well. Each was brilliant. Each was in ambition's grip. And New York was too small to hold two such men. In every contest, one of them had to lose. In the end, one of them had to die. Drama, if not history, required it.[7]

But what of the others? How could so many people, of so many different backgrounds and outlooks, agree that Burr was a villain? What was it about him that drew their relentless attacks, which in the end brought him down? His many enemies couldn't all have been wrong about him. But if they were right, if Burr was a villain, then the real mystery is not in his downfall, but in how he ascended to power at all.

Burr's rise to national fame is hard to explain because Burr himself is a puzzle. He was not one of the Founding Fathers, the elite little group who seemed to have been everywhere and done everything in the nation's early years: Washington, Adams, Jefferson, Franklin, Hamilton, Madison, and a couple of dozen others. He does not fit into the second rank of leaders whose friends and writings describe them well, men such as Rufus King, Alexander James Dallas, or Albert Gallatin. He never set forth a political philosophy, which some of the others did, or if he did, it is lost to us. Most of his papers disappeared or were scattered within a few years of his death. Getting a handle on him, much less a conventional label, is impossible. In this he is nearly unique among most leading lights of late eighteenth-century America. "Ask a question of the shade of Alexander Hamilton and you soon get an answer," a recent Burr biographer writes. "Ask one of the shade of Aaron Burr and, like a shout into an empty well, it sends back only a faint and mocking echo."[8] Yet there he is, in the thick of some of the country's grandest political battles. He very nearly became the nation's third president. The election was not merely close; it was a tie. His name is far more famous than those of some who *did* advance to the White House. We need to understand him, because what he did made a difference, but no matter how hard we try, we cannot. Neither could Burr, perhaps. He often wrote of himself in the third person, as if he were a friend, or maybe a distant acquaintance. "He is a grave, silent, strange sort of animal," he once described himself, "inasmuch as we know not what to make of him."[9]

Of course, we do know a few things about him—how he looked, for example. He often sat for portraits, and he was remarkable enough for people to take careful note of his appearance. "His stature is about five feet six inches; has a spare meagre form, but of elegant symmetry," one observer described him. "His complexion is fair and transparent; his dress was fashionable and rich, but not flashy."[10] This agrees largely with another description. "Under the medium height," it runs, "his figure was well proportioned.... The head was well, even classically, poised upon his shoulders; his feet and hands were peculiarly small; the nose rather large, with open, expanding nostrils; and the ears so small as to be almost a deformity. But the feature which gave character and tone to all, and made his presence felt, was the eye. Perfectly round, not large, deep hazel in color, it had an expression which no one who had seen it could ever forget."[11]

Everyone noticed the eyes. "They glow with all the ardor of veneal fire," goes another account, "and scintillate with the most tremulous and tearful sensibility—they roll with the celerity and frenzy of poetic fervour, and beam with the most vivid and piercing rays of genius."[12] The portraits do not do justice to the eyes themselves, but they do

Aaron Burr, 1802. *(Courtesy New York Historical Society)*

catch the intensity of his gaze, and the high, pronounced forehead. As to what was going on behind them, in that brilliant and restless brain, the eyes never told. They kept secrets well.

We know other things, too, some of them superficial, some not. He was always a neat and splendid dresser, who enjoyed intelligent conversation and elegant living. He was devoted to his wife and his daughter, both of whom bore the name Theodosia. He had the huge capacity for hard work that most successful people share. And though we rarely know what he thought, or why he did what he did, we know one thing beyond any doubt. Aaron Burr was a traitor.

His offense took place in his nineteenth year, in the summer of 1775, when he took up arms against his sovereign, George III. England's ministry never tried any of the Continental soldiers or officers for that particular crime; but what Burr and thousands of other subjects did around that time easily met one of its oldest definitions of treason: the levying of war against the Crown.

When Burr got word of Lexington and Concord, he was a frail, precocious young man of high social standing. If America had an aristocracy, then he was part of it. His mother's father was Jonathan Edwards, the most famous preacher the New World had yet produced. Edwards was best known for such chilling sermons as "The Eternity of Hell Torments," "The End of the Wicked Contemplated by the Righteous," and, of course, the famous "Sinners in the Hands of an Angry God," which left countless churchgoers in trembling knowledge of their own evil natures and what awaited them in the Pit. Burr's mother, Edwards's daughter, was also very pious, but it was a piety of a different sort. She was something of a mystic. Perhaps she passed on her second sight, her otherworldly perceptions, to her son (but without the religious strains), for his insight into human nature was profound. His own father, Aaron Burr Sr., was also a minister, and he served as president of Princeton when young Aaron was born. His cousin Timothy Dwight would later preside at Yale, and his brother-in-law, Tapping Reeve, would run the best law school that the young republic could boast. In the legal world, in religion, in academe, in blood, in all of the most important networks of the day, Burr had solid connections.

He was a brilliant young Princeton graduate, studying law with Reeve, when word of the early battles came. At that moment he decided he wanted adventure, and soon he got it. When he arrived in Massachusetts, he learned that General Washington had ordered an army to march on Quebec. Burr signed on, and the autumn of 1775 saw him follow Colonel Benedict Arnold into the Maine wilderness to take the stronghold by surprise. A friend told him not to go. "You will die, I know you will die," he told Burr. "It is impossible for you to endure the fatigue."[13] He was wrong. Burr survived and came back a hero.

It was his first great frontier adventure, the first imperial outreach for a nation not yet a nation—its first invasion, an effort in embryo to export revolution at a neighbor's expense. Quebec was like New Orleans. Each was a French city that sat near the mouth of one of the continent's greatest rivers, one of the key access points to the interior. Burr learned a lot on that trip. He also learned about frontier conditions. The way was long, the weather cold, the food scarce. Dog became a great delicacy. But Burr hung on, showing his mettle often enough, and before long he was one of Arnold's captains. He showed great courage under fire. In the final snowy hours of 1775 he marched on Quebec behind his superior, Brigadier General Richard Montgomery. When the general fell in a hail of grapeshot, Burr kept urging the men forward until a colonel took charge and ordered retreat. Burr then tried to carry Montgomery's body back with him in the blinding snowstorm, but the task was too much for him. Nevertheless, he had gotten the army's attention, and by the summer of 1776 he had drawn duty in New York on General Washington's staff.

That stint lasted only a few days. Something happened. No one knows what, exactly, but Burr was a bad match for Washington. Some say that Burr, the aristocrat, didn't bother to hide his disdain for the provincial Virginian whose skills he found unimpressive. Others claim that the problem was some sort of sexual scandal. Few famous Americans can match Burr's reputation for womanizing. But whatever the problem, Burr moved on fast, joining the staff of General Israel Putnam instead.

That summer would haunt his latter days. In September the British invaded Manhattan, threatening the army and cutting off a brigade. Burr went in search of it, found it, and led it to safety; he was no stranger to New York and he knew how to navigate the island. Tradition says that he first met Alexander Hamilton that day, for Hamilton was one of the trapped soldiers. Nobody knows. But Hamilton or no Hamilton, Burr's feat was impressive, and when Washington failed to point it out as such in the next day's orders, Burr took the omission as a slap in the face.[14] He began to grouse that his promotion was slow in coming. When at last he made lieutenant colonel in the summer of 1777, he wrote Washington, not in thanks but in reproach. "The late date of my appointment," he observed, "subjects me to the command of many who were younger in the service, and junior officers in the last campaign." He found this unacceptable, asking to be restored to "that rank of which I have been deprived."[15] Very few people dared speak that way to the imposing Washington, and fewer still were twenty-one years old.

Still, he did his duty. He led charges on British lines, using his pistols against them.[16] At an outpost of Valley Forge, when faced with a violent mutiny—a fragging, no less—Burr drew his sword and slashed the ringleader's arm so savagely that he nearly severed it.[17] But despite all the acts of bravery, he continued to cross Washington, whom he later called "a man of no talents. . . . one who could not spell a sentence of common English." The running feud with his commander-in-chief was perhaps the first in the long chain of events that would lead to his destruction.

At war's end Burr settled in New York and turned to the practice of law, and Hamilton did the same. Now that the shooting had stopped, law was a prime field for the ambitious. Between them the politicians and soldiers had made a mess of things. People were bankrupt, titles were clouded, and legal problems abounded. Soon lawyers were cleaning up all of the messes, but for a price, as always.

As the eighteenth century neared its close, New York, and particularly New York City, found themselves at the heart of powerful forces. Here the frontier, with its sources of supply and demand, was still fairly close to the Atlantic, close to where land and ocean met at the mouth of one of the East's finest harbors, into which flowed one of its most important rivers. The old Dutch landed aristocracy ruled the Hudson, but the explosion of commerce, the capital that was pouring in, and the rise of the merchant class were all beginning to throw the old ways into confusion. The sudden changes demanded skill and bred competence in the city's attorneys. The New York bar of those years is one of the best groups of legal talent that the nation has ever produced. For a young, ambitious man of charm and talent, practicing law at such a place, at such a time, was an excellent, exhilarating gamble, if he had what was needed. Both Burr and Hamilton did.

They were soon making names for themselves. The two men were on friendly terms with each other. Though they were often opponents in court, they were just as likely to represent the same side. They both appeared for the defense, in fact, in America's first sensational murder trial, *People v. Weeks*. The accused had allegedly abused his lover, then killed her, and thrown her body into a public well. People were sure of his guilt. During the trial the courtroom was packed, and shouts of "Crucify him! Crucify him!" rolled in from the street through the windows. Once Burr and Hamilton were done with the case, the jury returned an acquittal in minutes.[18]

Of course, whenever the two men worked together in court, the question was bound to arise of which one would have the honor of addressing the jury last. In *Weeks* the defense, cockily sure of itself, waived summation, avoiding the usual problem. But in another case, the story goes, Hamilton claimed the privilege for himself. Burr agreed without a fuss to be the next to last. When he began his closing argument, Burr mentioned every point that Hamilton had planned to make, quite literally leaving the other man speechless.[19]

Where Hamilton was intense and dramatic, Burr spoke slowly, clearly, concisely. He never buried his audience under a mountain of words, or drew the sword of sarcasm. He came across as a smart and straightforward lawyer, and he was good at listening—to clients and to everyone else. He gave them his attention, which never failed to please and flatter them. They loved him for it. Before long his income was princely, and he was hugely popular throughout the small but growing city, indeed, throughout the state, for he practiced law nearly everywhere.

The people were not the only ones watching. So were their leaders. In 1784 Burr found himself honored with a seat in the New York Assembly, the gift of the citizens, and five years later Governor George Clinton had made him the state's attorney general. Now his climb began for real.

In those days the state was a political jumble, with factions being more important than issues. As the New York of the landed Patroons gave way to commerce and capital, three extended families wrestled for supremacy. "The Clintons had *power*"—so went the saying—"the Livingstons had *numbers*; the Schuylers had *Hamilton*."[20] That just about sums things up. Hamilton, a poor West Indian immigrant, had married into one of the region's most aristocratic and well-known families, bringing all of his brains and energy to its ranks. Set against this combination was the more egalitarian clan of George Clinton, who served as governor for more than two decades, and somewhere in the middle were the distinguished Livingstons.

When the Constitution came into force in 1789, the families naturally jockeyed for federal office. Three families; two federal Senate seats. A deal soon developed between Schuylers and Livingstons to support each others' candidates, thus locking out the Clintons. But Hamilton went back on the deal. Philip Schuyler, his father-in-law, became a senator, all right. But then, at Hamilton's urging, the Schuyler group backed his friend Rufus King, and not the Livingston man, for the other Senate position. It was one of the worst mistakes that Hamilton ever made. The Livingstons broke with the Schuylers and joined with the Clinton crowd, and the new coalition soon gained total control of New York politics, locking the Schuylers out.

At first Hamilton neither knew nor cared. For him New York was a stepping stone to more important national power. He was an immigrant; he had no petty state or sectional loyalties. He was a born nationalist, even an imperialist. While Burr had antagonized George Washington, Hamilton cultivated him, becoming his chief military aide in the closing days of the war. Now Washington was president, and he promptly made the young Hamilton his secretary of the treasury and his most trusted adviser, and Hamilton, no slacker up to this point, began to shine as never before. Banking, commerce, credit, capitalism; he saw the wave of the future, and he meant for the United States to ride that wave. Soon he came to control Congress, which enacted almost all of his measures and policies into law. "I can not see that I can do any further good here, and I think I had better go home," one senator wrote in disgust. "Everything, even to the naming of a committee, is prearranged by Hamilton and his group of speculators."[21] In the thick of building the new government to his own personal specifications, Hamilton put New York out of his mind.

But not for long. While Hamilton became a national figure, Burr continued his climb up the New York political ladder. The two men, so much alike, who had run together for so long, were now moving in sharply different directions. Hamilton's bold new path had put them on a collision course.

The first salvo sounded in 1791, when the Clintons and Livingstons took their revenge. Philip Schuyler was up for re-election, and they meant to see that he lost. He did lose—to Aaron Burr. The Clinton/Livingston group chose Burr not merely for his own great abilities, but because he was something of a free agent. He was neither a Livingston nor a Clinton, and as such he was useful to both, with a public image of independence. Burr used their backing to make the leap to the national stage, but in doing so he drew Hamilton's wrath. War had been declared.[22]

By now Hamilton was building the nation's first real political party, which bore the name of the Federalists. He made it in his own image. Hamilton was an Anglophile, a rumored monarchist, and the childless Washington's heir apparent. He was obsessed with the need for commerce and merchant fleets and overseas markets and sources of supply. These were the foundations, he knew, of history's greatest empires. His program, his goal, was to make America such a power. The Federalists were merchants. What is more, they were merchants who were friendly toward England, a major trading partner. As the French Revolution grew in violence, the Federalists looked on in horror at the threat it posed to stable government, constitutionalism, Christianity, and business as usual. Not surprisingly, the party was strongest in the East, especially in the port cities, and the heart of its power was in Congregational, ocean-going New England. New York lay on the fringe of this Federalist bastion.

In the South and West another view flourished. There the farmers, large and small, distrusted a strong central government. They remembered the trouble that just such a government, the one in London, had caused just a few years before. They simply wanted to farm in peace, to build an empire of liberty, not an empire of commerce. Land was the key to self-sufficiency and thus to security. Since land was good, and plentiful, in the South and West, this other party took hold there. Distrusting England, supporting the bid in France for liberty and equality, it took the name "Republican." At its head were two Virginians, James Madison and Thomas Jefferson.[23]

The Republicans had a foothold in New York, which bordered on the frontier and had good Western farmlands. As the 1790s wore on, and the partisan fighting heated up, the state became the no-man's-land, the key point in dispute. It was neither New England, nor South, nor West; it had good land, a mushrooming port, and three families fighting for control; it had every trait of a battleground. By the end of the century, it was at the center of the Federalist-Republican struggle in every way. New York City, with its merchant heart, its outlying spread of small farmers, and its large number of assembly seats, was at the state's political center. And Burr was at the center of New York City. In the end, everything turned on him. It had to.

Burr was so central not just because he was a New Yorker, but because he was his own New Yorker. Neither Clinton nor Livingston, he was certainly no Schuyler. He was a Burrite, together with a small group of powerful friends. He was not quite a Republican, either. As a senator, he usually voted with the Republicans, but not always. Now and then he flirted with Federalists, enough to keep him in the center. That was the key to his power. It also made everyone loathe him.

Spymasters despise traitors and double agents, for all their usefulness, especially when they work for pay. The idea that someone would betray his own country for something as petty as money disgusts the professionals and those who believe in the cause. True, these people often have very valuable wares, so one must sometimes do business with them, but the odium remains. After Benedict Arnold tried to sell West Point to the British and then ran to them for protection, they gave him a brigadier general's commission, but they always kept an eye on him and treated him with faint contempt. One never knows who a traitor's next customer will be.

In the United States of the 1790s, with its vicious partisans, this is how everyone viewed Aaron Burr. The Republicans saw Federalists as closet monarchists who wanted to undo the American Revolution. Federalists feared that Republicans were Jacobins, extremists in league with France, who would set up a guillotine in the capital if someone gave them a chance. This was not hyperbole. The two parties hated and feared each other in a way that modern Republicans and Democrats can hardly imagine. Burr's great crime was to play games with both.

He was useful, all right. They couldn't simply ignore him. He had a lot of popular backing, in New York and elsewhere, for his fame as a lawyer was national now. And with proper courting, his vote could be had. He was not exactly for sale, though that would have made things easier. But he was flexible and hard to nail down, and that often made people angry.

At least partly because Hamilton ruled the Federalists, Burr tended to vote Republican, but the Republicans never fully trusted him. "They doubtless respect Burr's talents," explained one leading Federalist, "but they fear his independence of *them*."[24] Thomas Jefferson, now emerging as the Republican leader, never liked Burr, or so he said later. "I had never seen Colonel Burr till he came as a member of the Senate," he declared in 1804. "His conduct very soon inspired me with distrust. I habitually cautioned Mr. Madison against trusting him too much . . . under General Washington's and Mr. Adams's administrations, whenever a great military appointment or a diplomatic one was to be made . . . he was always at market, if they wanted him."[25] They never did. Washington remembered whatever it was that had made him dislike Burr during the war, and Adams thought him an intriguer.[26] Jefferson followed Washington's lead. In 1791, the young Senator Burr was writing a history of the Revolution, one in which he planned to stress the importance of the common soldier at the expense of the generals. To that end he wanted to look at some government records. Jefferson, then Secretary of State and custodian of the papers in question, refused him on Washington's orders. "It has been concluded," he told Burr, "to be improper to communicate the correspondence of existing ministers." This was around the same time that Congress wanted an explanation of a military debacle in the West, the rout of General Arthur St. Clair, from the president and his officers. They were suddenly on the spot, so they were being cagey about what they would reveal of executive business to anyone outside the executive branch. Burr might not know it, or maybe he did, but his request had put him on the fringes of the very first claim of executive privilege.[27] It was a rehearsal for his and Jefferson's future.

The rebuffs no doubt bothered him. He had power in New York, and a respectable place in the national capital, but he was never quite an insider, despite all of his family background and personal skills. Many people still liked him, of course, William Blount for one. He once did Blount a good turn. The Tennessean came to Philadelphia in 1796 as a senator, but Congress was slow to admit the region to statehood. Burr took the lead in breaking the roadblock, thus earning Blount's strong support. Blount, too, flitted back and forth between parties, so he could identify with Burr, and Burr with Blount. "It will be the true interest of Tennessee in particular and the Union in general," Blount told a friend that autumn, "to promote the interest of Jefferson–Burr for President and Vice-President at the ensuing election."[28]

Vice President: an office that one of its occupants would one day denounce as "not worth a bucket of warm spit."[29] But in 1796 things were different. Each of the first two vice presidents went on to become chief executive, so the post may have been fine with Burr. He failed to get it, though. He was not a strong enough force, and Jefferson won it instead, the Federalist John Adams getting the presidency. The parties both feared Burr too much.

Four years later things were different. The Federalists' popularity had peaked. They had become too autocratic, attempting to silence their enemies by trying them for sedition.[30] The Republicans had grown in power, turning into the white knights. Now, more than ever, New York was the focal point of the fight for national power. New England was solidly Federalist, and the South and West just as completely Republican, the seaport of Charleston excepted. Pennsylvania was faintly Republican, and New York was the swing state. Burr was from New York.

He got busy early in 1800. The state's legislators chose its presidential electors, so they were who Burr targeted. He ran an aggressive campaign for New York City's Republican slate, the candidates for the group of seats that would decide which electors would win and lose in the fall. He hand-picked the candidates, compiled lists of voters, and went after would-be investors. ("Ask nothing of this one," he noted next to a name. "If we demand money he'll be offended and refuse to work for us.") On election day he offered rides to the polls. Hamilton fought back, but the Federalist tide was receding. Burr and the Republicans won the election hands down.[31]

Given New York's importance, Jefferson wanted to reach out to it, to ally it to Virginia. What that meant was clear: his running mate had to be a New Yorker. Burr had done well, but Burr was not New York. Other factions lurked there. George Clinton was still governor, still a powerful man. Jefferson made inquiries. Before long the answers came back. "Colonel Burr is the most suitable person and perhaps the only man," a New York friend reported. "Such is also the opinion of all the Republicans in this quarter that I have conversed with; their confidence in A.B. is universal and unbounded."[32] The answer would seem to be Burr, not Clinton.

But Jefferson faced a problem. Burr was thinking about running for governor, a better job than vice president. On top of that, he blamed Jefferson for his loss in 1796. As he had understood it, Jefferson and his friends had failed to beat the bushes for him in the South as they said they would, dooming Jefferson to second place, himself to third, and making a Federalist president. Another well-placed New Yorker had told Jefferson as much. "Burr says he has no confidence in the Virginians; they once deceived him, and they are not to be trusted."[33]

Burr believed that he had made himself clear to Jefferson's closest advisors, that they knew that "his name must not be played the fool with."[34] Thus he accepted the nomination for the national ticket, though with reluctance. Then, unlike all of the other candidates, he set about campaigning.

Later, after the election, Jefferson made a slipup. He revealed, no doubt accidentally, that he had done little if anything in 1800 to see that the South voted for Burr. But that didn't matter by then. The South, and Republicans everywhere, did vote for Burr, as solidly as they had for Jefferson. The electors had heeded Burr's warning, and as a result, the two men had exactly the same number of electoral votes, and the nation had its first Electoral College crisis.[35]

The early electoral system had flaws. Each elector wrote two names without declaring which was his choice for president and which for vice president. No one knew that within a few years running mates and parties would appear, and that two men might run on a ticket, thus having a huge chance of getting the same number of votes. The 1800 election was the first tie. Because of the tie, the country fixed that particular problem of the electoral system, but the fix was not soon enough to straighten out the turn-of-the-century election.

No Republican wanted Burr as president. Only the electoral fluke had put him on a par with Jefferson. But now that he was there, he had a chance, for the tie meant that the House of Representatives would get to choose the president. And the lame-duck house was largely Federalist.

The Federalists lacked the clout to elect their own man, but they had power enough to block the Republican choice. The Republicans were clearly for Jefferson. The Federalists were not so sure. Jefferson, Burr—for them the question was which of the two they feared and hated more. Burr had beaten the Federalists in giving the Republicans New York. On the other hand, he had voted Federalist in the past, at least some of the time. He was unpredictable, a loose cannon, a loathed and despised free agent, but that meant that he could be unpredictable in the Federalists' favor, so most of them sided with Burr.

This was when Burr's reputation for intrigue moved into overdrive. He knew as well as anyone else that he was to have been vice president. He could have settled things once and for all, just by announcing that he would not serve as president. In that case the mantle would fall on Jefferson, foiling the Federalist scheme.

But Burr kept quiet. As weeks turned to months and inauguration day loomed, Burr said nothing either to give Jefferson the victory or to encourage the Federalists or the one or two wavering votes that could have made him the winner. The silence was nerve-wracking. On February 11 the House went into continuous session, holding vote after vote after vote, every one a deadlock. Finally James A. Bayard could take no more of Burr's hedging. As Delaware's sole representative, his choice was the choice of his state. After thirty-six ballots, believing that Jefferson was the safer bet, he finally gave in. Jefferson became president, with Burr his vice president.

One of Burr's many biographers claims that he was a man of principle. He was either "too timid or too gentlemanly"[36] to seize what chance had offered him. That is a rare view, both for historians and for the men who knew Burr. Burr knew he had the Federalists' votes, and that if he opened his mouth he could only alienate the supporters he had, could only make himself weaker. Machiavelli once wrote that in warfare neutrality is stupid. In the end both belligerents blame the neutral party for not taking sides. Better to back a loser, wrote the Florentine, than to back nobody at all. That way you have at least one friend, a friend who owes you something.[37] Burr knew better than to stay neutral for neutrality's sake. He had shown, and would continue to show, that he played the game well, so well that he earned that title "modern Machiavel." And he had ambition enough to be president. No; Burr stayed silent because he guessed, and rightly so, that in silence lay his last, best hope to be president. The downside was that both parties blamed him for doing it. If he had any friends in early 1800, he had almost none a year later.

☙

The summer of 1800 saw Burr at the height of his powers. Hamilton the Federalist was neutralized, Jefferson was more or less a friend, and Burr stood near the top of the political ladders of New York and the nation. Nine months later he was sliding downward, never again to climb. Jefferson resented his attempted political coup. Before long Burr found that he had no patronage. When he gave the new president lists of names he hoped to see in federal office, all of them Burrites of course, nothing much happened. Once or twice Jefferson went along and appointed a Burr lieutenant to New York federal office, but that was all. His refusal to find a job for Matthew L. Davis was a cast-down gauntlet. Davis was one of Burr's closest allies. Burr asked Jefferson what was going on. Jefferson's reply was curt. Burr's questions, he said, "fall within the general rule . . . of not answering letters on office specifically, but leaving the answer to be found in what is done or not done on them."[38] He might as well have written "You know full well what's going on." He was locking Burr out. Burr rarely got to see the president or any cabinet officer, except in passing on the street. "Burr is completely an insulated man in Washington; wholly without personal influence," one writer noted.[39] To one and all, Aaron Burr was bad news.

Things were rough in New York, too. When Jefferson made appointments there, he was not listening to Burr, but he *was* listening to George Clinton. By now the old governor was grousing that Burr had edged him out for the vice-presidential nomination. So Jefferson began taking good care of the Clinton/Livingston faction, even as it began to back away from Burr. Soon Burr was almost alone.

By 1804 he was desperate. As vice president he had played his usual game, siding first with one party, then with the other. It earned him only contempt. He had few cards left to play, but play them he did. As the election year began, he paid a rare visit to Jefferson. Exactly what he wanted was not quite clear; maybe an appointment to a diplomatic post, perhaps the president's backing in the New York governor's race. He seemed in effect to be offering to go into exile quietly, if only Jefferson would grant him a last political wish.

Maybe this was the key moment of Burr's remaining life, the instant that set him on the path to the frontier that waited to the west of the mountains, though he himself might not have known it. Nothing could restore him to the power that he had held a few years before; in that sense he had burned his bridges in the 1800 election. But a respectable life was still possible. Serving in England, or France, or Spain, would be nothing to be ashamed of. These were very important posts. The job as New York's governor was at least as important. Burr was capable; he could have handled any of them. A public life was his life's ambition. Without such an outlet, his brains and his energies would twist into new and possibly dangerous paths. He couldn't simply lie idle. If Jefferson had held out his hand at this moment in Burr's career, maybe things would have turned out differently. Jefferson refused.

Before long the Republicans nominated George Clinton as their vice-presidential candidate, and Burr began his campaigning for governor. The New York race was to be a strange one. Two forces had been knocked completely out of power. One was Burr. The other was the Federalist party. The Livingston/Clinton crowd was against both of them. Down now to his last card, Burr played it. He began to court the New York Federalists. The irony is that the thing that would bring these two wounded foes together was Jefferson's greatest triumph, a triumph that would presage Burr's greatest disaster: the Louisiana Purchase.

⸙

Even in 1802 the Gulf of Mexico was still Spain's lake. From the southernmost tip of Florida to the Yucatan, the coastline belonged to Carlos IV. He owned the cork in the bottle, too, the island of Cuba, which guarded all the approaches. The United States had gained a foothold in the Gulf in 1795, when Thomas Pinckney had wrung concessions from Spain in the agreement that bears his name. Pinckney's Treaty gave the United States a right of commercial deposit in the city of New Orleans. This allowed frontiersmen to do business with the seagoing vessels there: buying and selling, loading and unloading. But that right was only good for three years, after which Spain could withdraw it. Were that to happen, the West would be cut off again from the outside world. As for Spanish Florida, it, too, barred the way to the Gulf. The nation could not expand southward or westward, not while Spain held onto those lands.

This was a problem, but not a big one. Spain was weak and growing weaker. The United States would push it back in time—if some stronger power didn't get there first. Jefferson wanted the lands, all of them, and he was afraid lest the Spanish might prove "too feeble to hold them till our population can be sufficiently advanced to gain it from them piece by piece."[40] The greatest danger was that Spain would give the province back to the French.

France was perhaps the most powerful country on earth, and far more potent than Spain. Rumors of such a transfer had been on the winds for years. But in 1801, with Napoleon closing his fist ever more tightly around the French Republic, the danger began to grow in earnest. He was gaining control not only of France, but of Europe. Soon he turned his thoughts to New World colonies. In 1800 he signed a secret treaty with Spain, taking Louisiana.

Jefferson had always favored France. He had enjoyed his time as minister there, and he liked French republican principles. But Jefferson understood geopolitics. In 1802 he wrote one of his most famous and remarkable letters, famous because it neatly sums up the Mississippi problem, and remarkable for his sharply and suddenly reversed views on England and France.

> There is on the globe one single spot, the possessor of which is our natural and habitual enemy. It is New Orleans, through which the produce of three-eighths of our territory must pass to market, and

from its fertility it will ere long yield more than half of our whole produce and contain more than half our inhabitants. France placing herself in that door assumes to us the attitude of defiance. Spain might have retained it quietly for years. Her pacific dispositions, her feeble state, would induce her to increase our facilities there, so that her possession of the place would be hardly felt by us, and it would perhaps not be very long before some circumstance might arise which might make the cession of it to us the price of something of more worth to her. Not so can it ever be in the hands of France. . . . The day that France takes possession of N. Orleans fixes the sentence which is to restrain her forever within her low water mark. It seals the union of two nations who in conjunction can maintain exclusive possession of the ocean. From that moment we must marry ourselves to the British fleet and nation.[41]

Jefferson wasn't alone. His old archrival Hamilton was in nearly perfect agreement. "I have always held that the unity of our empire, and the best interests of our nation," he declared in 1802, "require that we shall annex to the United States all the territory east of the Mississippi, New Orleans included."[42] The two had even grander ideas. "Our continent must be viewed," Jefferson wrote as early as 1786, "as the nest from which all America, North and South is to be peopled." A decade later Hamilton went him one better, arguing that "We ought to squint at South America."[43] Mexico was tantalizingly close, just beyond Texas; but all of that would have to wait. New Orleans had to come first.

In 1802, with rumors flying that Bonaparte had taken Louisiana for himself, the Spanish government withdrew the right of deposit. Now the game began for real. The Republicans and the Federalists both shouted for action. The word *jingoism* was nearly a century away, but the feelings were already there. "Louisiana is ours," the writer Charles Brockden Brown claimed bluntly in early 1803, "even if to make it so, we should be obliged to treat its present inhabitants as vassals."[44] A New York newspaper said the same thing. "It belongs of right to the United States to regulate the future destiny of North America. The country is ours; ours is the right to its rivers and to all the sources of future opulence, power, and happiness."[45] Meanwhile, in the West, things were getting even uglier. William C.C. Claiborne, Mississippi's territorial governor, had to deal every day with the pressure of living in the danger zone near New Orleans and Florida.

For him, Spain's revocation of the right of deposit was the cherry on top. "We would be justified to ourselves and to the world," he fumed, "in taking possession of the port in question and reclaiming, by force of arms, the advantages of which we have been unjustly deprived."[46] Hundreds of miles to north and east in Washington, the Republicans knew very well how Westerners felt about the valley and the river that ran through it. "The Mississippi is to them everything," Secretary of State James Madison told a fellow Easterner. "It is the Hudson, the Delaware, the Potomac and all the navigable rivers of the Atlantic states formed into one stream."[47] Now that the right of deposit was gone, and France was about to take center stage, Thomas Jefferson had to act.

Jefferson wanted to act. He was an expansionist. He believed in an empire of liberty, a self-sufficient farming continent that Europe could not threaten. He had spoken in his first inaugural address of what the nation already controlled: "a chosen country, with room enough for our descendants to the thousandth and thousandth generation." But by then Americans were already to the banks of the Mississippi. Not at every spot on the river, not yet; still, the nation's growth was remarkable. Jefferson had even greater things in mind: "a rising nation, spread over a wide and fruitful land . . . advancing rapidly to destinies beyond the reach of mortal eye."[48] This could only mean Florida, Louisiana, the trans-Mississippi West, a West that would be a Republican stronghold, far from the Federalist maritime states of New England. But in early 1803, with a possible French crisis building, his orders to American diplomats were restrained: negotiate to buy only New Orleans from France, or at least re-secure a right of deposit.

Jefferson's man in France was a Livingston from New York, Robert R. Livingston. As minister to France he had a hard job. England and France were at peace for a time; Napoleon was turning his energies to building a New France in America. The world's Great Powers had always been either strong continental military states or else maritime nations with vast overseas colonies, large merchant fleets, and strong naval fleets to protect them. France was clearly one of the former; Napoleon wanted it to become the latter as well. Louisiana was to be his starting point, along with the Caribbean— sources for sugar, cocoa, coffee, molasses, and many other tropical goods, goods that could feed and clothe his armies. Livingston had to reckon with this man and his New World designs, and Napoleon was a man to be reckoned with. "There never was a government in which less could be done by negotiation than here," he declared. "There is no people, no legislature, no counsellors—One man is everything. He seldom asks advice, and never hears it unasked—his ministers are mere clerks, and his legislature and counsellors parade officers."[49]

But most of Livingston's dealings would be with Charles-Maurice de Talleyrand-Périgord, Napoleon's foreign minister. Talleyrand was a survivor, a holdover from Royalist and Jacobin days, an urbane chameleon whom Napoleon once described as "a silk stocking filled with mud." He was a useful man, but a dangerous one, whose morals changed with the fashions. Talleyrand was there in the audience room when Livingston first met Napoleon amid the hubbub of court and the splendidly-attired Europeans. The first consul asked the plainly clad American if he had ever been in Europe before, and Livingston told him no. "You have come to a very corrupt world," Napoleon said. He turned to Talleyrand. "Explain to him that the old world is very corrupt. You know something about that, don't you?"[50]

Talleyrand was infuriating. He was not inclined, any more than Napoleon was, to part with the Isle of Orleans. For a while he even refused to admit that France had a deal with Spain. Livingston was at a loss, weeks away from America, while the turmoil that was Europe changed almost every day. He tried cajolery; he tried threats. He argued that France could not afford colonies. He explained that refusal to deal might make an enemy of the United States. He warned of the backwoodsmen and their lust to take New Orleans by force. More than once he spoke of the chance of an Anglo-American alliance.

Perhaps the message got through, but it probably wasn't enough. Napoleon wanted an overseas empire that was good enough to challenge Great Britain's. Already he had an army on Santo Domingo, commanded by his own brother-in-law, fighting to put down a massive slave rebellion, led by "the black Napoleon," the slave Toussaint L'Ouverture.[51] When they were done with that little island, the soldiers would go to Louisiana. That was when fate intervened.

The revolt in Santo Domingo was a great, bloody business. Toussaint and the slaves were a match for the French, and what they couldn't handle, the *vomito negro*, the yellow fever, easily did. In late 1802 Napoleon heard that his brother-in-law Leclerc was dead, while the rebellion lived on. The soldiers who were to garrison Louisiana were dropping like flies in the Caribbean.

While this was going on, the English were preparing for war. Napoleon's fleet in Brest, which was to sail for New Orleans, could just as easily make for an English port. So His Britannic Majesty's Navy put to sea, preparing to blockade Europe. The fragile peace was breaking down. England and France were about to fight the last and greatest of a string of imperial wars—world wars some of them—that stretched back for more than a century, which would decide the fate of Europe and the New World, too.

Nobody knows exactly why Napoleon did what he did next; he had too many possible reasons. Louisiana would have been hard to keep after England and France went to war. England's navy could lop it off, the same way it had lopped off New France not fifty years before. Spain could not hold it. The Americans wanted it. If they got it they would be happy with France, and they would never let England take it away. They would be willing to pay money for it, money that Napoleon could use against England. And if Napoleon didn't sell, then the United States might side with England against him. Selling suddenly seemed the smart thing to do, but the decision still hurt. "Damn sugar, damn coffee, damn colonies!" he is supposed to have sworn when he made it. In April 1803 Talleyrand let Livingston know that Louisiana, all of it, was for sale.[52]

The offer was not a total surprise. Livingston had made suggestions and Jefferson had entertained hopes. The president even commissioned the Lewis and Clark expedition before he heard of the French offer, in the belief that he would need to know something about the province. But when Livingston heard the proposal, it was so good, and the price so low, that he instantly leaped at the chance. Soon he and James Monroe, a Virginia expansionist friend of Jefferson's, had signed a treaty that went far beyond their instructions. When the word arrived in Washington, on the eve of the Fourth of July, bedlam ensued. At first Jefferson worried about the constitutional niceties of expansion, but not for long, and the deal went through.

The results were far-reaching, for Jefferson and the nation. Napoleon had sought to rebuild France's maritime colonial empire, and lost. Jefferson had sought to push the U.S. frontier down the road to continental supremacy, and won. The Republicans were behind him, of course, and even most Federalists sided with him. A few Republicans thought him too high-handed, acting more like a Federalist. Some of the more extreme Federalists sounded like the Republicans of the old days, harping on Jefferson's usurpation of power and claiming that no republic of such a huge size could survive. "We rush like a comet into infinite space," griped one of them.[53] Soon, they warned, the nation would split in half down the Appalachians, with Westerners going their own way.

The idea didn't bother Jefferson, or at least he said that it didn't. "Whether we remain in one confederacy, or form into Atlantic and Mississippi confederacies, I believe not very important to the happiness of either part," he said. "Those of the Western confederacy will be as much our children & descendants as those of the Eastern."[54] To another friend he wrote that if those who lived in the valley should "see their interest in separation, why should we take side with our Atlantic rather than our Mississippi descendants? It is the elder and the younger son differing. God bless them both, & keep them in Union, if it be for their good, but separate them, if it be better."[55]

Jefferson had just doubled the country's size, with a little help from Napoleon, and removed a serious foreign threat to American national security. He could afford to make light of some remote fears of secession. But a more immediate secession threat was building on the near side of the mountains, a direct result of the Louisiana Purchase. It was to be Aaron Burr's last hope in the East.

The Purchase did more than increase the country's size and security. It also guaranteed Jefferson's re-election. It was a huge coup for the Republican Party, and not just in terms of reputation. The Republicans had always been strong in the West, and the Federalists nearly nonexistent. Now the West was larger than ever before, stretching for thousands of miles. The Federalists had nothing to offer it. They had no hope at all there. By 1804 Congress had set up two trans-Mississippi governments, the Territory of Orleans to the south and the Louisiana District to the north, the latter based at St. Louis.[56] These meant new government offices to fill, and Jefferson filled them all with Republicans. Patronage meant votes. The Federalists, now dominant only in New England, became a still smaller minority.

Throughout much of American history, from the very beginning, in fact, when geographical minorities had problems with federal laws, they often talked of secession. The idea is that each state joined the Union willingly, so each should be able to leave the same way. The last, most famous secession attempt was in the 1860s, and it caused the bloodiest war that the county has ever fought. But secession was an old concept by then. Some say that Jefferson was the one who took the first step. When the Federalists passed the Alien and Sedition Acts in 1798, Vice President Jefferson condemned the oppressive laws in secret. His attack took the form of the Kentucky Resolves, a set of protests that the Kentucky legislature adopted, but which Jefferson wrote. In those resolves, Jefferson spoke once more like a young revolutionary. "The several States composing the United States of America are not united on the principle of unlimited submission to their general government," reads the first sentence. "Whensoever the general government assumes undelegated powers, its acts are unauthoritative, void, and of no force . . . ."[57] Scholars say that this was a far cry from secession, and so it was, on its face. But these same scholars tend not to mention that when the colonies seceded from the British Empire in 1776, Jefferson was the one who explained why, in America's most famous document.

Now Jefferson was on the receiving end. Locked out of power in Washington, the New England Federalists still controlled their own state governments. A few of them despaired of continued life in the Union, a Union ever more in thrall to the Republican South and West. The Purchase showed the Federalists that their loss in 1800 was no temporary setback. Never again would they be a majority. Secession of the New England states, a new Northern federal union, seemed the only way out to some.

The secessionists were few enough. Most Federalists were against the idea. So the ringleaders looked for allies, especially to their south in New York. To them Aaron Burr seemed ideal. As for Burr, he needed the Federalists as much as they needed him in the battleground of New York, if he were to win the governor's race. He was down to almost no options. But he knew the secessionists were in the minority. So he played the game that he knew so well, and tried to keep everyone guessing.

William Plumer was in on the plot. The New Hampshire senator dined with Burr one day in early 1804. Two other would-be secessionists were at the table as well, Timothy Pickering and James Hillhouse. The talk was very earnest. Plumer recalled it some time later. "Mr. Hillhouse unequivocally declared that it was his opinion that the United States would soon form two distinct & separate governments," he wrote. "On this subject Mr. Burr conversed very freely— & the impression that his observations made on my mind, was, that he not only thought *such an event would take place but that it was necessary that it should.*"[58]

Burr's usual hedging might well have won the secessionists, but he needed the rest of the Federalists. Alexander Hamilton knew that, and he meant to see that Burr didn't get them. During the spring of 1804 he hit Burr with everything he had. He was sure that Burr was just using the Federalists to get himself back into power. Once there, said Hamilton, Burr would become "the most dangerous chief that *Jacobinism* can have."[59] Meanwhile, Hamilton came out in strong support of the Union. "Dismemberment of our Empire," announced the imperialist, "will be a clear sacrifice of great positive advantages, without any counterbalancing good."[60] And if Burr won, warned Hamilton, "a dismemberment of the Union is likely to be one of the first fruits of his elevation."[61] But Hamilton didn't hate Burr because Burr might destroy the Union. Hamilton hated Burr because Burr was Burr. This was when people began to say that Hamilton had voiced his "despicable" opinion of Burr.[62]

A few days later, Burr lost the election. He had played the last card to no avail. He had nearly another year left as vice president, but he was as lame a duck as the country has ever seen.

Now the great drama took place along the banks of the Hudson. The headwaters had built and flowed for a long time, finally to reach the end of their travels just beyond the Heights of Weehawken, New Jersey, across from Manhattan. In June Burr wrote to Hamilton, demanding "a prompt and unqualified acknowledgment or denial" of the despicable opinions that Burr had been hearing about.[63] Hamilton refused. His answer was that of a lawyer, which of course he was, though his public career sometimes overshadowed the fact. The man who had told of the insult, he said, failed to describe "to whom, when, or where" the comment was made. "'Tis evident," he declared, "that the phrase 'still more despicable' admits of infinite shades, from very light to very dark. How am I to judge of the degree intended?" he asked Burr. "Or how shall I annex any precise idea to language so indefinite?"[64]

Theodosia Burr Alston. *(Courtesy New York Historical Society)*

Back and forth the letters flew, while the Hudson rolled on imperturbable, Burr demanding explanations and Hamilton always refusing. Before long Burr issued the challenge.

A dozen mysteries surround the duel, the most famous in American history, but three tower over the rest. What was the opinion that Hamilton uttered? Why did Burr challenge Hamilton now? And why did Hamilton accept? Both men seemed to go out of their way not only to make the duel happen, but to make it happen at this particular moment. Burr knew of Hamilton's hatred long before this, and he could have issued a challenge at any time. Hamilton could have denied making the insult. He could even have admitted it and apologized. He would have been no worse off, and maybe Burr would even have let the matter go . . . unless what had been said was so dreadful that Burr would still have challenged him. Perhaps that was it. No one knows what the sentiment was, but some have suggested that it involved both Burr and his daughter Theodosia. She was attractive, brilliant, and charming, a twenty-one year old beauty in 1804, and the apple of her father's eye. Maybe she was more than that. The two were unusually close, especially after the death of Burr's wife. One of the best guesses, then, is that Hamilton claimed that Aaron and Theodosia were caught in the throes of incest—perhaps even claimed that it had been going on since Theodosia was nine years old.[65] Burr could never have let a comment like that go unpunished.

As for why Burr challenged when he did, the only explanation is that having lost the governor's race, partly because of Hamilton, he had nothing left to lose. Perhaps he wanted to take Hamilton with him into the shadows. Perhaps he had to vent the hurricane of his frustration. Whatever his reasoning, the timing couldn't have been coincidence.

The duel took place on the morning of July 11, at the top of the New Jersey cliffs that overlook the Hudson. The view from Weehawken today is spectacular, with Manhattan sparkling across the river, one of the capitals of the world. It was a fitting place for two of its greatest architects to destroy each other's lives. Both pistols fired; nobody knows which sounded first. Hamilton missed; Burr did not. Hamilton died the next day.

The funeral was almost Wagnerian. Not even Washington's matched it for ceremony or size. Hamilton had been in his prime, his genius recognized even by his greatest enemies. His death, at the hands of the vice president of the United States, shocked Americans North and South.

But the shock was less in the West. Life there was rougher, and often shorter, where the rule was kill or be killed. People out there didn't even follow the *Code Duello* too closely. Often duels turned into bloody brawls involving shotguns, knives, and horsewhips. No one there thought any less of Burr for defending his personal honor in any way that he wished, especially against a *Federalist*, a hated name in the Western Country.

The Western Country. Already Burr had turned his thoughts to the place before he pulled the trigger. The Louisiana Purchase, the event that helped bring him to Weehawken, had opened up another world, a distant world beyond the mountains. Perhaps the New England secessionist plot got him thinking as well. Once, not too long before, the Hudson had been the frontier of America. Burr had fought along it in his youth to make the states independent. But now that frontier lay inland, along and beyond an even more powerful river, where new possibilities waited. So it was that before his term as vice president came to a close, Aaron Burr came to a new realization. He had played his last card in the East, but the deck had been reshuffled. The game was not over. He would play the next hand in the West.

Part Three

The Plan

*A*nthony Merry was run-of-the-mill, or at least most Americans thought so. He wasn't even an ambassador, merely a minister plenipotentiary of His Majesty's Government. But that was not his fault. England only sent ambassadors to other Great Powers, and the United States didn't qualify. Europe's envoys in Washington were all mere ministers, and Merry was no different.

A few people said nice things of him. They called him "a plain, sensible man," "clearsighted and vigilant," and "easy, polite, and very civil," but they said other things too. Senator William Plumer opined that Merry "was neither the scholar nor man of talents," and the minister's own secretary once called him "slow and methodical," not exactly a glowing tribute.[1] Everyone seemed to agree that while the man was smart enough, he had no imagination, no initiative. That was a problem. The United States was of growing importance to England, just as it was to France, and England was weeks away. For the English representative in America, initiative was a basic requirement, and Merry utterly lacked it. John Randolph of Roanoke once treated the minister to some of his biting wit. If you asked Merry the time of day, the Virginia Republican said, he would answer "I will write to my government for instructions."[2]

Merry got too little credit. He was a career diplomat who had done good service from Amiens to Madrid, and he had served at Paris, too. The United States was no prize posting. The New World was quite new to him ("perfectly savage" was how he described life in Washington), and he faced several highly delicate international problems. Sometimes, given the things he heard, he *did* need to write for instructions, and to let Whitehall know of important developments. In the summer of 1804, one of those moments arrived.

On August 6 Merry composed a brief dispatch to Lord Harrowby of the Foreign Office, labeling it "Most Secret" and translating it into cipher. He came straight to the point. "I have just received an offer from Mr. Burr the actual vice president of the United States," he began, "to lend his assistance to His Majesty's Government in any manner in which they may think fit to employ him, particularly in endeavoring to effect a separation of the Western part of the United States from that which lies between the Atlantic and the mountains, in its whole extent."

Merry had known Burr since late 1803, having met him when he first arrived in America. Carefully he tried to describe him to his London superiors. He mentioned "the Profligacy of Mr. Burr's character," and he observed that "he is now cast off as much by the democratic* as by the Federal Party." But Burr was still influential, he wrote; at least he still had connections. This fact, thought Merry, when combined with "his great Ambition and Spirit of Revenge against the present Administration, may possibly induce him to exert the talents and Activity which he possesses with Fidelity to his Employers."[3]

The unimaginative Merry said nothing about how extraordinary Burr's proposition was. Most likely he thought that it would speak for itself. Nor did he mention the duel or Hamilton's death of less than a month before, although the whole East Coast was abuzz with the news. He might have thought it irrelevant, and maybe it was. Burr had started to show an interest in the West several months earlier, before the Republicans dumped him, before he had lost the governor's race. But Merry's letter is the first hard evidence of what Burr might have been considering.

Others had talked the same way before, and Merry probably knew it. His friend George Hammond had been minister here when Genêt was stirring up trouble. William Blount had once approached Merry's predecessor, Robert Liston, in nearly exactly the same way as Burr had now approached Merry. But no one could dismiss such proposals as just a lot of hot air. The American Revolution had shown everyone, on both sides of the Atlantic, that successful secession was possible, if the right men were in charge and stirred the cauldron correctly. Merry was right. Burr still had a few powerful friends. He himself was powerful because of charm and intellect, if not in political terms. In light of these things, Merry seemed to be putting something

---

* "Democratic" was another, more sinister name for the Republican Party. It referred to the democratic principals of the French Revolution, stirring up memories of mob rule and the Reign of Terror, as did "Jacobinism."

between the lines of this most secret dispatch. Despite the tradition of would-be Western secessionists, Aaron Burr, the dispatch hinted, might be the man who could actually bring it off.

⊱✿⊰

Burr was a dangerous man. Hamilton had said that until the very end. But though he called Burr dangerous, and many other things, too, he had never called Burr stupid. Neither did anyone else. Some people may be a threat to others because of low intelligence, but Burr was not one of them. His danger lay in his brains. Knowledge of what went on in them has always been hard to come by, both for people who knew him and for the historians. One reason is that few things that he wrote survived. His friend and early biographer, Matthew L. Davis, gave papers of his to friends as mementos once Burr had gone to his grave. Burr himself no doubt made sure that some writings didn't outlive him. Others wrote down what he said to them from 1804 to 1807, but once Burr was on trial for treason their papers grew hard to find, and their memories tended to waver. Nobody wants to portray himself as the ally of a traitor. To make sorting out things even harder, Burr tailored the story he told to whomever happened to be listening, playing upon the desires and fears of his audience. If we had all of the burned and scattered letters and records back from the ashes of time, if we knew beyond doubt that everyone told the truth, we would still have a story shot through with conflicts and question marks. No one will ever know what Burr was really up to.

Burr himself was probably not quite sure in the spring and summer of 1804, even before he gunned down Hamilton. His political career was in ruins. Both parties had deserted him. His New York power base was gone. A man of rich tastes, he had let his finances crumble. And the martyred Hamilton in death was able to do what he never could in life, dealing Burr a mortal blow that was a political *coup de grace*. Several weeks after the duel, the state of New Jersey would indict the vice president for murder. Across the Hudson, a grand jury indicted him for violating a recent antidueling law.[4]

Things were bad in the East, but the West offered Burr many options. Land speculation there might restore his wealth. Relocation there could return him to political power. Others had gone there and come back as congressmen, even after failure back East. Then there was the lure of Latin America. Jefferson hadn't yet wrested the Floridas from Spain, much less Texas or Mexico. And, of course, the cauldron that was the Mississippi Valley was always simmering, threatened by sea and by land. Louisiana might be big, but it was wild and unpeopled. The frontiersmen might have the Mississippi, but with France and Spain and England at war, and the United States a very weak country, New Orleans might fall to an enemy. The foreign lands that ringed the valley were thus both threats and targets. And Burr, with the talk of New England secession still fresh in his ears, could hardly forget the stories that had been floating back from the West for years, stories of filibustering* and plots of disunion. Burr could have been mulling any or all of these thoughts when, a few weeks before the duel, he heard from an old friend and comrade-in-arms, none other than James Wilkinson.

Wilkinson and Burr went back a long way, all the way back to 1776, when they fought to conquer Canada. They had not seen each other for a while. Wilkinson now had his hands full as general-in-chief of all U.S. Army forces. Most of his regular soldiers and officers were out in the West, since the Spanish menace there was the main landward threat to the nation's security. He had had the honor of receiving New Orleans from the French barely six months before. He had seen the sullen crowds there stare with lethargic anger at the American flag as it was run up the staff, getting the clear message that the Creoles cared little for their new masters. He knew that Spain was unhappy, too. Napoleon had promised that he would never part with the province, and right away he had gone back on his word. In short, things out West were unstable, and that interested Wilkinson, not just professionally but personally, for he had not yet found the money or glory he wanted, and he was always on the lookout for both. That was probably one of the things that brought him all the way from New Orleans to New York City, to visit Burr under cover of darkness. "To save time, of which I need much and have little," he had written Burr before the sun had hidden itself on May 23, "I propose to take a bed with you this Night, if it may be done without observation or intrusion—answer me & if in the affirmative, I will be with [you] at 30' of the 8th hour."[5]

Nobody knows for certain what the two men said to each other that evening, but it had to be about the West. Wilkinson was perhaps

---

* Filibuster is another odd word that needs some explanation. It derives from the Dutch term for freebooter, that is, a pirate or plunderer.

the most important and prominent Westerner; he had had dark designs on the Valley for years; and just a few weeks after this secret meeting, Burr told Merry that he had plans for disunion.

Despite Merry's dispatch, Burr could not have been certain. He needed time to think and plan, and in the face of the duel he had neither. As the outcry arose at Hamilton's death, he had to get away. On the morning of July 21, he took a boat across the Hudson to New Jersey. It was the start of a long, long journey.

※

Captain Thomas Truxtun, a retired American naval officer, was seething. A Federalist through and through, he was as mad as any good Federalist at the Republicans' rise to power. More than once he snarled about "the tyranny exhibited to the friends of the former administration."[6] For Truxtun it was personal. Once, just a few years before, he had been a national hero, commanding the forty-four gun frigate *Constellation* in the naval war against France, defeating the swift frigate *L'Insurgente* and mauling the fifty-four gun *La Vengeance.* He had commanded whole squadrons (hence his usual title of commodore) and had sailed as far as Canton. He was one of the great captains of the young American navy. The Republicans, though, had spurned him, and spurned the navy, too. They saw no need for sea power. In 1802, while trying to fit out his new ship *Chesapeake,* he finally lost his temper. He wrote to the secretary of the navy, a man who knew little about navies and less about tact, carrying on about his severe lack of men and supplies. If the administration would not support him, Truxtun wrote, "I must beg leave to quit the service."[7]

He should have known better than to make a threat that he could not keep. The secretary accepted his resignation. Astonished, Truxtun tried to backpedal. He claimed he was half-mad with fatigue when he wrote the hasty letter. He wrote to John Adams, Timothy Pickering, and even Aaron Burr about how bad his treatment had been. In early 1804 he wrote Jefferson, threatening to go over the president's head and take his case to the public. Nothing worked.[8] Two years after the government showed him the door, Truxtun seemed to be on the beach for good. He was bitter, forlorn, and angry.

On Sunday morning, July 22, Truxtun was at work in the study of his home Pleasant View, in Perth Amboy, New Jersey, preoccupied with thoughts of what had happened between Burr and Hamilton. He

Thomas Truxtun. *(Courtesy New York Public Library)*

had no problem with dueling; he had even considered calling out the secretary of the navy for treating him badly. As for Burr and Hamilton, he had to admit that under the *Code Duello*, Burr had been quite justified in issuing the challenge. On the other hand, he had been a great admirer of Hamilton, as any good Federalist should be. It was all quite troubling. Then a servant interrupted him; a caller was here to see him. Truxtun said be would be down shortly, but he lost track of the time somehow. Now his wife came in and told him his caller was Vice President Burr.9

That got Truxtun's attention. He came to the door and spied a boat drifting just offshore, with Aaron Burr in it. The New Yorker was playing things safe, with all of the talk of indictments. But Truxtun welcomed him in, and gave him a hot cup of coffee.

Burr knew just how Truxtun felt about the Republican president. He knew how capable Truxtun was. Nothing in Truxtun's later account suggested that he and Burr talked of the West during this particular visit. But Burr had other friends in New Jersey. His call on Truxtun, an estranged and capable naval officer, could not have been coincidence, especially in light of what happened in the weeks and months that followed. One can almost see those hypnotic eyes of Burr's taking in Truxtun's gestures, sizing up the man as he listened to him talk, factoring in his impressions as he pondered his options.

After a twenty-four-hour stay Burr moved on, filing Truxtun's name away in his brain. He would see Truxtun again, but for now he had to keep moving. Truxtun returned to whatever he was working on, probably half-desperate thoughts of how to regain his commission, interspersed with bursts of partisan rage.

Quickly Burr made his way to the Philadelphia home of his friend Charles Biddle, one of the commonwealth's leading men. Anthony Merry was in town, too, as was a former British soldier named Charles Williamson. The latter was now an American citizen, and lately a frontier land agent. Burr knew him rather well, having served now and then as his attorney. Williamson still had something of the soldier in him, and something of the British subject as well. England and France were at war again, the final and most desperate round of the Anglo-French Wars, and Williamson wanted in. His plan was to raise a levy of men throughout the United States and use them to hit the French in the Caribbean. Spain was France's ally, and it could be a target, too, especially Spanish Florida. Williamson was fairly sure he could find enough men to go along with him. During the summer of 1804, both in New York and Philadelphia, he discussed his ideas with Burr.[10]

Burr obviously got ideas that season, from Williamson and Wilkinson both, and he was anxious to develop them. Soon after he came to town, Williamson called on Merry. By the end of the following month, Merry had written to Whitehall, and Williamson was aboard an England-bound ship to present his idea to the Admiralty, where he had a powerful friend or two.

Williamson looked to the South, to the Floridas and beyond; Merry wrote of the West. Williamson planned an attack on foreign lands; Merry described an upheaval in American politics. But both involved disaffected Americans who longed for adventure in wilderness worlds far from the reaches of civilization. The plans, if we can call them that, were still half-formed at best. Burr had other things on his mind. He shared rumors of assassination attempts with his daughter Theodosia. "These, I assure you, are mere fables," he told her. "Those who wish me dead prefer to keep at a very respectful distance."[11] By "respectful distance," he probably meant out of pistol range, since he had shown how good he was with one of those. He also talked of his love life, which he often told his daughter about in surprising detail. Lately he had been half-heartedly courting a Philadelphia widow, but the affair was now winding down. "If any male friend of yours should be dying of ennui, recommend to him to engage in a duel and a courtship at the same time," he advised Theodosia.[12] This was just a dalliance, though; his real concerns lay on the boundaries of America, and at its heart as well. He still had the job of presiding over the Senate, but Congress would not meet for months. So Burr set out on the next leg of a trip far to the South, to the very border of the place he and Williamson talked about, a place where he could get away from the hubbub about the duel, the smoldering world of Spanish East Florida.

※

The coast of Georgia was once called the debatable land. The English had first come in force in 1733, in response to Spanish moves north from St. Augustine. Now, in 1804, the sparse population hugged the coasts, the roads were bad, the rest of the nation was far away, and the Spanish were as near as they ever had been.

St. Simons Island had once been the high-water mark of the Spanish Empire on the East Coast of North America. In 1742 a small battle had happened there between the forces of Spain and England. The melodramatically named Battle of Bloody Marsh had sent the Spanish back southward, never again to move north. Now St. Simons, just a few dozen miles from the Florida border, was secure, though remote and largely cut off from the rest of the United States. It was home to several plantations. The main crop was long-staple cotton, which grew only along the far southern coasts. Short-staple cotton, which along with the cotton gin would give birth to the Old South of moonlight and magnolias legend, was not yet omnipotent inland. On St. Simons, however, with its humid, subtropical climate, the plantations were already growing.

One of the local plantation owners was Pierce Butler. He was a signer of the Constitution, a slaveowner, and a friend of Aaron Burr, none of which seemed to him to be mutually inconsistent. In late August he welcomed Burr as a guest to his home on the Hampton River. St. Simons was hundreds of miles away from New York, New Jersey, and their respective grand juries, so Burr could take his ease for a while, and from here he could venture into Florida. He had an interest in seeing it, probably because of his talks with Williamson. He may also have liked what he saw of Butler's operation and the profitable cotton crop. Some U.S. citizens were already living below the St. Mary's River, so Burr decided to go and see for himself whether the place was ripe for intrigue or investment.[13]

His original plans called for a tour of West Florida, which lay on the far side of the Appalachicola River. It would have taken weeks, but it would have been worth the trip, for that was what the Mississippi frontiersmen lusted after, and he had even gotten a Spanish passport that would have let him go see it. But nature foiled his plans. Soon after he came to Butler's plantation, a massive storm, a hurricane in fact, hit St. Simons with such ferocity that old island legends still mention it. Butler's house, fronting on the river, nearly washed away. For weeks Burr was trapped, and by the time he could travel again, West Florida was out of the question. Congress would meet in December, and he planned to be there for it. He only had time to look around the coast of northeast Florida. Then he went back to St. Simons, and from there by canoe up through the coastal rivers, weaving through the barrier islands, heading for South Carolina and a visit with Theodosia.

He was traveling incognito, under the strangely revealing name of King, but when he arrived in Savannah, people found out who he was, and they gave him a warm reception. After New York hostility and Philadelphia indifference, the show of public support must have been ambrosial, and no doubt it entered into his calculus. The South, and by extension the West, which shared a lot with it, seemed quite happy about Hamilton's death. Burr's reception in Carolina was happy as well, bringing a reunion with his daughter and grandson, and his son-in-law Joseph Alston. The latter was one of the Alston crowd, a family of big-time slaveowners and speculators, and Burr's relations with him were good. The Alstons had money, and this could be useful. Filibustering meant men, supplies, and weapons, and the key to them all was money. Patriotism might draw some, but self-interest would be the motive for most. By now Williamson was well on his way to England. He might be there already, for all that Burr knew. Merry's dispatch was en route as well, but months might go by before Burr heard from either of them. Meanwhile, here was Alston, a ready investor to whom he was linked by the blood of his grandson. The discussions must have been interesting.

The visit could not last forever, no matter how strong Burr's feelings were for Theodosia and little Gamp. The Senate would soon be in session, and with New York closed to him he planned to go out with a flourish, in his chair at the chamber's center. In October he set out for Washington.

※

Thomas Jefferson usually tried to present himself as an easygoing, straightforward man of republican virtues, a man of no ill will, with the greater good always in view. His writing was mild and expansive, rarely sharp, usually bland, especially when he had to discuss unpleasantries. Sometimes he comes across as a little bit vague, even slightly bewildered at the political storms that often swept around him. But Jefferson was no fool, not more than Aaron Burr was. Few fools rise to be president. Fewer still enjoy such a good track record in office. In his eight years as chief executive, not once did Jefferson need to veto a law. His terms, on the whole, were successful. That could mean but one thing. Thomas Jefferson was a supremely capable political animal, all the more dangerous for seeming not to be one. And Jefferson could take things personally. He often saw an attack on Republican principles as an attack on himself. When someone declared political war on him, Jefferson could have strong reactions, for all his blandness of tone.

One thing that always got Jefferson going was the system of federal courts. Lawyers and judges were usually conservative sorts, always looking to the English common law. That was bad enough. Jefferson was no great friend of the likes of Coke or Blackstone. But since his first term had begun, things had been even worse. In their last days of power, the Federalists had packed the nation's benches with their own kind, where they would be safe from the popular backlash. Presidents, congressmen, come and go, but a federal judge holds his job for life—or, in the Constitution's more technical words, for a term of "good Behaviour," which has turned out to be much the same thing. The Republicans might own the House and the Senate, and the executive branch as well, but the Federalists held the federal benches, for as long as the judges could keep breathing.

Take John Marshall, for instance. He had been the Supreme Court's chief justice and a thorn in Jefferson's side since early 1801. He was Jefferson's distant cousin, and the two men hated each other. Marshall, too, was low-key and affable, but very truly so. Nearly alone of all of the early great American figures, Marshall comes across in his writings as a really likable man. A smart man, too, a logician; the early Republic had no shortage of brains. "When conversing with Marshall, I never admit anything," Jefferson wrote. "So sure as you admit any position to be good, no matter how remote from the conclusion he seeks to establish, you are gone. So great is his sophistry you must never give him an affirmative answer or you will be forced to grant his conclusion. Why, if he were to ask me if it were daylight or not, I'd reply 'Sir, I don't know, I can't tell.' "[14]

In 1803 the chief justice had deftly escaped a dangerous legal trap. In his opinion in *Marbury v. Madison,* he won a war with the Republicans by eagerly losing a battle. Federalist William Marbury, a would-be justice of the peace, asked the Supreme Court to order the executive branch to deliver his signed commission. Marshall knew that if his court said yes, then Jefferson and Madison would ignore the court order and maybe impeach him and his fellow justices for good measure. If he said no, the court would become a toothless laughing stock. Marshall's solution was elegant. He ruled that the court *had* to say no, because the act of Congress that supposedly empowered it to say yes was an unconstitutional one. Marbury never got his commission; but by denying Marbury, Marshall claimed for himself and his fellow judges the power to strike down the laws of the Republican Congress.

All of this infuriated the Republicans. Thoughts of impeachment swirled around, refusing to die away. Impeachment: now *there* was a way to remove the Federalist judges. But even Republicans knew that they needed to find a legal justification, a Federalist weak point, for drawing such a dangerous sword. In 1804, having re-elected Jefferson while maintaining their hold on Congress, they found one, in the form of Samuel Chase.

Chase was an old, intemperate Supreme Court justice. On that bench he usually kept his nose clean, but when he rode circuit he was a terror. He and his fellow justices spent a lot of their time in the saddle, making the dreary rounds of the federal circuit courts that sat from Massachusetts to Georgia. They hated that part of their job. The Federalists had voted in 1801 to put an end to the practice, but the Republicans restored it the following year. So Chase kept on riding circuit, getting himself into more and more trouble.

The problem was that he was too political, a dangerous thing for a judge to be. His first big misstep came in the 1800 trial of John Fries. Fries was a rabble-rouser, or so most Federalists thought; when he helped break a couple of tax protesters out of a Pennsylvania jail, they put him on trial for treason. True, people in Pennsylvania were angry, and the air echoed with threats against the government and the sound of marching troops, but Republicans tended to think that things such as riot and unlawful assembly weren't quite as bad as treason. Chase thought otherwise. When the *Fries* trial began, he told the defendant's lawyers up front that the alleged acts were treasonous, without waiting to hear their arguments. This gutted their case, and the judge was obviously prejudiced, so they resigned rather than do battle in a kangaroo court. Fries thus had no counsel for his trial, which ended with a guilty verdict and a sentence of death. Then Chase went after another Republican, James Callender, for libeling the president, conducting a trial that was almost as bad as Fries's, muzzling and bullying the defendant's attorneys and railroading the trial through the court. The Federalists owned Congress and the presidency then, but a few years later things were different. In 1803 Chase delivered a charge to a Baltimore federal grand jury, a charge in which he accused the Republicans of mobocracy, abolishing federal judgeships, and threatening the courts' independence. This was too much for the Republicans. Whatever the truth of Chase's comments, they now attacked the courts' independence in a more direct way. They impeached Chase.[15]

An early edition of *Black's Law Dictionary* defines "state trial" as "a trial for a political offense." The defendant in such a trial, of course, depends on whose politics have been offended, but regardless of that, the term also suggests a high-profile proceeding and a notorious target. An impeachment of a Supreme Court justice for partisanship on the bench surely fits the description. The Chase impeachment was not quite the first state trial in America, though like the *Fries* trial it may have come close. But the Chase affair was the most dramatic one up until then, and presiding over it all was Vice President Aaron Burr.

Burr gave every sign of enjoying his last few weeks in the spotlight, taking a certain malicious pleasure in having his way. He had charge of all the arrangements. He set about following the precedents from the recent impeachment of Warren Hastings, India's governor-general, whose trial had lasted for several years. One of the precedents was a stern one. Before the proceedings began, and with Chase still absent, he saw that someone had provided an armchair for the accused. He told the sergeant-at-arms to remove it. "Let the judge take care to find a seat for himself," a senator heard him say.[16]

Then things got underway. Chase appeared and asked for a seat, and Burr chided him for being presumptuous. "In Great Britain," he pointed out, "when an officer is impeached, & Appears before the House of Lords—instead of having a Chair the Accused falls on his knees & rises not till the Lord Chancellor directs him."[17] The whole scene was a little bizarre—the crowd, the colorful banners, the wrangling over a chair for a feeble old man who had once signed the Declaration of Independence—and in charge of it all was Burr, with a thundercloud hanging over his head. "It was the practice in Courts of Justice to arraign the *murderer* before the *Judge*," one newspaper reported, "but now we behold the *Judge* before the *murderer*."[18]

Normally Burr behaved himself better than this, but he had many things on his mind. He could never forget for a moment now what people thought of him. During a break in the trial, the Senate debated a bill that would have given him the lifetime privilege of using the mails without postage. Some of the members opposed it and didn't mind saying so while Burr was in the chair. Others said debate was improper while Burr was there to hear it. Just then Burr felt a bad headache coming on. He told the Senate that the pain might well keep him absent the following day. With that the Senate postponed the debate.

The next day the gloves came off. Republicans generally supported the bill, and they accused the New England Federalists of fighting it because Burr had gunned down Hamilton. But the Federalists raised different objections. James Hillhouse, one of New England's would-be secessionists, was blunt. "The Vice President is an ambitious man—he aspired to the presidency," he reminded and warned the chamber. "Disappointed ambition will be restless. You put arms into his hands to attack government—He may disseminate seditious pamphlets, news papers & letters at the expense of the very government he is destroying."[19] Despite Hillhouse's warning, the Senate approved the bill, though it later stalled in the House. As for the warning itself, it showed that fears of the man were very much afoot.

Those fears were justified. Burr was busy, behind the scenes as usual. James Wilkinson was in town for much of the winter, and he and Burr met often, hunched over maps of Mexico. Every so often

Wilkinson sent for surveys and reports of the far Southwest. Now that Louisiana was in American hands, he and many frontiersmen wanted to make it a springboard. In time the Mississippi Valley would be rich in farms and produce, but for now a lot of backwoodsmen wanted to take the short route to glory and wealth, and in their view that meant marching on Mexico. Wilkinson had come across many such men, and he doubtless told Burr about them. A large group of them in New Orleans called themselves The Mexican Association. And they were not alone. All up and down the river were men who would like nothing better than to strike out even farther west. "The Kentuckians are full of Enterprize and although not poor are as greedy after plunder as ever the old Romans were," a Western general and soon-to-be federal senator wrote to Wilkinson that season. "Mexico glitters in our eyes—the word is all we wait for."[20]

Despite all the talk of Mexico, Burr had other irons in the fire. During these weeks he saw Anthony Merry. The previous summer Charles Williamson had been his go-between, but now he met with the minister face to face. He was blunt about wanting guns and support, and money, too, of course. This time he went into greater detail about what he claimed he was planning. "The Inhabitants of Louisiana seemed determined to render themselves Independent of the United States," Merry reported to Whitehall. "The Execution of their Design is only delayed by the Difficulty of obtaining previously an Assurance of Protection & Assistance from some Foreign Power and of concerting & connecting their Independence with that of the Inhabitants of the Western Parts of the United States, who must always have a Command over them by the Rivers which communicate with the Mississippi."

Merry went on at even greater length.

It is clear that Mr. Burr (altho he has not as yet confided to me the exact nature & extent of his Plan) means to endeavor to be the Instrument for effecting such a Connection—he has told me that the Inhabitants of Louisiana notwithstanding that they are almost all of French or Spanish origine, as well as those of the Western part of the United States, would, for many obvious reasons, prefer having the Protection and Assistance of Great Britain to the Support of France, but that if His Majesty's Government should not think proper to listen to this overture, Application will be made to that of France who will, he had reason to know, be eager to attend to it in the most effectual Manner, observing, that Peace in Europe would accellerate the Event in question by affording to the French more easy Means of Communication with the Continent of America, though, even while at War with England, they might always find those of sending the small Force that would be required for the Purpose in question.—he pointed out the great commercial Advantage which His Majesty's Dominions in general would derive from furnishing almost exclusively (as they might do thro' Canada and New Orleans) the Inhabitants of so extensive a Territory, where the Population is increased with astonishing Rapidity, with every Article necessary for their Consumption: while the Impossibility of the Country, in question, ever becoming a Naval Power, (since it would have only one bad port, that of New Orleans, where no large Vessels can pass,) and, consequently, of any Jealousy or ill will arising from that Cause, would ensure the permanent & beneficial intercourse abovementioned.

The threat about going to France was strong medicine. By the spring of 1805, England was in the fight of her life with Napoleon Bonaparte. Trafalgar had not yet happened. The French sphere of influence was already dangerously large, and Burr knew how England felt about that. He was doing all that he could to draw Great Britain's attention. As for the price Great Britain would have to pay, he tried to keep things reasonable:

In regard to Military Aid he said, two or three Frigates & the same number of smaller Vessels to be stationed at the Mouth of the Mississippi to prevent its being blockaded by such Force as the United States could send, and to keep open the Communication with the Sea would be the whole that would be wanted; and in respect to Money the Loan of about one Hundred Thousand Pounds, would he conceived be sufficient for the immediate Purposes of the Enterprize altho' it was impossible for him to speak at present with accuracy as to this Matter.

Two or three frigates: only a fraction of England's naval power, but enough to match any naval force that the United States could hope to throw against them. Burr must have been getting lessons from Truxtun. As for the hundred thousand pounds, Burr's promised commercial gain for England would more than offset that. Merry ended putting in his own tuppence worth. "If a strict confidence could be placed in him," he suggested, "he certainly possesses perhaps in a much greater Degree than any other Individual in this Country, all the Talents Energy, Intrepidity and Firmness which are requisite for such an Enterprize."[21] Not one woman or man in a thousand would put any trust in Burr. Merry had to know that. But the plan was so sweeping, so imperial in vision, that he simply had to report it.

Burr, with his always chaotic finances, was sure to skim some of the money, or so we have to believe. Any man who proposes the dismemberment of his own nation is probably not above cooking the books of a revolution. He also looked for other sources than Merry, one of them being a major enemy of England. Carlos Martinez de Yrujo, Spain's minister to the United States, knew his way around the capital and American society. He had been on hand when William Blount had tried what Burr was trying now. He had seen it all before, and here was Burr, arousing his suspicions.

Burr could not have told Yrujo of his plans. That would have been sheer lunacy. He merely asked for a passport to visit Mexico. Yrujo had obliged him the previous summer with permission to travel the Floridas, but now Yrujo said no. Burr couldn't have told him what was going on, but somehow Yrujo found out. He had no intention of helping Burr invade his own empire's territory, if that was what Burr was planning. Soon he was writing to other Spanish officials, warning that Burr was a British agent.[22]

The would-be British agent still had duties as vice president, which included presiding over the Senate and suggesting candidates for government jobs. After cold-shouldering Burr the previous spring, and for most of his first term in office, Jefferson was now courting him, hoping to influence him in his handling of the Chase proceedings. Suddenly Burr managed to win the appointment of family and friends to federal office, and not just any federal office, but to the new governments in the Western Country. Earlier the few appointments he got out of Jefferson were in his home state of New York, but now his focus was half a continent distant. His stepson became a New Orleans judge, and his brother-in-law a territorial secretary. The prize went to James Wilkinson: the army's commanding general became the governor of Louisiana as well.[23] Later Jefferson drew fire for giving an important civilian post to a serving military officer, but as usual he had a defense. "I did not think myself departing from my principle," he explained, "because I consider it not as a civil government, but merely a military station."[24] His real reason was different. He wanted to make Burr happy.

Jefferson's subtle bribery accomplished little, if anything. Burr kept showing studied indifference to the political combat around him. Day after day went by. As he watched the proceedings he remained "remarkably testy." One senator said that "He acts of the tyrant—is impatient and passionate . . . he is in a rage because we do not sit longer."[25] When the Senate split one afternoon as to whether to stay in session, Burr voted against an adjournment, but two or three members wearily wandered out of the chamber. Calling their act "improper & indecent," Burr demanded an apology. "The conduct of Mr. Burr is really extraordinary!" burst out one of them.[26] Yet the train of petty tyrannies grew longer each day. He threatened to replace the senators' chairs with benches. He scolded the members for eating while in their seats. He reprimanded one of the defense counsel for wearing an inappropriate coat.[27] Captain Queeg would have been proud of him. He seemed bent on squeezing every last drop of authority from his role as presiding officer, even if that meant some browbeating, before his power turned into a pumpkin on inauguration day.

Burr's fixation meant long hours in the chair, with hours of interminable testimony. To fight off the inevitable boredom, he probably spent time looking over some of the major players in the drama, who now strutted and fretted before him. The foremost of the managers, the members of the House of Representatives who acted as prosecuting attorneys, was John Randolph of Roanoke. One of the Virginia Randolphs, he was smart and silver-tongued, but screechy of voice, which marred the overall effect, as did his scarecrow-like body. He was a devoted Republican, so much so that he was starting to think Thomas Jefferson not enough of one, and he hated Chase with a passion. Randolph was a major reason why this trial was happening, and Burr had plenty of chances to watch him in action. Another manager was Caesar A. Rodney of Delaware, somewhat new to the scene, but playing an active role. Virginia's Charles Lee, a former U.S. attorney general, appeared now and then for the defense, but Chase's lead counsel was his fellow Marylander Luther Martin. Martin was no public speaker, but he knew his law as well as anyone in the country, and it showed. He hated Thomas Jefferson as much as Randolph despised Chase, so his appearance was not merely business. It was duty and pleasure too. In the nation's early years, the personal was the political more often than not.

Among the senators Burr could spot his good friend Jonathan Dayton—Dayton of New Jersey, whose term would end at the same time as Burr's. Soon he would be heading for a new life in the West. Dayton, like the managers and the lawyers, was there most of the time, but if Burr grew tired of watching the regular group, he could always take in the steady stream of witnesses. Among them was another Randolph—Edmund, who like Lee had served as U.S. attorney general, at least before a financial scandal drove him from Washington's cabinet. Another witness was George L. Hay, one of the Virginia lawyers who had fallen afoul of Chase during the *Callender* trial. Hay was here to tell the Senate what appearing before Chase could be like if an attorney took different political views. Still another who came to give evidence was Chief Justice John Marshall, who failed to display his usual easy temperament. Marshall knew what was in the balance. If a Republican Senate convicted Samuel Chase, the Federalist courts were in trouble. The country would see a great many more impeachments. Marshall, smelling danger, had even backed away from his holding in the *Marbury* case to try to placate the Republicans, but it might not be enough.

Burr saw all of these men and more as the days of the trial plodded on. Little could he or they have begun to imagine that barely two years later they would assemble again for another state trial, most of them with vastly different roles. Judges would become defendants, witnesses judges and advocates, and prosecutors jurymen. One thing, though, would be the same. Burr would be at center stage, though he would not have to share that role with Chase.

With three days left in Burr's term, the time for the vote arrived. The Senate acquitted Chase, though a majority voted guilty on three of the charges against him. The two-thirds vote required for conviction saved him, as it has saved others since then. With the end of the trial, some of the rancor disappeared. "Mr. Burr has certainly, on the whole, done himself, the Senate & the nation honor by the dignified manner in which he has presided over this high and numerous court," wrote Senator Plumer, who had blasted Burr before.[28] Now that this remarkable man was reaching the end of his public life, some people could afford to be generous.

The following day, March 2, 1805, Burr took leave of the Senate. He made a small speech as his last public act. He spoke of the need for the rule of law, and the Senate as the supreme repository of that rule. This chamber, he said, was "a sanctuary; a citadel of law, of order, of liberty." He went still further. "If the Constitution be destined ever to perish by the sacrilegious hands of the demagogue or the usurper, which God avert," he declared, "its expiring agonies will be witnessed on this floor." The words held a terrible irony, especially in light of what would come after.

The end had arrived. Burr strode out of the chamber, the world now all before him. "In New-York I am to be disfranchised," he wrote to Joseph Alston, "and in New-Jersey hanged. Having substantial objections to both, I shall not, for the present, hazard either, but shall seek another country."[29]

His quest now began in earnest.

⁓

Roads, even ruts in the woods, were the only way. The rivers went only so far inland before meeting the mountains and drying to trickles. Long before disappearing, they sprouted rocks that kept boats from moving farther upstream. All this was why New Orleans was crucial. It was the only easy way out of the West. One or two passes, the Forks of the Ohio, for instance, and the Cumberland Gap, allowed Easterners overland access to the West, but they were few and far between, and the roads through them were terrible.

Even the Philadelphia-Lancaster turnpike, along which Burr found himself jouncing in the spring of 1805, had its problems, and it was the most advanced road in the country. Built a decade before for a half-million dollars, its sixty-six miles of rock surface were passable in all weathers, but it came at the cost of a very rough ride. Most preferred to walk or use a horse, but those with luggage had to deal with carriages. The stages stopped at an assortment of inns and roadhouses that sometimes offered the meanest of shelter and food, and even worse companions. Pickpockets, whores, and murderers infested these swaths in the woodland. They were the worst and the saddest signs of "civilization." They had thrived even in the wilderness, but the roads concentrated them the way that a trickle of honey draws flies. The roads were the vanguards of cities stabbing out into a pristine land.

This was the path that Burr had to take if his plans, or any of them, were to work. Talking about the Western Country was one thing. Experiencing it was another. In Washington, Philadelphia, and New York Burr could study maps and write friends and intrigue and scheme all he wished, but in the end he had to see the frontier and meet the people who alone could bring him back from oblivion. Released from vice presidential duties, he set out to get the lay of the land.

He would stop first at Pittsburgh. It was actually the jumping-off point, the place where he could leave carriages and horses and trails behind and take to the Western Waters. Then the whole web of frontier rivers would be his. After Pittsburgh he need never set foot on land again, if that was what he wished, until he came to the Gulf of Mexico, thousands of riverine miles away.

Burr knew about rivers and their importance. He had lived most of his life near the Hudson, large, long, and of vital strategic importance to all of North America for the previous hundred years. But the Hudson could not have prepared him for *La Belle Rivière*. The Ohio's length, its depth, its crystalline clarity, made it simply matchless. Others might be longer, or wider, or even prettier, but there was only one Ohio, the beautiful river that would carry Burr into the heart of the West.

Soon he was on it, sliding slowly downstream in a floating palace while the world moved backward around him. A patchwork of vessels checkered the Western rivers in the days before the steamboats. Bateaux, keelboats, canoes, even galleys for a time back when Spain owned the Mississippi, and, of course, the flatboats. Long and wide, often lashed to others of their kind to make little waterborne towns, they were an easy way to take bulk goods down the river. But Burr's was no regular flatboat. "Sixty feet by fourteen," he described it, "containing dining room, kitchen with fireplace, and two bedrooms."[30] From this mobile base he would strike out to conquer Western hearts and minds.

He could not help but notice all the traffic on the Ohio, and its relative safety now that the army had beaten and herded the tribes north and west and out of the invading whites' way. Daily he had the chance to note the river's navigability and the commonest types of goods he saw on its boats. All this was probably useful, maybe even worth the trip all by itself. But he had other things to do than watch the banks and the boats. The West had its share of bigwigs by now, and he needed to meet with them.

First on his list was Matthew Lyon. A firebrand, a near-fanatical democrat, that was Lyon through and through. He had once represented Vermont in Congress, during the Federalist years. He once got into an argument on the floor of the House with Connecticut's Roger Griswold, spitting in Griswold's face. A few days later Griswold charged into the chamber and began to hit Lyon with a stick. Lyon defended himself with a pair of fire tongs. The two men stumbled and spun through the chamber while others looked on aghast. That had been in 1798. Not long afterward the Federalists went after Lyon for violating the Sedition Act. They convicted him and sent him to jail. Now Lyon was back, having moved to Kentucky and won a new seat in the House.[31]

Lyon's comeback in the West was a tonic for Burr; if Lyon could do it, so could he. But Lyon could serve as more than just an inspiration to Burr. He now had Western connections, connections that Burr would like to tap into. Burr wanted to talk to him. He caught up with Lyon for a while in Pittsburgh when he got there in late April. He wanted to get the congressman together with James Wilkinson, whom he hoped would soon arrive from Washington, but Lyon had other plans. "My business would not admit of my waiting one moment for the company of any ceremonious gentleman," he fired back at Burr. "In all the journeys of my long life, I had not waited half an hour for the company of any man." With that the Spitting Lyon of Vermont, as some people called him, was on his way to Kentucky.[32]

As soon as he could get his boat ready, Burr started out after him. Wilkinson hadn't shown, and Burr couldn't wait any longer. He scribbled a note to Wilkinson, asking him to try to catch up with him in Louisville. "Make haste," he told the general, "for I have some things to say which cannot be written."[33]

Thirty-six hours later he overtook Lyon's boat, and the two vessels lashed together. The Burr and Lyon boats floated along in tandem for a few days, long enough for Burr to speak of any number of things. Lyon was Burr's acquaintance but he was also Jefferson's friend, or at least a strong supporter. He had voted for Jefferson instead of for Burr in the tie of 1801. Burr was probably careful about what he said; instead he used his old tactic of listening to Lyon and what he had to say. Most of it was about Lyon's views of Burr's political chances if he followed Lyon's lead and moved west. But Lyon had things that Burr wanted, or he would not have pursued the man downriver so hard. Whether or not he got them from Lyon is another story.

Burr had come west, and had chased down Lyon, for more than political advice. Other things awaited him in Cincinnati. The rivers were key to movement in the world beyond the mountains, and he was seeing that now for himself, and not just hearing others' reports. The

Ohio was second only to the Mississippi in importance. Navigation up and down its length was excellent, except in one place, the Falls, at Louisville. There the river narrowed and freshened, and rocks choked the current. Whoever could make a way around this spot would be both rich and famous. Naturally Burr was interested in taking on such a project.

Before he left Philadelphia, Burr had already joined a plan to dig a canal around the falls. Several prominent citizens, many of them Burr's friends, would have a stake in the company that was forming. They were to meet in Cincinnati in May, another reason for Burr's sprint down from Pittsburgh. The planned meeting was no secret, and neither was its purpose. The Philadelphia papers reported that this was the reason for Burr's journey west. They were partly right, at least, but Burr, exploring his options, had other plans too.

Clausewitz had not yet written his classic treatise on war—he was busy researching it firsthand, in fact, while Burr was exploring the West—but Burr knew by instinct some of the principles that the Prussian would write about. An armed strike from the West, whether aimed at the federal government or at the dominions of Spain, would have to rely on men. If a blow were to fall, it would be down to the south somewhere, almost certainly at New Orleans. The logistical problem, then, was to move men there from the centers of population, from Kentucky, Ohio, and Tennessee too. The river Burr was traveling would be crucial for that. It opened the way to points as far east as western New York, and the major rivers of Tennessee emptied into it. What Burr needed, in Clausewitsian terms, was a secure base in the Old Northwest, lying among its towns, somewhere on the watery highway along which men and supplies would pour, yet a place that was safe and out of the way. One early May evening he found it, as the twilight drew back like a curtain to reveal a large and serpentine island spreading itself before his approaching boat.

Harman Blennerhassett was guileless and good natured, and he was a bumbler, too. A less likely conspirator never lived. But on this beautiful evening he had the bad luck to own the magnificent tract in the middle of the Ohio on which Burr was about to land. It was his refuge from the world's slings and arrows. He haled from Killorglin in County Kerry, Ireland, but he had dabbled too much for his own good in a political association that called a little too loudly and vio-

Blennerhassett Mansion. *(Courtesy Blennerhassett Island Historical State Park)*

lently for Irish independence from Britain. For that reason, and for one or two others, he had fled his homeland some years ago. He knew something of law, and botany, and a good many other subjects of science, and in time he found his way west with his wife. Harman and Margaret hoped to pass their days in an idyll, he in his botanist's garden, she on horseback, studying nature and lavishing their attentions on each other. Their island, one of the largest on the Ohio, showed the benefits of Harman's wealth, for he was heir to Castle Conway. He had built a new home here, a beautiful frontier mansion, with acres of cultivated wilderness that promised them years of peace. He was forty-one; Margaret was but twenty-eight or so. She, too, was Irish, and an Irish beauty at that. Tall and willowy, with eyes of blue and a romantic and athletic temperament, she was simply breathtaking, with a dark loveliness that sang of queens of Eire. She had been a teenager when Blennerhassett first courted her, and the two came together like magnets, soon producing a couple of sons. She was one of the finest sights on the Ohio, and many a man must have fancied himself in Blennerhassett's place as, night by night, he shared her warm and comfortable bed. Some of these men might have had different thoughts had they but known that Margaret was not just his wife but his niece as well. The incest was another reason why Harman and Margaret had gotten as far from civilization as they could. They might have gone farther still had they but known that their retreat had put them squarely in Aaron Burr's path.[34]

As his flatboat glided out of the gathering darkness, the Blennerhassetts went to meet him and invite him to dinner. Burr carried a letter of introduction from a mutual friend, having never met Blennerhassett before. For his part Blennerhassett was flattered to be receiving the attentions of a former vice president. As is so often the case, the discussion at dinner went unrecorded, but we can reconstruct it based on their later correspondence. Burr probably made vague allusions to some of his tentative plans, the invasion of Mexico most likely, but that evening he was probably more interested in the island than in his host and hostess.[35] Their retreat could be his redoubt, if he came to need one. He gave hints of his interest, and Blennerhassett probably suggested that his fortunes were beginning to wane, and that a move farther west, to Louisiana perhaps, might be a pleasant change. He and Margaret took Burr for a man of influence whom the nation still valued. They probably couldn't appreciate Burr's total political ruin, and Burr did not disillusion them. If other witnesses are believable, we know that he often hinted that his plans for foreign conquest had official support.[36] At evening's end Burr declined the offered bed, and the Blennerhassetts walked him back to the shore of their little kingdom. As he prepared to board his boat, he stumbled and fell on the sand of the bank. He arose and dusted himself off, saying half to himself "That's an ill omen."[37]

With that the first meeting of Blennerhassett and Burr was over. Despite the stumble, Burr was undeterred, and soon he was on his way again. A few days later he was in Cincinnati, at the home of his friend John Smith, one of Kentucky's federal senators and a man with good connections among Spanish officials in Florida.[38] Jonathan Dayton was there too. Dayton, like Lyon, had come from the East. Unlike Lyon, he was now a private citizen, his term in the Senate having just ended. But he was still influential, and he was still Burr's old friend. As for cutting a way around the Falls of the Ohio, soon Dayton, Burr, Smith, and others were discussing their canal-building plans. Of more immediate interest to Burr was the capital his fellow developers brought to the project. His other plans needed men and supplies, but they also needed funding, which was crucial to everything else. Merry hadn't come through yet, so Burr was looking elsewhere. Soon the canal company had a subscription against which Burr borrowed $25,000, a massive sum in those days. And when Burr and Dayton weren't discussing canals, they were talking of other things. Their friendship went all the way back to Princeton, and to the march into Canada. Now they planned another march, past the places where government came to an end. Burr would let Dayton as much into his confidence as he let anyone, including James Wilkinson, and Dayton would be one of Burr's most important lieutenants.

One thing is odd about the people whom Burr consulted. A number of them had had something to do with William Blount's old scheme. Lyon and Dayton had both had ringside seats. Dayton had been Speaker of the House, and had signed his name to the articles of impeachment against Blount. Lyon had spat at Griswold during the floor vote to elect impeachment managers for Blount's prosecution. Burr's discussions with Anthony Merry were eerily similar to Blount's approach to Merry's predecessor. All of these connections with Blount, true, were largely incidental. The American political scene was small, and some of the same names invariably popped up. But the list of Burr contacts with Blount connections was growing, as Burr's next major meeting would show.

❧

Andrew Jackson was a Celt. The fierce blue eyes and fair complexion said so, as did his name.

That wasn't unusual in the West. The early English settlers were from Teutonic, Puritan stock. By the time the lowland Scots, the Scots-Irish, the Highland Scots, and the Irish—each more Celtic than the last—began to arrive in force, most of the good Eastern lands were full of earlier settlers. The Anglo-Celts moved inland, along the base of the mountains, finding the passes and becoming the vanguard of westward expansion. The frontier was full of Scottish and Irish names: Jackson; young Sam Houston, his protégé; Henry Clay, the well-known Kentucky attorney; Allen B. MacGruder, Kentucky's federal land agent; John McKee, the federal Choctaw agent; and William C. C. Claiborne, the governor of the Mississippi territory, not to mention James Wilkinson and thousands of others. Fiercely individualistic, driven by a love of the land and a longing for more, as at home in the woods as their far-distant forebears, the Anglo-Celts seemed made for America. Just as the Anglo-Saxon and German tribes had once faced Rome across Hadrian's Wall, the Rhine, and the Danube, so now their descendants eyed one another, first across the Mississippi, then across the Sabine, and later across the Rio Grande. Two thousand years earlier, Roman technology and organization had given the Empire the upper hand, but now the roles were reversed. In America the Spanish forces had only muskets, while the Celts to the north had rifles, and frontier individualism was an asset and not a liability. The woods belonged not to massed infantry but to the lone hunter and fighter, men such as Andrew Jackson.[39]

Jackson hated the Spanish. He hated the English, too, and the Cherokee, and the Choctaw and the Creek and the Seminole. At one time or another he fought nearly all of them, sometimes two or three at once. Jackson, more than most, was an American, proud to the point of arrogance, patriotic past the point of passion, intolerant of any force that even seemed to stand in the way of his young, strapping nation. Scrawny and frail at first glance, he had a will of steel, a temper fit for the Furies, and a physical and mental toughness that is almost beyond belief.

He had once been William Blount's lieutenant, and he remembered his conspiracy well. He had been in the Senate during Blount's impeachment, judging his old master favorably. He didn't blame Blount one bit for wanting to destroy New Spain. Now, seven years later, he showed every sign of wanting to kick the Dons out of Florida and throw them all the way back to the gates of Mexico and beyond. As commander of Tennessee's militia, near the front lines of the Spanish-American hot zone, he was in a position to make it happen. The Spanish were terrors whom he meant to destroy. "They have taken an unjustifiable & insulting position on the East side of the river Sabine & within the Territory of New Orleans!!!" he told his troops in 1803 when tensions were running high. "Acts thus daring as well as degrading to our national Character & constituted rights demand prompt satisfaction . . . ."[40] Soldier, lawyer, Tennessee leader, hater of everything Spanish—here was a man Burr could use.

Soon Burr was moving south towards Nashville and Jackson, crossing from the Ohio and Kentucky lands to the world of central Tennessee. He could not hope to be incognito. Everywhere he went along the frontier, people greeted him with bands, parades, and parties. He was one of the most important people ever to have come to the west of the Appalachians—Jefferson never did—and what was more, he had slain Hamilton, the great Federalist enemy. His reception in Nashville in late May 1805 was not much different than the ones before. A cannon salute welcomed him for a visit that lasted for several days. Throughout the festivities Jackson was there. Burr stayed with him, gaining his trust in the process. "A man of intelligence," Burr described him, "and one of those prompt, frank, ardent souls whom I loved to meet." Jackson held a continuous open house, summoning the most important citizens from miles around to come and meet Burr. The high point came with a ball that Jackson gave in his distinguished guest's honor. As the charismatic New Yorker and the dashing Tennessee general entered the room, everyone fell into a hush at the breathtaking sight. On a less public level, Burr heard with approval of Jackson's racehorse Truxtun. The commodore reigned supreme at sea, Jackson boasted, and the steed that he had named for him was peerless on land.[41] Knowing the affinity that Jackson felt for his old friend probably heartened Burr. It was an omen that offset the stumble he took on Blennerhassett's Island.

Before long, Burr had to get moving again. His new friend gave him a boat to take him down the Cumberland, back to his Ohio River flatboat. Three days after that, he finally caught up with James Wilkinson.

The general was at Fort Massac, not far below the Cumberland's mouth. He had recently seen both Dayton and Smith, and now he spent several days with Burr. Much went unwritten that season. Even the letters of introduction that Wilkinson penned for Burr were guarded. "To him I refer you," he wrote to one friend, "for many things improper to letter, and which he will not say to any other."[42] All of the circumspection is maddening, but at least it shows that the two men were up to something.

Armed with his missives from Wilkinson, and traveling on a barge that he got from the general, Burr now met the Mississippi, taking it in for the first time. Where the Ohio emptied into it, the two streams ran in parallel down the same channel for miles, the Ohio's clear blue-green on one side, the muddiness of the Father of Waters on the other. Burr could see the sandbars, the sawyers, the miles of wilderness and heavily wooded banks, and occasionally a village or town ringed round by forest or canebrake. And all up and down the river he saw the countless boats and rafts, bearing goods and people south. Everything in sight showed him just how far from the rest of the world the Mississippi Valley really was.

He stopped in St. Louis, and later in Natchez. St. Louis was the heart of Upper Louisiana, the only sizable town on the river's middle or northern reaches. Between it and the southern settlements was pretty much one long unbroken forest. He emerged from that stretch at Natchez, where Governor Robert Williams of the Mississippi Territory warmly greeted him. Then, two months after leaving Philadelphia, he came at last to New Orleans.

Here was the place, so utterly different from New York City, that would be the center of anything that Burr meant to do in the Western Country. At once the town's ways made themselves felt on visitors. The languid, tropical heat fell like a blanket, with air so humid that it could be seen. A babble of voices rang through that air: Spanish and French, African and Indian tongues; the faces and figures—the Creoles, the grizzled backwoodsmen in homespun and leather, selling corn or bear hides, the dusky quadroons, the clouds of mosquitoes and gnats that swirled around all of them, the hustle and bustle along the quay as ships tied up and cast off, some of them bound for the British Isles, or war-torn Europe and the British blockade, others for the Gold and Ivory Coasts, the fine mansions and churches, the tolling of Catholic bells and the telling of Rosary beads, the whisper of mantra-like prayers in the heat, the music and filth of the streets, and underlying it all, the smoldering tension, and the ceaseless, indifferent flow of the river. New Orleans was not just any town; it was the essence of diversity, a little world on the front lines of a war that was waiting to happen, a war between empires and cultures.

The Spanish were getting closer. Up on the Ohio people talked of them; lower down, in Tennessee, Jackson railed at them. Now Burr stood at the muzzle of the gun barrel that was West Florida, and he could feel the Spanish all around him. The backwoodsmen wanted West Florida as much as they had wanted New Orleans. Several rivers ran through it to the Gulf, paralleling the Mississippi rather than feeding it. To the bear hunters of the territory above it, those streams were just as important as New Orleans's river.[43]

The most aggressive expansionists said that West Florida had been part of the Louisiana Purchase, but France had been noncommittal. When Robert Livingston asked Talleyrand about the boundary lines, the French minister said with a verbal shrug, "You have made a noble bargain for yourselves, and I suppose you will make the most of it."[44] So the frontiersmen intended to do just that, and the Jeffersonians

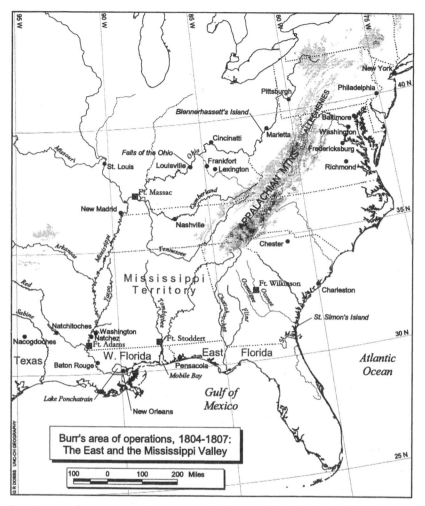

Burr's area of operations, 1804–1807: the East and the Mississippi Valley.

too. In early 1804, Congress passed the Mobile Act, which recognized the extreme western part of Florida as United States territory and directed the president to extend federal jurisdiction over the area "whenever he shall deem it expedient."[45] The Spanish quite rightly flared at this, Minister Yrujo denouncing it loudly. In New Orleans a Spanish officer, Juan Ventura Morales, had much the same reaction. All of the Floridas, he sputtered, "are the absolute property & domains of the King of Spain, having been conquered by his royal arms from the English nation."[46] Spain had not sold the Floridas to France, he insisted, so France could not have sold it to the Americans.

A lot of Americans didn't care what the Spanish authorities thought. If Spain could take it from England by force, then England could take it back by force. Spain was weak. England was strong. Mobile Bay would be an excellent naval base for the world's greatest maritime power, or a fine anchorage for an invading fleet. Even French intervention was possible. Napoleon, already regretting the sale of Louisiana, was starting to take a harder line toward the United States, and Spain was his puppet-ally. Better for the United States to relieve Spain of its burden, and shore up New Orleans's flanks.

A problem crouched to the west as well as to the east. Spain owned land on the other side of New Orleans too, and the borders there were equally hazy—perhaps even hazier. Louisiana reached at least to the Sabine River, a hundred miles west of the Mississippi. The stretch between the Sabine and West Florida was barely more than that. An enemy need only seize the bottleneck to hold the whole valley, half of the Union, hostage. The frontiersmen, not to mention the expansionist crowd in Washington, thought that the safety margin was far too small, and the question of borders far too open, to settle for such a boundary line. So they argued that as part of the Purchase the United States had gotten all of Texas, everything to the Nueces or even the Rio Grande.

Some looked even farther than that. Mexico was a major player in the worlds of sugar and cotton production. Louisiana understood sugar, and the whole South was coming to know about cotton, so Mexico was attractive. The province would also be a great market for the produce of the valley. But the real lure was the silver mines, thousands of them in all, three dozen of them world-class, together producing as much or more silver as the rest of the world put together. Precious metals, markets, and land; no wonder the shadowy Mexican Association had sprung into being in New Orleans. Even Governor Claiborne may have belonged, the way that he talked. "The Marching of a few thousand Troops to the Western Frontier of Louisiana," he swore, "would make Spain tremble for her Mexican possessions."[47] Another member was Burr's old friend Edward Livingston, a transplanted New Yorker. Most of the city's new imperial masters thought very much the same way.

The Spainish no doubt knew it. Having made the biggest land deal in history, a deal that Spain denounced as illegal, the United States was now behaving very badly about it, pushing its claims past the limit. In West Florida, disgruntled American filibusters attacked Spanish-owned Baton Rouge in an effort to "liberate" it. In Washington, Paris, and Madrid, American diplomats threatened war, and when they weren't busy threatening they added insult to injury by trying to bribe Spain to part with the Floridas. So threats against Mexico would come as no surprise, even though designs on Texas and East and West Florida were of more pressing concern.

The Spanish had no intention of taking such things lightly. As Burr was moving down the West's rivers, a Spanish force was advancing on New Orleans from the opposite point of the compass, past the Sabine and to the banks of the Arroyo Hondo, not far from the Mississippi. Other troops, from Havana and Mexico, reinforced Texas and Florida. Claiborne countered by putting his militia on alert and dispatching warnings to Washington, half a continent away.[48]

Spain knew it couldn't hold Florida if the United States was really determined, but it would not knuckle under to bribes and threats of force. It would make the brash young republic become an open aggressor. Texas and Mexico seemed safe enough; they were larger and farther from America's reach. Thus Spain had nothing to lose by stubbornness, if Florida was already lost. When America's chargé d'affaires at Madrid made another in a long line of protests, Spain's de facto prime minister, Manuel de Godoy, played the fatalist. "You may choose either peace or war," he responded. "It is the same thing to me."[49]

Burr knew about most of this. In fact he was counting on it. War between Spain and the United States would fan the flames of conquest. He would be able to find recruits, equip a force, and march on Mexico with no opposition at home, certainly none in the Western Country. If he chose the wilder plan of separating the West from the Union, wartime would be the best time. Many Westerners, militiamen too, would be more loyal to their region than to a far-away federal government. Yorktown had proved that. The regular army was minuscule, and it couldn't hope to fight Spain and a coup at home all at once. And on top of that was the Creole hatred of Anglos.

Thomas Jefferson, the author of the Declaration of Independence, the supreme assailant of empire, had shown himself as North America's first great imperialist. Not only had he bought Louisiana, thus ignoring the region's right to self-determination as completely as had the Spanish and French; he had then signed a bill denying self-rule to the people there, Creoles and others who had awakened one morning to find themselves in a different country than the one they had gone to bed in. "Our new fellow citizens," he declared, "are as yet as incapable of self-government as children."[50] Instead they came under the rule of federally appointed officials. All this was old hat to them, for they had never had much of a voice at all in whoever happened to own them. But it still grated, and this time their political masters were of a totally different culture, in everything from language to religion. So the resentment began to build.

Florida, Texas, Mexico, the slow-burning Creole anger—all of these forces swirled around Burr as he started to woo New Orleans. The place was simply a tinder-box. The problem was not in starting a war or a revolution, but in stopping one. All he need do was strike a match and half a continent would go up in flames. He got to work fast.

He started by meeting with Livingston, dining with Claiborne, and introducing himself to well-known adventurer Daniel Clark. He saw everyone who mattered. Clark would be useful; he was one of the Mexican Association's leading figures, although he denied it. Burr also approached Juan Ventura Morales, the intendant of Spanish West Florida. Perhaps he thought the man could be useful somehow. Burr even breached the walls of the local Ursuline convent. Not even lady-killer Hamilton had managed such a feat, but Burr wasn't interested in overcoming the sisters' virtues. Rumor had it that they were as keen on the idea of liberating Mexico as anyone in New Orleans. The clergy there, they believed, could stand some shaping up. "The bishop conducted me to the cloister," Burr explained to Theodosia. "We conversed at first through the grates; but presently I was admitted within, and I passed an hour with them greatly to my satisfaction. None of that calm monotony which I expected. All was gayety, *wit,* and sprightliness. . . . We had a repast of wine, fruit, and cakes. I was conducted to every part of the building. All is neatness, simplicity, and order." But Jonathan Edwards's grandson, no doubt on his best behavior while in the cloister, gave signs of a troubled conscience about things going on in the outside world. "At parting, I asked them to remember me in their prayers, which they all promised with great promptness and courtesy . . . ."[51]

Burr had come nearly as far as he could from his comfortable New York world and still be in the United States. He had spent three weeks in New Orleans, but it was time to go home. Now he faced the problem that confronted all of the Western rivermen. Home was upstream. He would have to fight the current, his former friend and ally, for thousands of miles, or else go another way. He chose the Natchez Trace, a poorly marked road barely sixteen feet wide. It ran from Natchez to Nashville, 500 miles of it, through swamps and Indian lands, following animal trails for a lot of the way. Wilkinson had been one of the commissioners who won the right from the tribes to develop the Trace. "This road being completed," he had predicted, "I shall consider our Southern extremity assured, the Indians in that quarter at our feet & the adjacent Province laid open to us."[52] That had been in 1801, and though many people had used it since then, it still wasn't much of a road. It ran through what Burr described as "a vile country, destitute of springs and of running water—think of drinking the nasty puddle-water, covered with green scum and full of animalculae—bah!" But even this leg of the trip was useful. The long trail through the wilderness confirmed for Burr just how cut off from the rest of the world that Old Southwest was. If this was the closest thing to a military road, then army movements on land would be sluggish. It meant that initiative was crucial. Whoever struck first down here would be in a strong position, since reaction times would be slow. Still, he was happy to see the end of it. "I was glad to get on the waters of the Tennessee," he wrote, "all fine, transparent, lively streams, and itself a clear, beautiful, magnificent river."[53]

In Nashville Burr stayed with Jackson again. Then he moved on, heading west to St. Louis and north as far as Vincennes. In St. Louis he spoke to Judge Rufus Easton, asking him questions about the town's little army garrison. Burr seemed very interested in whether any of its officers would be fit to command a march on Santa Fe, the commerce and traffic center of the northwestern realms of New Spain.[54] At Vincennes he met with William Henry Harrison, out from Virginia to serve as the territorial governor. Wilkinson had written a letter of introduction for Burr, asking Harrison to consider appointing him as Indiana's territorial delegate to Congress, but this feeler that Wilkinson and Burr cast out came in the end to nothing.

By November Burr was at last back east of the mountains, having traveled thousands of miles to their westward. He had learned much that he hadn't known about the place and its people. Perhaps he now had a concrete plan, or at least thought that he had. He had looked, and listened, and in consequence was perhaps beginning to make up his mind. Some things, though, were still up in the air, funding, for one. Whatever he wanted to do, he simply had to find the money to do it and that couldn't wait much longer. For most of the following winter and spring of 1806, he would be busy trying to interest financial backers and others. Meanwhile something new was happening. Burr, the listener and watcher, now came to realize that *he* was being watched.

⚘

Keeping a secret out west was impossible, especially if it had something to do with filibustering or setting up a new country. From the days of Genêt and before, everyone always blabbed. The trouble was usually alcohol. George Rogers Clark was a lush. Blount landed in trouble because one of his men got drunk. Self-important braggarts, soldiers on the make, and traders who ran their mouths were everywhere. The odd thing was how people ignored all the rumors.

Burr was too smart not to know all of this. Blount, now dead, had once been his friend, and his impeachment had caused a sensation. Everyone in the country knew the story, just as everyone now knows of Iran-Contra or Watergate. Stories about Wilkinson were also around, and Wilkinson was one of the country's most prominent men. Burr had to know that rumors were inevitable, but not necessarily fatal. He may even have gambled on the chance that rumors could be harmless, maybe even helpful.

He was one of the best-known men in the country, better-known even than Wilkinson. He talked with a great many people, and they in turn talked with others, repeating what he had said. Every step he had taken out west was notorious. He couldn't have escaped all the attention, and he gave no signs of trying. Yet he talked of filibustering, of separating the West from the Union. Even if he hadn't yet made up his mind which, if either, plan he would try, they were dangerous subjects to speak of, and so only one conclusion is possible: Burr was trying to hide in plain sight, muddying the waters with conflicting reports of what he was up to, reports no wilder and no different from the ones that had bubbled up for years. With all of the talk came publicity.

The nation's early newspapers were different from ours. The syndicates, the wire services, the dispassionate reporters who write in clinical phrases—all of these were things of the future. Small local papers were the fashion, published by men who relied on tidbits of gossip, and whose party allegiance showed on every page. Because information traveled so slowly, the papers often built stories out of the feeblest whispers. When political topics came up, vitriol flowed as freely as ink, and when things were calm, some editors weren't above stirring things up. Rumors connecting Burr's name with talk of western uprising would be too good to ignore.

The first report came in August, while Burr was still on the frontier. The Federalist *Gazette of the United States,* a Philadelphia paper of long standing, began guessing what Burr might be up to. "How long will it be," asked the editors, "before we shall hear of Col. Burr being at the head of a revolution party on the Western Waters?" The paper insinuated that Burr was raising a frontier army, and that soon a convention of the western states would meet "to form a separate government." It went on to ask the disturbing question of what would become of "the forts and magazines in all the military ports at New Orleans and on the Mississippi." The editor had heard about filibustering plans, too. "How soon will Col. Burr engage in the reduction of Mexico, by granting liberty to its inhabitants and seizing on its treasures, aided by British ships and forces?"[55]

Other papers were asking the same questions before long, as were people both west and east. One story that popped up in the Southern editions from Richmond to Charleston for the next few months linked Burr with the Yazoo speculators. Several years earlier, the Yazoo land companies, named after an Old Southwestern river and made up largely of state legislators, bought huge tracts of western lands for almost no money from the states in whose legislatures they sat. The scheme was fraud on a massive scale, and the voters threw out the scoundrels and rescinded the sales, but not before title passed. Suddenly the ownership of much of the Old Southwest was in doubt, and the speculators were fighting, trying to win in court. Now, a decade and more later, the lawsuits were still going on, and the papers were pointing out that an independent western nation might help solve the problem by giving flat-out title to the land jobbers.[56]

The idea was certainly plausible. If Burr really meant to start a new government, he needed as many people as possible with him. Those without money could still offer other types of support. Some of what the papers said was simply speculation; other stories started with leaks from sources unfriendly to Burr. The fact is that Burr talked a lot, and about dangerous things. A security leak was inevitable. But now that Burr was back in Philadelphia, an even greater threat arose.

"He is meditating the overthrow of your Administration," Thomas Jefferson read one day in December 1805 in an unsigned letter he had received. "Yes, Sir, his aberrations through the Western States *had no other object*. A foreign Agent, now at Washington knows since February last his plans and has seconded them beyond what you are aware of. . . . Watch his connexions with Mr. M _ _ _ y and you will find him a British pensiner and agent."[57]

This was one of the first of a good many warnings that Jefferson got about Burr. A few weeks later another one came, in the form of a letter from Kentucky's Joseph Hamilton Daveiss. Daveiss was the commonwealth's federal district attorney and John Marshall's brother-in-law. The Marshalls were a strongly Federalist bunch; another of the chief justice's kinsmen, Humphrey Marshall, had led the West's charge against Blount and the threats of western separatists. Now Daveiss got into the act, warning Jefferson that Burr was plotting much the same thing with people out in Kentucky. At first Jefferson took some interest. "The information is so important that it is my duty to request a full communication of everything known or heard by you pertaining to it," he told Daveiss, "and particularly of the names of all persons whether engaged in the combination, or witness to any part of it." For the next few months Daveiss made a string of reports to the president, but Jefferson soon lost interest. A lot of the names that Daveiss mentioned were those of good Republicans, which is one reason why Jefferson let the whole thing go, at least according to some.[58]

Jefferson let other things go as well that year, and they later came back and bit him. North Americans weren't alone in trying to free the New World from Spanish control. Francisco Miranda, the cultured, well-traveled Venezuelan, made Latin-American liberation his life's goal. He had toured both Europe and the United States; he had friends on both sides of the Atlantic. Even as Charles Williamson and Anthony Merry were talking to London about British backing, so, too, was Miranda. He wanted to give Venezuela its freedom, and for that he needed the usual: men and supplies, weapons and ships. Whitehall said no. So Miranda decided to try the United States.

He arrived in early November, just when Burr was returning from the West. He began outfitting ships in New York, paid for by New

York investors. He wanted his people's independence; the investors wanted new markets. The match was a natural. Miranda also wanted official assistance. In December he met with James Madison, and at about the same time he dined with Jefferson. Although what he wanted was government help, Madison told him that he wasn't going to get it. That being the case, Miranda tried for something else. He wanted the government to look the other way while he launched his expedition.

Jefferson, though an expansionist, preferred to win new lands without force of arms. "Peace is our passion," he had written at the time of the Louisiana Purchase. The French minister in Washington, General Louis Marie Turreau, put it more cynically. Jefferson's policy, he wrote, was "to conquer without war."[59] Not that Jefferson was opposed to force; for most of 1805 and much of 1806, he danced on the edge with Spain. He bristled whenever Spanish patrols skirted near New Orleans. His December 1805 Congressional message was a belligerent one. The Spanish intended, he told the Congressmen, "to advance on our possessions until they shall be repressed by an opposing force. . . . The protection of our citizens, the spirit and honor of our country, require that force should be interposed to a certain degree."[60] He knew, though, that bloodless conquest was less expensive and good for business when it was an option. Better to take advantage of the death struggle between England and France by going after Spain, the Sick Man of the Americas, without a war than by making a misstep and bringing the wrath of the British fleet or Napoleon down around his ears. What was more, Americans could get rich from neutrality in the Anglo-French war. Miranda saw a hint of this during one of his Washington interviews. "We will feed them all while they fight," Jefferson told him. "If they pay for it," a cabinet member added. "To be sure," agreed Jefferson.[61]

But neutrality had its own price. The United States must adhere to the rules of international law that governed neutral countries, and enforce its own laws as well. One of the latter was the Neutrality Act, enacted in the wake of Genêt. It barred American citizens, and everyone else, from setting out from United States territory to attack another country at peace with the young republic. Miranda was planning to break this law, and he wanted a wink and a nod from the government. Going by what he told others, he got it. Just before Christmas, two vessels packed with contraband weapons put out to sea from

New York, headed for the Caribbean, and Miranda followed them in a larger ship, the eighteen-gun *Leander,* in early February.[62]

Within days of hearing the news, Jefferson ordered a criminal investigation. Before long the government indicted two men for violating the Neutrality Act: investor Samuel G. Ogden and New York Port Surveyor William S. Smith. Jefferson went ahead and fired Smith even before the indictments came down. Based on the president's reactions, Miranda either was wrong in thinking he had his backing or else didn't mind misleading others. But during the trials the defendants subpoenaed Madison and the other department heads, trying to get the whole story, insofar as there was a story to get. Nothing came of the effort. The department heads were scattered around the country by then while Congress was in recess. Treasury Secretary Albert Gallatin did take time to observe that a defendant could paralyze the entire federal government by forcing executive branch high officials to participate in a criminal trial.

As it turned out, the cabinet officers' help wasn't needed. Ogden and Smith won acquittals, largely, claimed Jefferson, because the marshal had packed the jury with Federalists. The marshal's name was John Swartwout. He was one of the handful of people whom Jefferson had appointed at Burr's request back when Burr had become vice president. Jefferson now fixed what had obviously been a mistake: he fired Swartwout too.

The president's enemies, including the press, clamored that Jefferson had gone back on his word to Miranda. That was unfair. Jefferson had given him no word to keep. But critics claimed that silence had been consent. Jefferson learned a hard lesson that spring. Inaction and action were one and the same to the public. By not disavowing Miranda up front, Jefferson seemed to the people to give his support. He wouldn't forget the lesson, but it took a while to sink in.[63]

⁂

Jefferson and Madison weren't the only ones to meet with Miranda. Burr ran across him in late 1805, when both were in Philadelphia. "Detestable" was how Miranda described him. As for Burr, he saw Miranda as a competitor, probably envying him his resources, most of which came from his own home state. "The bare suspicion of any connexion between him and me would have been injurious to my project and fatal to his," he later wrote.[64] Instead of getting all tangled up with Miranda, then, Burr busied himself with pushing the British for a decision as to whether they would back him. In late November of 1805 he saw Anthony Merry again. Now his price had gone up. Merry told London that he was asking for "two or three Ships of the Line—the same Number of Frigates and a proportionable Number of smaller Vessels" to conquer Louisiana and the Floridas too. And of course there was the matter of money. "According to an estimate he had made," Merry reported, "he could not do without a loan of one hundred & ten thousand Pounds." In New Orleans Daniel Clark was to be able to draw on the funds. In return Burr promised much, harping on the small arms and artillery that he had found stashed around the Western Country and mentioning all of the "persons of the greatest property and influence" whose support he had won. It was a strong pitch, but in the middle of it Burr slammed into a brick wall. The British minister had to tell him that he had no word from the Foreign Office, after reporting on Burr's plans for more than a year. This was a crushing blow. Without money and command of the sea, conquest would be difficult, whatever Burr's target of choice. He asked Merry to try again, and Merry agreed.[65]

At about this same time, Burr had a meeting with Jefferson. Neither ever said what took place, but probably Burr was fishing for information. Jefferson had no reason to give it, but Burr probably learned that tensions with Spain seemed to be easing. This was good news for Jefferson and bad news for Burr. During a Spanish-American war, filibustering would be patriotic. In peacetime it was a crime. With less chance of a war and no word of support from England, Burr had to rethink his plans.

First was the ever-present problem with money. Whitehall's long silence warned Burr that he might never get an answer at all. He would need other sources, then. As luck would have it, he received word in early 1806 from his new friend Harman Blennerhassett, with whom he had been corresponding. Blennerhassett was no longer rich, but perhaps his credit was good, and he offered Burr all that he had. "I hope, sir," he said, choosing his words with care, "you will not regard it indelicate of me to observe to you how highly I should be honored in being associated with you, in any contemplated enterprise you would permit me to participate in." From other comments he made, the "enterprise" would seem to have been Mexico, or possibly the Floridas. He felt sure that the country would call on Burr's talents if war with Spain broke out, and he wanted to be there for Burr when it did. "I shall await with much anxiety the receipt of your reply," he closed. Burr had the man hooked.[66]

Burr roped in his own son-in-law, too. The Alstons were not merely adventurers—they were rich ones. Theodosia's husband Joseph was a wealthy man, and his political career was hitting its stride. Now in his late twenties, he was a member of the South Carolina legislature; in 1812 he would become governor. Before long Burr had gotten commitments from Alston, commitments of about $50,000.[67]

Burr even tried to shake down the *Spanish* government. Now the tale grows fantastic. In early December his good friend Jonathan Dayton approached Carlos Martinez de Yrujo. He told the pompous Spanish minister nearly everything—the conversations with Merry, the Mexico and Florida plans, all that Burr had spoken of to his various listeners. Burr later said that the idea was to lay a smokescreen.[68] Yrujo was a perennial thorn in America's side, but he had good connections. He could read the papers as well as anyone else, and he may even have been the one behind some of the early rumors. Dayton wasn't giving away any secrets. His goal was to make Yrujo think that Burr had abandoned his plans of invading New Spain. Obviously Dayton and Burr wouldn't be asking Yrujo for money to help overthrow his own empire. Instead Dayton planted a new idea in Yrujo's mind, telling the minister that Burr's goal was not just Western secession, but something still more ambitious: the capture of Washington, D.C.

Yrujo listened, spellbound, as Dayton sketched out the plans. Burr was currying favor among friends. He would use them to infiltrate the city. When the word came, Burr's men, heavily armed, would seize Jefferson, the banks, and the arsenal too. Burr would then dictate a peace to the state governments, and if he ran into trouble he could get to the navy yard with the funds from the banks and sail for New Orleans, which he would then lead to independence. The Union's power would be broken, and New Spain would be safe. All that Burr needed to make it happen was . . . money, money from the Spanish Crown.

Yrujo bought it. He wrote his masters in Madrid, trumpeting the coming "dismemberment of the colossal power which was growing at the very gates" of Spain's New World empire.[69] He even gave Dayton and Burr a few thousand dollars to get the ball rolling. But Madrid saw things in a different light. The whole story was too wild to be true. Dayton and Burr were playing Yrujo, playing him like a flute, or so it would seem—except for one thing. Burr approached several others with almost exactly the same story, and the men he approached were warriors, the men whose skills of violence he would need to do what he was threatening.

About the same time as Dayton was courting Yrujo, Burr fell in with General William Eaton. Eaton was quite a character. He was the original Lawrence of Arabia, even more so than T. E. Lawrence himself, with more than a touch of James Bond thrown in. He first began his climb to fame in the West in the 1790s, where he had fought under General "Mad Anthony" Wayne in the Battle of Fallen Timbers. Then he moved on to Georgia on special orders from the secretary of war to keep an eye on the unsteady three-way border of the Creek Indian Nation, Spanish Florida, and Georgia. He had orders to pay special attention to the hotheaded Georgians, who seemed ready to invade both of the other two. He was something of a spy, refusing to tell the local militia commander what he was really up to. While he was on the border, his commanding officer court-martialed him for profiteering. Eaton went over his head and took his case to the secretary of war. Timothy Pickering, in charge of War and later State, had taken him in hand, and for a time he became the arch-Federalist's special agent. When Blount's scheme exploded in 1797, Pickering gave Eaton the job of capturing one of Blount's top men in New York, which he did with daring and flair. He made midnight rides, military arrests of civilians, and break-ins of doubtful legality, all of which he pulled off like a pro. Afterward he found himself on his way to the troubled North African shore, where he spent the next few years as a one-man C.I.A., toppling unfriendly governments, propping up pro-U.S. rulers, marching cutthroat armies hired in Egyptian back alleys across the vast North African deserts, becoming a national hero—and running up huge bills in the process. In 1805 he returned to America, where Congress snubbed his demands for reimbursement. That got Eaton angry, as angry as Truxtun, and that made him a good target for Burr.[70]

They talked all winter long. Burr could see that Eaton resented the government, and he played on that theme. He told Eaton of his designs on Mexico, and on the Mississippi Valley as well. He even told Eaton his plans for Washington, and Eaton later described them. "If he could gain the marine corps, and secure to his interests the naval commanders, Truxtun, Preble, and Decatur, he would turn

Congress neck and heels out of doors, assassinate the President . . .
and declare himself the protector of an energetic Government." Eaton
objected. The country wouldn't stand for it, he insisted. Burr answered
that "he knew better the dispositions of the principal citizens of the
United States than I did." Eaton wasn't convinced; the label "usurper"
would destroy Burr, he warned. "He smiled at my want of confidence," Eaton recalled, but still the general fought him. Even if the
plan worked at first, he couldn't take on the whole nation. "If he
should succeed at the seat of government," he warned the former vice
president, "his throat would be cut in six weeks by Yankee militia."[71]

But then Eaton quit objecting. He decided to win Burr's confidence by pretending to go along with him. The plan worked; Burr
kept on talking.

Burr talked to Thomas Truxtun, too, but more about Mexico than
about Washington. Burr was starting to give up on the British fleet
he had tried to get, and he had to have sea power if his plans in the
Gulf were going to work. Burr now talked of reconnoitering Carta-
jena and Vera Cruz, and got his friend to speculate on Havana's vul-
nerability. Finally he asked Truxtun flat out if he would be willing to
command a naval expedition for him. "I asked him if the Executive of
the United States was privy to or concerned in the project," Truxtun
asked Burr in return. "He answered me, emphatically, that they were
not. . . . I told Mr. Burr that I would have nothing to do with it." Burr
kept on going, observing "that in the event of a war he intended to
establish an independent Government in Mexico; that Wilkinson, the
army, and many officers of the navy, would join. I replied, that I
could not see how any of the officers of the United States could join.
He said that general Wilkinson had projected that expedition, and
that he himself had matured it; that many greater men than Wilkinson were concerned, or would join; and thousands to the westward."
Truxtun still said no.[72]

Burr also went after western officers. Despite what he said to
Truxtun, he often told others, or let them believe, that he would have
government backing. Blennerhassett was one of these. Another was
Edward Tupper, an Ohio militia general whom Burr had met while
making his western tour. Near the end of 1805 Tupper wrote him to
offer his services if war broke out with Spain. Spanish-American tensions were still high enough to make a war likely and Burr's official

involvement possible, at least in the eyes of people who didn't know better. Burr wrote back and asked Tupper to consider raising a regiment for use against the Floridas.[73] At about this same time he wrote Andrew Jackson with exactly the same request. He asked the Tennessee general for a list of the names of his chosen officers. "I will send it to the Department of War," he promised, "and believe my advice would be listened to."[74] He had said as much to Tupper. Maybe he even believed it. This was about the time of his autumn visit with Jefferson. But despite all of the contacts and all of the talk, things were looking grim for him.

Despite Jefferson's warlike message of December 1805, an uneasy peace continued to rule. Small border marches and skirmishes flickered along the Sabine like the soldiers' nighttime campfires, but that was as far as things went. That was bad news for Burr. "We are to have no war with Spain, except in ink and words," he wrote at the turn of the year.[75]

Even worse news was the silence from England. Burr talked a good game with everyone from Merry to Eaton, but he couldn't move without money. Money was probably the main thing he was after, whatever wild plans he came up with. He had originally planned to head back west in the spring of 1806, but as the equinox came and went, everything but his mouth was on hold. In the middle of April he wrote Wilkinson in dismay. "The execution of our project is postponed till December," he said. "Want of water in Ohio rendered movement that way impracticable."[76] Things looked so bad that Burr even began fishing for a federal job again (fat chance *that* was). That spring he met with Jefferson for what turned out to be the last time. He reminded Jefferson of his offer, way back in 1800, to give up his try for the presidency if Jefferson would agree to give him a major appointment, perhaps as minister to Paris or the Court of St. James, or even cabinet rank. Then he moved on to threats. He said, recalled Jefferson, "that he could do me much harm; he wished, however, to be on different ground; he was now disengaged from all particular business—willing to engage in something—should be in town some days, if I should have anything to propose to him." Jefferson could read newspapers as well as anyone else. He knew the rumors. He knew that Burr had been busy out west. Burr's threat hung in the air around him. But he didn't give in. He told Burr that he must know that "the public had withdrawn their confidence from him," and that in light of that fact an appointment was out of the question.[77] Burr left the president's mansion having gained nothing at all, but having had nothing to lose.

Burr also threatened Merry. As the spring of 1806 turned to summer, the two had their final meeting. Still no news from England for Burr, the British minister told him, and the conspirator "lamented exceedingly that I had not, because he and the persons connected with him at New Orleans would now, though very reluctantly, be under the necessity of addressing themselves to the French and Spanish Governments." More hot air, perhaps. But as far as Merry could tell, Burr seemed dead set on tearing the West from the Union. English assistance or not, the attempt was going to happen. "His last words," Merry reported, were that "with or without such support it certainly would be made very shortly."[78]

Of course Burr had a fallback. That spring and summer, he arranged to buy a third of a million acres of land in the Washita River Valley, which lay in the southern reaches of Louisiana, to the west of the Mississippi. Clouds had surrounded the title for years. A decade earlier a Hollander, Baron de Bastrop, got the land from the Spanish Crown, well before Napoleon bought or sold Louisiana, which complicated things. Burr had probably heard of the place during his first trip in the West. Now he set about buying it. Whatever might happen with Spain and the boundary dispute, the lands would still be there, waiting for settlement and development, offering a fresh start, and lying close to New Orleans and the Texas and Florida borders. "This much I will tell you," he supposedly told Senator John Smith later in 1806, "if there should be a war between the United States and Spain, I shall head a corps of volunteers and be the first to march into the Mexican provinces. If peace should be proffered . . . I shall settle my Washita lands, and make society as pleasant as possible."[79]

Then, in April, amid the long string of setbacks, the moment arrived. In mid-March a small Spanish army moved up from Texas and passed the disputed Louisiana border. The soldiers took up a position just a few miles from the westernmost American settlements and well to the Sabine's east. A smaller group had been there before, and U.S. troops pushed them out. Now, less than a month later, they were back in force, more than six hundred, a sizable frontier army.[80]

By late April, Washington had the news, and so did Burr. Jefferson decided to show that he would not back down. Soon the orders were going out to reinforce the American station at Nachitoches on Louisiana's southwestern border, for deploying troops and gunboats to New Orleans, and finally for General Wilkinson to get from St. Louis to the trouble zone "with as little delay as possible." If the Spanish meant business, so, too, did Jefferson.[81]

As Burr got wind of these things, he started gearing up fast. He redoubled his recruitment and funding attempts. He flitted between Philadelphia and Washington, letting more friends in on his plans. He contacted Yrujo again, this time directly, and in June came his final threatening visit with Merry. Yrujo's answer was the same as the British minister's; he could not offer support. Burr was dismayed but undeterred. He found lieutenants. He wrote Blennerhassett, telling him that he was on his way. He sent several agents to New Orleans by sea, to keep the Mexican Association in the loop. Now, more than ever, a single spark would do it.

Dayton was busy, too. Of all of Burr's contacts, he knew the most about what the man planned, and he was the most committed to it. Rumors were afoot about Wilkinson, and in July Dayton wrote him. "It is now well ascertained," he told the general, "that you are to be displaced next session." (It wasn't.) "Prepare yourself, therefore, for it. You know the rest. You are not a man of despair, or even despond, especially when such prospects offer in another quarter. Are you ready? Are your numerous associates ready? Wealth and glory! Louisiana and Mexico!"[82]

The rumblings were getting too loud for Washington to ignore, but ignore them it did. Maybe it was because so many conspiracies had flared up and faded along the frontier for so long. Most had just been a torrent of talk. But this time things were different. War had never been so close, not in twenty years, and the frontier never so ready and crowded. Burr's plans were no secret. The only problem lay in figuring out which of them he intended to execute. By July, Jefferson had been getting warnings for months, in addition to reading the papers. Even William Eaton tried to alert the president. After his discussions with Burr he had gone to see Jefferson and advised him to appoint Burr to London, Madrid, or Paris as a means of getting him out of the way. "I thought colonel Burr ought to be removed from the country," he explained, "because I considered him dangerous in it." Maybe Eaton was doing the patriotic thing, or maybe he was on an errand from Burr, for his suggestion resembled the one that Burr himself had made to Jefferson. Eaton swore that "it was through no attachment to him that I made that suggestion, but to avert a great national calamity which I saw approaching; to arrest a tempest which seemed lowering in the West; and to divert into a channel of usefulness those consummate talents, which were to mount 'the whirlwind and direct the storm.' " Whatever side that Eaton was on, he was still a portent of danger, yet Jefferson did nothing other than to tell him blandly that such posts were too important for the likes of Burr.[83]

Yrujo did something, though. He may not have been sure what Burr was going to do, but he figured that whatever it was, it would be bad for Spain. Whether or not Burr pulled off western independence, the American West was a threat to Texas and Florida, and maybe Mexico. As Burr made his final arrangements, the Spanish minister sent to Madrid for a secret agent who could follow Burr's movements. Soon José Vidal was on his way to America in response to the minister's summons. The chase was about to begin.[84]

By the summer of 1806, Aaron Burr had done all he could with the few resources he had. Blennerhassett, Alston, and a handful of others had backed him financially as best they could. England and Spain had said no. But he felt that he knew the frontiersmen. Burr liked to talk of history, to compare what he was about to do to mankind's past moments when new empires came into being. He surely recalled what an angry mob had managed to do when it stormed the Bastille not long before, and the days of Concord and Lexington. These things weren't delusions; they were current events. Burr had lived some of them himself. But whatever his thoughts were about, they clearly involved the West, where people were ready for conquest and war. Those feelings were his strongest resource. They were almost all that he had, but they could easily be all that he needed. Just scant years ago they had created the United States, had beheaded a king, had spawned Napoleon's empire, had plunged all of Europe into the greatest war that it had known in two thousand years and more. What might they do along the frontier, the heart of North America, where government was thousands of miles distant and fortune favored the bold?

In late August he set out from Philadelphia, headed once more for Pittsburgh and the Ohio's headwaters. The planning was over. The execution was about to begin. A few weeks later Vidal arrived from Spain and followed him into the heart of the West. And all the while in Washington, Thomas Jefferson did nothing.

Part Four

The Execution

*W*ilkinson was in a tight spot.

In Nachitoches in October 1806, he had a Spanish army in his front, civilian hotheads to his rear, and bloodthirsty officers at his side, all of them itching to fight. He couldn't even begin to decide where to start sorting everything out.

His troubles had started when he'd received orders from Secretary of War Henry Dearborn. The Spanish were threatening New Orleans, Dearborn had told him, and Wilkinson had to stop them. "You will . . . take upon yourself the command of troops in that quarter," Dearborn ordered the general. "You will, by all the means in your power, repel any invasion of the territory of the United States east of the river Sabine, or north, or west of the bounds of what has been called West Florida."[1]

When Wilkinson had gotten these orders in mid-June,[2] he was in St. Louis, and he was reluctant to leave its comforts for the wilds of western Louisiana and the woes that it promised. Dearborn had told him to get moving "with as little delay as practicable," but Wilkinson took his own sweet time. Meanwhile, down south things were cooking along. Don Antonio Cordero, the Spanish captain-general in charge of Texas and points north, was pushing things to the limit, as was Colonel Simon de Herrera, the senior officer with the army on the Sabine. Herrera had troops well to the river's east a lot of the time, and that was provoking American forces.[3] "If you should attempt to continue these troops within the territory of the United States," had warned Colonel Thomas Cushing, the U.S. commander on the ground before Wilkinson arrived on the Sabine, "it will be my duty to consider you as an invader of our territory, and to act accordingly."[4]

In New Orleans, Governor Claiborne wasn't helping. He sent his own warning to Herrera. "If the officers of Spain should persist in their acts of aggression," he growled, "your excellency will readily anticipate the consequences; and if the sword must be drawn, let those be responsible whose unfriendly conduct has rendered it indispensable."[5] Claiborne obviously meant the Spanish, but he should have looked to the beam in his own eye. It takes two to tango, though, and the Spanish seemed willing. Wilkinson knew something about Herrera. Cordero had ordered him east, and Wilkinson said that "if the Spaniard possesses a drop of true Castilian blood, he will not recede from his avowed orders and solemn determination."[6] Nobody would back down, in short; war was all but certain.

In mid-September Wilkinson had finally reached Nachitoches and begun to take stock of the situation. He had men, but supplies were low. The Spanish were barely fifteen miles away, and they were mounted. They had no artillery. But they could move faster than he, in attack or retreat. Reinforcements were moving up from a Texas town better known then as Béxar and now as San Antonio. Things were going badly.

Wilkinson had no problem with the idea of conquest. Just a few weeks before, in July, he had ordered Lieutenant Zebulon Pike into the western wilderness, far into New Spain, on an errand much like Lewis and Clark's, to explore the Red and Arkansas Rivers all the way to their headwaters. While Pike was at it, he was to reconnoiter Santa Fe, and to report on anything of military interest. Such news would be useful for invaders.[7]

But outright war would be bad, not just for Spain and the United States, but for Wilkinson too. He was still a Spanish pensioner, an important source of intelligence whom most Madrid insiders knew only as Agent Number 13. The Spanish would not take kindly to his biting the hand that fed him. They weren't paying him to make war on them. For that matter, the United States government wasn't paying him to commit treason. Payment: *that* was the common theme with Wilkinson. Duty was fine, as long as it paid. And right this minute he was having trouble serving two masters. He was about to disappoint one of them—he didn't know which one just yet—and he would soon be the poorer for it.

As if all this weren't enough, he had the problem of Burr to consider. He thought a lot about Burr, maybe too much, maybe even now, on this early October day when he sat at Colonel Cushing's table discussing the latest Spanish movements. Burr had pushed him for months to launch an invasion of Mexico, an invasion that Wilkinson had been longing to make. The general was still considering it, if war should erupt. "A blow once struck," he advised Dearborn, "we should make every advantage of it, and if men and means are furnished, I will soon plant our standard on the left bank of the Grand River."[8] If war did break out, however, where would Burr fit in? He hadn't found much backing so far, at least not that Wilkinson knew, though he had heard little from the New Yorker in the past several weeks. In the spring he had asked Burr about the lack of funds. "What has become of the grand expedition?" he asked Burr. "I fear Miranda has taken the bread out of your mouth. I shall be ready before you."[9] What good were Burr and his vaunted eastern connections if he couldn't bring in the British or deliver the money? Without them he was useless.

And he couldn't stop worrying about his wife. Ann was a frail woman, too frail for this rough frontier life, though she had always been game. She would have been better off if she had stayed in Philadelphia instead of marrying him and coming out west. Now she was deathly ill, hovering "over the grave" as he put it,[10] so that on top of everything else, with all that he had to consider, the Spanish, the would-be filibusters, the battle that was about to start, he couldn't get her out of his mind. . . .

A brawny young man with a shock of blond hair entered the room, interrupting Wilkinson's thoughts. He asked to see Colonel Cushing, and Cushing arose to greet the newcomer, who handed him a letter. It was a message from Jonathan Dayton, introducing two men, Samuel Swartwout and Peter V. Ogden. The bearer then identified himself as Swartwout. He was the younger brother of John Swartwout, the New York federal marshal and loyal Burr supporter whom Jefferson had recently fired.

Cushing introduced Swartwout to Wilkinson, and the three men sat down at the table. Swartwout explained that he had come from New York to volunteer to fight the Spanish. The talk turned to other things too, most of them mundane, some of them about Swartwout's business dealings in New Orleans. Then Cushing was summoned away for a while, leaving Swartwout alone with Wilkinson.

They only had a few minutes. Swartwout pulled a sealed envelope from his pocket and handed it to the general, telling him that it was from Burr. Burr? Where was he? Wilkinson asked. Philadelphia, Swartwout answered, or at least that was where he had been in late July when he had given Swartwout this letter. At that moment Cushing returned and Swartwout changed the subject. He eventually left Cushing's, and so did Wilkinson.[11]

That evening, back in his own quarters, Wilkinson opened the envelope that Swartwout had given him. He found a letter written in cipher. The system was fairly simple, and fairly common too, using the 1800 edition of Entick's *New Spelling Dictionary* as the key.[12] A lot of people used such codes for confidential messages. Burr and Wilkinson had established their system a few years earlier. But the fact that Burr had used a cipher at all for this letter showed without doubt that this was only for Wilkinson's eyes. Since Burr had talked so openly to so many people about so many dangerous things, whatever this message contained had to be *really* dangerous.

Wilkinson set about deciphering it. Now and then the words gave him some trouble, but gradually the meaning grew clear. As the message formed on the page, Wilkinson realized that everything in the West was about to change completely. He started to read this amazing, extraordinary letter. "I have at length obtained funds," it began, "and have actually commenced . . . ."[13]

~

Aaron Burr rode down a trail in western Pennsylvania, chatting eagerly with the little group riding with him. On this fine August day, two months before Wilkinson's receipt of his letter, great things were happening. To the east of the mountains' high wall in New York, one of his chief lieutenants, a shady character named Comfort Tyler, was gathering men and buying supplies. Burr had lined up a Pittsburgh merchant to deliver more goods before long. Another staff member of his, the French colonel Julien de Pestre, was riding alongside him here on the road from Pittsburgh as he scouted around for new talent. Burr had written Blennerhassett that he was on the way to his island; but first he had this detour to make so he could drop in on an old friend.[14]

George Morgan was a former comrade-in-arms, and a former client too. Since the end of the war with the British he had retired to the West, to Washington County, so far into Pennsylvania that he was nearly in Ohio. He had worked for a time with the Spanish, founding the town of New Madrid on the Mississippi's far bank, but now he was happy to stay at Morganza, his country home outside Pittsburgh. Morganza was where Burr was now heading, in the company of Morgan's sons John and Tom. John, the elder, was also an officer, a New

Jersey militia general, and that had drawn Burr's attention. He soon sent up a trial balloon, remarking that the Union was bound to break up one day. Then he started to ask pointed questions about the Washington County militia. All of it came as a surprise to John.

George Morgan was proud of Morganza. With Burr and de Pestre on hand, he was getting to show it off. The conversation stayed lively at the midday meal, and Morgan began getting expansive, dreaming of what the West would become. "After dinner," he later recalled, "I spoke of our fine country. I observed, that when I first went there, there was not a single family between the Allegheny mountains and the Ohio; and that by and by we should have Congress sitting in this neighborhood, or at Pittsburgh." Burr's reaction was strong. "No, never," he said, "for in less than five years, you will be totally divided from the Atlantic states." He referred to the taxes the realms of the West had to pay for the privilege of being colonies, and he asked why it should have to pay them. "Great numbers were not necessary to execute great military deeds," he argued. Westerners could free themselves. "All that was wanting was a leader in whom they could place confidence, and who they believed could carry them through." The Union was bound to break up.

"God forbid!" answered Morgan. "I hope no such things would ever happen, at least in my time."

But Burr kept going. "With five hundred men," he claimed, "New-York could be taken . . . with two hundred, Congress could be driven into the Potomac River." De Pestre nodded; it could be done.

That was enough for John Morgan. "I'll be damned, sir," he snapped, "if you could take the little town of Cannonsburg with that force." Burr kept his cool. "Confine yourself to this side of the mountains and I'll not contradict you," he told the westerner.

Things were getting uncomfortable. Having a killer as guest was bad enough, but having a traitor was worse, and Burr was talking treason. Burr should have seen that the Morgans weren't happy, but he refused to let up. After his words with John, he left the room, but as he withdrew he caught Tom Morgan's eye and gestured with his head towards the door. Tom trailed after him. Once outside, Burr asked Tom what he planned to do with his life. Tom mentioned his law studies, but Burr was dismissive. He said, recalled Tom, that "he was sure I could not find employment for either body or mind." Tom didn't understand. "He said that under our government there was no encouragement for talents . . . . He asked me, how or whether I would like a military expedition or enterprise?" Tom was young, with a youngster's interest in battles and fame, but he had seen how his father and brother had acted when Aaron Burr started talking. "It would entirely depend upon the object or cause for which I was to fight," he said carefully.

The answer was not what Burr had expected or hoped for. "I wish you were on your way with me," he said, but then he stopped pushing Tom. He decided to try a different approach. Later that day he went with John and some others to see the Morgans' mill, apparently saying some things along the way. When the group came back, John went to his father and warned him. "You may depend upon it," he told him. "Colonel Burr will this night open himself to you. He wants Tom to go with him."

John was right. Evening fell, Burr retired, and most of the others went to bed too, but George stayed up to read with his wife. Later, around eleven, she heard Burr coming down the stairs. "You'll have it now," she warned her husband, and then Burr appeared, candle in hand, as she slipped off to her room.

Burr sat down next to Morgan, and drew a book from his pocket. He glanced through it for a moment—one can imagine those eyes of his, large and luminous in the firelight—and then he asked Morgan if he knew "a Mr. Vigo, of Fort Vincent, a Spaniard." Yes, answered Morgan, he knew him. Vigo had been part of a western plot in 1788 to break up the infant Union. Morgan had helped put an end to that plot. It was, he told Burr, "a nefarious thing to aim at the division of the states." Morgan was emphatic. "*Nefarious.*"

That brought Burr up short. He thrust the book into his pocket again and went back to his room, leaving his host in the dark.

Burr had struck out with Tom and with George, but the next day he tried John one last time. The young general went with him as far as little Washington, near Pittsburgh, and took a walk with him there. The talk kept turning to martial affairs. "Colonel Burr asked me," said John, "if I thought I could raise a regiment in Washington county; or whether I could raise one with more facility in New Jersey." John's answer went unrecorded.

Washington was the home of David Bradford, one of the leaders of the Whiskey Rebellion. That had been twelve years ago, but people remembered it well. It was just the sort of western uprising that Burr kept talking about, an armed western protest against federal taxation. Burr said that he knew several men who had been in on that uprising. One of them, he said, had once told him "that if he were ever engaged in another business of the kind, he pledged himself it should not end without bloodshed." Burr spoke of that talk with approval. "A fine fellow," he called the man, and with that he was on his way.

That clinched it for John. "It was on these circumstances," he said, "that I advised my father to apprise the president of the United States that something was going on." On August 29, George Morgan wrote to President Jefferson.[15]

⚜

Before long Burr was on Blennerhassett's Island again. The tempo was picking up. He was making deals with merchants, setting men to grinding corn, recruiting adventurers left and right. Some of his plans revolved around the Washita lands, but not all of them, to hear him talk. He held conversations with Blennerhassett; soon his host was writing newspaper columns, under the name of Querist, suggesting the breakaway of the West and talking of marching to Mexico.

That seemed fine with Burr. The time was ripe for publicity. The valley was abuzz with rumors; so much the better for recruitment attempts. Burr gave no signs, just yet, that all of the gossip bothered him. He himself kept talking to friends, and they kept on talking in turn. He had established headquarters of sorts in Lexington, where Theodosia and Joseph Alston came to stay for a while, but he was on the move all the time. By early September he was downriver in Cincinnati, staying with his friend Senator Smith. A week later he moved inland to Frankfort for a visit with Senator Brown. Then it was on to Nashville to renew his acquaintance with General Jackson.

Jackson and Burr had something in common; they were fellow duelists. If Burr's bloody battle with Hamilton is the most famous duel in American history, Jackson's fight with Charles Dickinson is probably the second most famous, the western counterpart to the Weehawken duel. It had happened in the spring of 1806, just a few months before Burr's second visit to Nashville. It started over a horse race between Jackson's prized Truxtun and another well-known steed. At the last minute the challenger went lame and backed out, and soon ugly things got said, first about gambling debts, then about wives, and finally about honor and cowardice. It ended with an over-dose of testosterone and a shooting match at twenty-four feet.

Jackson took a hit square in the chest and then calmly took aim at Dickinson. "Great God! Have I missed him?" Dickinson yelled in shocked disbelief, backing away from Jackson. "Back to your MARK, sir!" Jackson's second shouted, and then Jackson gunned Dickinson down. The bullet lodged next to Jackson's heart held no power over his will. Fearless, and almost invulnerable: here was a man Burr could use. And Jackson had other qualifications as well.

In any list of expansionists, Jackson's name stands at the top. He had wanted revenge on the Spanish for years, had wanted to push them back and make Texas and the Floridas United States provinces beyond any possible question. Anyone who knew him knew that, too. Jackson was ready to go. Now here was Burr in Nashville again, telling Jackson what he wanted to hear about the hated Dons, and making arrangements in Tennessee. He was just as popular, just as honored, as he had been when he was here before. In between the balls and the visits, he talked a lot with Jackson. Giving the general thirty-five hun-dred dollars, he asked for five riverboats, and Jackson obliged him. Before long the lanky Tennessean had engaged a business partner to build the boats and gather the supplies Burr had ordered. As for Jack-son, he himself took care of supplying the men whom Burr would need before long. He issued a proclamation to his militia forces, put-ting them on alert. "The late conduct of the Spanish government," he wrote, "added to the Hostile appearance & menacing attitude of their armed forces, already incamped within the limits of our government, make it necessary that the militia under my command, should be in complete order & at a moment's warning ready to march."[16]

Jackson could barely restrain himself. He wrote with greed of a strike against Santa Fe and Mexico, of the conquest of East and West Florida and "all Spanish North America." It would all be terrific fun. The war that was about to start, he wrote, "will be a handsome theatre for our enterprising young men, and a certain source of acquiring fame."[17] Not just fame for his soldiers; fame for himself as well. No one, not Burr, not even Wilkinson, wanted it more than Jackson did. But they were less particular than he as to exactly how they got it. War was one thing; treason was another, at least for Jackson. He had no problem with invading other countries. He did it more than once, and under shady circumstances. But treason? Separating the West from the Union? That was out of the question. At least he said it was. "I hate the Dons," he frankly confessed. "I would delight to see Mexico reduced, but I will die in the last Ditch before I would yield a foot to the Dons or see the Union disunited."[18]

But Jackson wrote that in November, weeks after Burr's early fall visit. Well before he penned it, rumors were thick as flies. Jackson devoted most of his life to two overriding goals: American expansion and the Union's safety. But this former William Blount lieutenant was more than an American; he was a frontiersman. Perhaps that autumn was his life's defining moment, when he decided that disunion was wrong. Burr did lead Jackson to believe that his plan had War Department backing, and maybe somehow disunionist rumors hadn't reached him in Nashville. But whatever else may have been true, one thing is clear: he was helping Burr out for quite some time before he disavowed disunion. Burr was promising him his long-wished-for chance at the Dons, and maybe that was all that mattered.

But the rumors were getting hard *not* to hear, no matter how much people tried. As far away as the East Coast people were talking of the flotilla of gunboats that Burr was building along the Ohio and Cumberland. Gunboats, these sources said, not merely troopships. Stories were spreading of sharpshooters who would hold the Allegheny passes and prevent any federal meddling. Vidal, Yrujo's secret agent, reported to his master that he had found a hundred men under a colonel in Pittsburgh ready to head downriver and take Mexico.[19]

If the rumors were wild in the East, they were rampant in Kentucky. Before long John Smith was warning Burr from Cincinnati that things were out of control and asking him exactly what he was up to. He heard about what was going on upriver on the island. People saw all the hustle and bustle up there, and they didn't like what they saw. They were meeting and protesting, and Wood County, Virginia, which had jurisdiction, had called up its militia to defend against whatever might happen.[20] Smith was watching closely. "It is believed by many," he wrote to Burr, that your design is to dismember the Union. . . . I must confess, from the mystery and rapidity of your movements, that I have fears, let your object be what it may, that the tranquillity of the country will be interrupted . . . ."[21]

Clearly Burr hadn't told Senator Smith his story about disunion, and he didn't do so now. "I was greatly surprised and really hurt by the unusual tenor of your letter," he shot back. "If there exists any design to separate the Western from the Eastern States, I am totally ignorant of it; I never harbored or expressed any such intention to any one . . . ."[22] That was a lie. Maybe Washita *was* now his goal, but he had been saying otherwise. And even now Blennerhassett kept talking of Mexico, or even a march on Washington. Maybe Burr really had changed his plans, but maybe he was blowing more smoke. That was the problem; his stories were confusing, his actions ambiguous. No one knew, for sure, just what was happening, except for Aaron Burr.

But many people thought they knew, and one of them was Joseph Hamilton Daveiss, Kentucky's U.S. attorney. Daveiss had smelled something wrong a year earlier, and he'd tried then to warn the president. Jefferson had asked him for further reports. He could prove that. But his subsequent letters went without answer, while weeks became months and Burr kept on working.

The silence was bothering Daveiss. He started to fear that someone had intercepted his letters somewhere on the wild western roads; but he feared even more that they had made it through to Jefferson, and that the president was ignoring them. He was, after all, a Republican, and Daveiss a Federalist. The attorney wanted to know what was up. In July he sent a letter by private hand to Jefferson. Still no answer came, and now Daveiss knew for sure. The president was his enemy. "He saw that I now understood him," he explained the following year. "He hates every man on earth, who he thinks fully understands him."[23]

Angry, afraid, Daveiss now wrote to James Madison. "It is my duty, as a citizen," he told the secretary of state, "to support my government in a matter of this nature, and to communicate all I may hear or know about it: of this I am determined to acquit myself, no matter what regard the government may give it." That letter brought results. Daveiss soon had a terse letter from Monticello. Jefferson acknowledged receiving all of Daveiss's reports, but he suggested no action, disclosed no intelligence, and gave no hint that he was taking any steps.[24]

"Good God!" burst out Daveiss at this. "Was ever anything so astonishing! So unaccountable!" He now knew he had no backup, but he knew too that he had to stop Burr. He figured that Wilkinson was in on the plan, and as for the militia, as far as he knew, it might defect en masse to Burr. So force was out of the question. Daveiss thus turned to the only weapon he had, the power of the law.

On November 5 he went after the New Yorker in court, but even here he faced some tough going. First was the fact that he could not prosecute Burr for trying to break up the Union. Nothing on the statute books, as far as he could tell, made such a thing a crime. He had to settle for charging Burr with violating the federal Neutrality Act by preparing to invade New Spain. Even so, he tried to cast as wide a net as possible in the words of his complaint. "Burr seems to conceal in great mystery, from the people at large, his purposes and projects," he alleged in the charges.[25]

On December 2 Aaron Burr came unbidden into court, accompanied by lawyer Henry Clay. Here he was at the bar for all to see, ready to try to defend himself. Daveiss had a grand jury, but he couldn't find the key witness. He wanted to put Davis Floyd in front of the jurors. Floyd was one of Burr's major suppliers, his quartermaster, in fact, and his evidence would go far to show that Burr was building up stores enough to feed and equip a small army. But Floyd was far away in Vincennes just then. Without him Daveiss's case was weak, and he was afraid to go forward. "The scheme would gather strength by a failure," he thought, "so the jury was discharged."

A week or so later Daveiss got word that Floyd had returned to Kentucky, so he summoned another grand jury, this time filing complaints against Burr and his friend John Adair, who had just recently left the United States Senate. Burr was in Louisville when he got the news, and he asked for Clay's help again.

Henry Clay, though still in his twenties, was one of the state's brightest young stars. He had just been elected to serve out the rest of Adair's U.S. Senate term, and his life was about to get busy. But Burr wanted and needed young Clay. "It would be disagreeable to me to form a new connection," he told the young hotshot. "I shall . . . insist on making a liberal pecuniary compensation," he added, trying to get the lawyer's attention. It wasn't merely a matter of time or money, though. Clay was now a senator, or he would be soon, and he worried about getting his hands dirty by representing a rumored secessionist or a possible pirate. He told Burr so. Clay had a great future ahead of him as a charmer and an attorney, but Burr was already a master at both; Clay's youth and virtue were no match for Burr's age and treachery, and now Burr started to use them. The client wrote his counsel a vehement letter resembling the one he had sent to Smith. "I have no design, nor have I taken any measure," he said, "to promote a dissolution of the Union . . . I have no design to intermeddle with the Government or to disturb the tranquility of the United States . . . I have neither issued nor signed nor promised a commission to any person for any purpose. I do not own a musket nor a bayonet nor any single article of military stores." The litany of "nots" continued, and then he shifted ground. "My views have been fully explained to and approved by several of the principal officers of Government, and, I believe, are well understood by the Administration & seen by it with complacency. They are such as every man of honor & every good Citizen must approve."[26] Burr could be convincing. That was one of his strong suits. So Clay signed on again, and in early December the second round started.

Daveiss now had his grand jury, and he had his witness too. He didn't have Adair, but that was all right; he wouldn't need him or Burr until the grand jury indicted. But Burr was here anyway, and Henry Clay too, along with lawyer John Allen. So was Judge Harry Innes, and he was a problem for Daveiss. Innes was a Kentuckian from way back—so far back, in fact, that he had been one of the little group of James Wilkinson's that had intrigued with Spain for the commonwealth's independence before it was even a commonwealth. That had been twenty years earlier, when Wilkinson first went to New Orleans and took his pledge of allegiance to His Most Catholic Majesty, and Daveiss was sure that Innes hadn't changed.

The courtroom was packed when Innes began his grand jury charge. It was a fairly tame speech, not at all like the violent political diatribes that Samuel Chase and other Federalist judges had given. Chase's impeachment had ended a lot of that. But still Innes made his point. "Gentlemen of the grand jury," he cautioned them, "I require you to consider well the situation in which you are placed. You are said to be the bulwark standing between the chief executive power and the citizen to shield and protect him against oppression." He warned the jurors not to listen to hearsay, or allegations of any other criminal acts except those that Daveiss complained of, and not to consider acts from other judicial districts. In short, he hemmed in the angry Daveiss as tightly as the law would allow.[27]

When Innes had finished, he allowed Clay to address the court. "The only apprehension which Colonel Burr has on this occasion is the danger of delay—he fears nothing else—he dreads nothing else," the crack lawyer explained. "He has already suffered considerably in the prosecution of his private concerns by attending to the investigation of this fanciful conspiracy, and I hope he will not be made to suffer more."[28]

"I understand the drift of this thing," Daveiss broke in. "I know the manoeuvers both of Colonel Burr and his Counsel." Burr and Clay were here to prevent an indictment. If they succeeded, he explained, "their triumph will be glorious . . . the popularity of Colonel Burr will increase, and . . . he will be regarded as the object of a malicious prosecution." But Daveiss met Clay head on. "The attendance of Colonel Burr has not been required here," he said flatly. "His presence was perfectly unnecessary; it was not at my instance or solicitation that he has come forward. It was a voluntary act both of him and his counsel. I hope, therefore," he said pointedly, "that neither he nor his counsel will interfere." Daveiss then told the grand jurors that he would be happy to help them weave their way through the bewildering facts and law that they faced.[29]

Clay hit back hard. Daveiss had tried to silence him by claiming that neither Burr nor his lawyers had any legal standing here. Now Clay, who claimed a voice for himself, tried to deny one to Daveiss. A prosecutor had no business examining witnesses in front of grand jurors. Not in *this* court he didn't. That practice lay far in the future. This was Kentucky, in the American republic, and Clay appealed to republican virtues to silence the Federalist lawyer. "You have heard of inquisitions in Europe," he told the jurors and everyone else. "You have heard of the screws and tortures made use of in the dens of despotism, to extort confession; of the dark conclaves and caucuses, for the purpose of twisting some incoherent expression into evidence of guilt. Is not the project of the attorney for the United States, a similar object of terror? But all will not do; all the art of the attorney will not effect his purpose. I call upon him to produce a single instance where the public attorney has been accustomed to examine the witnesses before the grand jury; to sound the jurors and enter into all their secrets."

Clay was just getting started. "The woods of Kentucky, I hope," he continued, "will never be made the abode of inquisitors, or our simple establishments exchanged for the horrid cells of deception and tyranny. The groans of the suffering victims of priesthood and persecution under the lash and block, shall never be heard in our courts of justice. These instruments of monarchy shall never be made the means of extorting evidence under our free and happy government."[30]

Daveiss was quite an attorney, but he had his hands full with Clay. Then Burr himself, one of the nation's most capable lawyers, opened fire on him. He had not argued a case in years, and now he drew on all the pent-up skills that had been pacing, like restless tigers, the confines of his mind. He was here to *help* Daveiss, Burr said. Daveiss must know, he told the crowded room, "that every exertion in my power was used to aid and assist him in procuring testimony, he knows well that several witnesses have attended particularly at my request whose evidence otherways, he might have experienced a difficulty in procuring. Under these circumstances I trust the court, jury, and those present can never entertain an idea that any attempt is made on my part to suppress evidence." He was sympathy itself, the soul of reason and cooperation. Then: "But while it is my earnest desire to assist the attorney in the investigation of my conduct and my actions, still I am opposed to any innovation or any infringement which he may attempt in the ordinary forms of prosecution." Now he moved into high gear. "I am willing to submit to any regulations which are sanctioned by law," he proclaimed. "I am ready at all times to consent that law and equity shall compose the scale by which my actions are to be tried," he insisted. "But I shall never agree that the forms of justice and the dearest rights of my country are to be invaded in this case or any other where I have an opportunity of defending them."[31]

Daveiss had no chance at all. Innes sided with Burr and with Clay, and Daveiss knew that it meant the end of his cause. What was so plain to him was to the grand jury all innocence. "It is somewhat like Catiline's conspiracy," he urged. "The same means and address are used; and the same kind of desperate characters engaged in the scheme. Men without fortune or expectation, save from some revolution."[32] The jury couldn't see this. Despite the Wood County hubbub, the preparations all over the state, it went out of its way to vindicate Burr. "The grand jury are happy to inform the court," it reported, "that no violent disturbance of the public tranquility, or breach of the law, has come to their knowledge," and that neither Burr nor Adair was doing anything the slightest bit criminal.[33] The Neutrality Act did not require acts of violence, but Daveiss never got a chance to stress that. The cheers of the courtroom crowd were too loud. All he could do was protest. "You remark in history," he fumed, "that there are times in which whole nations are blind: this seemed to me to be one. It appeared as if Mr. Burr had wrought a spell or enchantment on the whole people and their magistracy."[34]

Burr was free to go, and a day or two later, after a magnificent ball in his honor, he did, heading towards Nashville again. Daveiss could only watch helplessly as the preparations on the Ohio continued. "I left Frankfort," he wrote glumly later, "expecting Mr. Burr would succeed in the first instance, and it would only cost the lives of a few thousand men, divided between the sword and climate to reinstate us."[35]

✦

Andrew Jackson was worried. Kentucky wasn't the only place where people were talking of treason. Stories were spreading in Tennessee, up the river, along the Natchez Trace, and Jackson didn't know what to make of them. He wanted his chance at the Dons, of course, but . . .

Then, in early November, Captain John A. Fort came to call on Jackson, bearing from a mutual friend a letter of introduction. Fort was on the way from New York cross-country to New Orleans. After spending a day or two with Jackson at the Hermitage, Fort happened to mention a plan to capture New Orleans and to break the Union in half.

Capture New Orleans?

Jackson pushed the stranger for details. Fort saw right away that he had said too much to the wrong man. He tried to backpedal, but that made Jackson angry. No one who saw Jackson angry ever once tried to stand in his way. When Jackson got going, the Furies themselves possessed him. So Fort started talking. The plan, he said, was one of grabbing New Orleans, invading Mexico, "and uniting the Western part of the union to the conquered country."

"How would it be accomplished?" asked Jackson.

"By the aid of the Federal troops," answered Fort, "and the general at their head."

Wilkinson . . .

Now Jackson could see everything. "It flashed upon my mind," he wrote later, "that plans that had been named of settling new countries, of Punishing the Dons, and adding Mexico to the United States . . . were only mere coverings to the real designs." Had Burr been playing him with his talk of invading New Spain? Jackson needed more information. Where, he asked Fort, had he heard all these things? From General Wilkinson? Fort said no. What about Burr? Fort could tell him little about Burr, having never had much to do with him. Then how, flared Jackson, did Fort know these things? Fort gave in and told him John Swartwout . . . Swartwout, Aaron Burr's very good New York friend.

That was enough for Jackson. "Knowing that Colo. Burr was well acquainted with Swartwout it rushed into my mind like lightning that Burr was at the head."[36]

Jackson had had little schooling, but he was smart and shrewd, and he was a soldier. He knew the geostrategy of the Old Southwest as well as anyone alive. Right away he set his thoughts down on paper. He had to get word to New Orleans and Washington, and he sketched out a terrifying scenario. "First a difference exist between our government and Spain, their minister at open war with our executive," he began. That much was true; Yrujo had only contempt for the government, and it for him. "A designing man forms an intrigue with him to regain the purchased Territory." Jackson might not know that Burr had met with Yrujo, but it was an excellent guess. "This designing man intrigues with the general of your army," he told officials in Washington, "and he is fully into the measure." Jackson hated and distrusted Wilkinson. He could believe anything of the man, even treason. He continued: the Spanish, "under pretext of defending their frontier . . . march[ ] a formidable force within two hundred miles of New Orleans." This was exactly the case on the Sabine. "The two armies are near enough to make arrangements to form plans of cooperation." (Wilkinson had been corresponding with Colonel Herrera and Captain-General Cordero for weeks.) "At this moment a descent is made from the Ohio and upper Louisiana on New Orleans, which is in a defenseless situation, two thirds of its inhabitants into the plan." Jackson no doubt knew all about the Mexican Association. "The town falls an easy prey to its assailants, and the two armies . . . with the aid of Spain shut the Port against the exportation of the West and hold out allurements to all the Western World to Join and they shall enjoy free trade and profitable commerce." It was a brilliant piece of synthesis for a man without direct knowledge of most of it. "The above plan," Jackson declared, "would jeopardize the Union, and be the most likely to insure success. . . . I may be mistaken," he warned, "but I as much believe that such a plan is in operation as I believe there is a God."[37]

Quickly Jackson fired off this dispatch to Washington, and then he wrote Governor Claiborne down in New Orleans. "Put your town in a state of defense," he told his old friend. "Organize your Militia, and defend your city as well against internal enemies as external . . . I fear you will meet with an attack from quarters you do not at present expect. Be upon the alert—keep a watchful eye on our General . . . ."[38]

Jackson also wrote Jefferson directly about his fears for New Orleans, even as Daveiss was trying to frustrate Burr's plans in court. But Jefferson didn't listen to Jackson any more than he had listened to Daveiss, or anyone else who had warned him of Burr. Meanwhile the preparations on the Ohio continued. Yrujo's agent Vidal reported that men were arriving in Pittsburgh from the East by the hundreds; boats were abuilding, and caches of provisions were growing. Then, a month after Jackson shouted alarm, Aaron Burr came back to Nashville.

&

James Wilkinson sat in his headquarters on the Sabine, reading by candlelight. He had finished deciphering the letter that Samuel Swartwout had brought him that day, and now all the words were clear on the page. Of the mass of correspondence and records that the Burr Conspiracy produced, this piece of writing would become the most famous. But that was later. All Wilkinson knew now was that it changed everything for him.

> Your letter post marked 13th May, is received [it read]. I have at length obtained funds, and have actually commenced. The Eastern detachments, from different points and under different pretence, will rendezvous on Ohio on 1 November.
>
> Every Thing internal and external favor our view. Naval protection of England is secured. Truxtun is going to Jamaica to arrange with the admiral there and will meet us at Mississippi. England, a navy of the United States ready to join, and final orders are given to my friends and followers. It will be a host of choice spirits. Wilkinson shall be second to Burr only and Wilkinson shall dictate the rank and promotion of his officers.
>
> Burr will proceed westward 1 August—never to return. With him go his daughter and grandson. The Husband will follow in October with a corps of worthys.
>
> Send forthwith an intelligent and confidential friend with whom Burr may confer; he shall return immediately with further interesting details. This is essential to concert and harmony of movement. Send a list of all persons known to Wilkinson westward of the mountains who could be useful, with a note delineating their character. By your messenger send me 4 or 5 of the commissions of your officers which you can borrow under any pretence you please, They shall be returned faithfully. Already an order to the contractor to

forward 6 months provisions to points you may name. This shall not be used till the last moment, and then under proper injunctions.

Our project my dear friend is brought to the point so long desired. I guarantee the result with my life and honor, with the lives, the honor and the fortune of hundreds, the best blood of our country.

Burr's plan of operation is to move down rapidly from the falls on fifteenth November, with the first 500 or 1000 men in light boats now constructing for that purpose; to be at Natches between the 5 and 15 of December, there to meet you; then to determine whether it will be expedient in the first instance to seize or pass by [Baton Rouge]. On receipt of this send me an answer. Draw on me for all expenses.

The people of the country to which we are going are prepared to receive us—their agents, now with me, say that if we will protect their religion and will not subject them to a foreign power, that in three weeks all will be settled.

The gods invite us to glory and fortune. It remains to be seen whether we deserve the boons.

The bearer of this goes express to you. He will hand a formal letter of introduction from me.

He is a man of inviolable honor and perfect discretion, formed to execute rather than to project—yet capable of relating facts with fidelity and incapable of relating them otherwise; he is thoroughly informed of the plans and intentions of   and will disclose to you as far as you shall enquire and no further. He has imbibed a reverence for your Character and may be embarrassed in your presence—put him at ease, and he will satisfy you.[39]

Burr had committed himself in writing. He had made his intent explicit, and he had said he was now acting and not merely talking. The letter meant all of these things. It also meant that Wilkinson had to put up or shut up. Wilkinson thought for a while, and then he put up.

One of the first things that he did was also one that Jackson was predicting. He wrote Captain-General Cordero and proposed a settlement. The last thing he wanted now was combat with the Spanish force bristling in his front. He had to work with, not against, them if the plans were to succeed. Letters flew back and forth for a time among Cordero, Herrera, and Wilkinson. By early November the Spanish agreed to their part in the plan. Wilkinson, on his own initiative, had avoided a war, gotten Spain to see reason, freed up his forces, and given himself a broad range of action. Now he could march on New Orleans.

President,	O	Navy,	96
Vice President,	Θ	Peace,	Γ
Secretary of State,	T	War,	٦
of War,	Γ	Treaty,	•—⊸
of Navy,	⅃	Convention,	:—•
of Treasury,	L	Commerce,	∿∿∿
Senate,	⏤┐	British Minister,	T
House of Representatives,	⎾⎽	French Minister,	Ṱ
Congress,	⬚	Spanish Minister,	Ṭ
Federal,	ꙗ	Appropriation,	V̶88
Anti-federal,	ꙗ	Reduction,	V̶88
Administration,	⊶⊶	Eastern,	⊛
Military establishment,	88	Southern,	⟨‡⟩
England,	▢	Middle,	⊕
France,	▣	British,	⊡
Minister,	T	Spanish,	⊡
Major General,	V͜	French,	▣
Brigadier,	V͜	Canada,	▣
United States,	⊏⊐⊐	Louisiana,	▣
States,	⊏⊐	Posts,	⊂⊐
Republican,	76	Garrisons,	⊂⊏⊐
Aristocratic,	89	Western,	⊛
City of Washington,	⌂	Mississippi,	┼┼┼┼
Election,	⊂⊐	Ohio,	⎓╫
		New Orleans,	┼┼┼┼

Burr,	13, 14, 15, 16.
Wilkinson,	45.

Partial key to the Burr-Wilkinson cipher. *(Report of the Bacon Committee, 1811)*

But the settlement was not what Jackson foretold. Wilkinson had no plans to bring Herrera along. What he had done was to make a de facto treaty, an agreement that he would stay east of Arroyo Hondo, while the Spanish pulled back west of the Sabine. Between them would lie no-man's-land, several miles of neutral ground. Both armies pledged to keep out of it until Washington and Madrid came to terms.

Wilkinson had been in bad shape. But now he had a way out of the trap. He had feared getting on Spain's bad side by attacking, and getting on Washington's too, by doing nothing or giving ground. For months he thought that he would have to do one or the other. But now he had a third option. Burr's letter had given it to him.

Burr was threatening Mexico. Burr was threatening the Union. Whatever he was planning, both Spain and the federal government had reasons to condemn him. By declaring war on Burr, Wilkinson could pose as his country's savior while shielding Mexico from invasion. He could keep drawing his Spanish pension as Agent Number 13 and retain his prized role as brigadier general. All he need do was betray Aaron Burr. With the Neutral Ground Treaty he had changed the rules. With the Spanish threat now neutralized, he could throw the United States Army at Burr.

Wilkinson did more in October than treat with Spain. He also pumped the courier Swartwout for as much information as he could get. He ordered Colonel Cushing to be ready to march. Burr's letter was more than two months old when Wilkinson got it; Burr could be anywhere by now, and with a force larger than Wilkinson's own. New Orleans was the natural target, so even as he struggled with bringing the Spanish to terms, Wilkinson sent word to the city to beef up its feeble defenses. It had only a few; Wilkinson had drawn nearly everything west with him, leaving the place wide open. Now that he planned to stop Burr's force, he knew that that had been a mistake. He had to defend New Orleans, but moving an army is a difficult thing, especially along the frontier. Until he could get his forces there, all he could do was write letters of warning. So write them he did, starting with a couple to Jefferson, leapfrogging the chain of command. "Sir," the first one began,

> A numerous and powerful association, extending from New-York through the Western states, to the territory bordering on the Mississippi, has been formed with the design to levy and rendezvous eight or ten thousand men in New Orleans, at a very near period: and from thence, with the co-operation of a naval armament, to carry an expedition against Vera Cruz. . . .
>
> A body of the associates is to descend the Allegany River, and the first general rendezvous will be held near the rapids of the Ohio, on or before the 20th of next month; from whence this corps is to proceed in light boats, with the utmost possible velocity for the city of New Orleans, under the expectation of being joined in their route, by auxiliaries from the State of Tennessee and other quarters.

It is unknown under what authority this enterprise has been projected; from whence the means of its support are derived, or what may be the intentions of its leaders, in relation to the territory of Orleans; but it is believed that the maritime co-operation will depend on a British squadron from the West-Indies, under the ostensible command of American masters.[40]

But Wilkinson refused to name names, omitting mention of Burr and everyone else. His official explanation was that in the unlikely event he were wrong about the plot, he did not want anyone's reputation to suffer. Wilkinson was a cool liar. He had to be. Only someone who was in on the plan could know all the things that Wilkinson knew. Though the general had now turned on Burr, he might betray himself as well with the depth of his own knowledge. Protecting himself was his main problem now—that and protecting New Orleans. But right now New Orleans was the bigger one. He sent letters there too, just as inflated as the ones he sent Jefferson, hinting at pending disasters beyond the readers' imaginations. He told the garrison commander at New Orleans to repair fortifications, build up supplies and buy a train of artillery from the French surplus there.[41]

By rounding on Burr, Wilkinson had shielded the Spanish, and he meant to collect. He sent a rider, his own aid-de-camp, in fact, all the way to Mexico City with a message for its government. He described the threat that Mexico faced, an "infernal combination . . . of backwoodsmen from Kentucky and the settlements along the Ohio," the same backwoodsmen and settlements that the Spanish had dreaded for years. "On my own responsibility and by my own private means I have taken and shall continue to take such measures as will enable me to check the commotion that threatens destruction to the realm of Mexico," he crowed to the Spanish viceroy. "I am risking my life, my good name, and my property by the means I have adopted." All the general asked in return was a modest reimbursement, more than a hundred thousand pesos. Surely that wasn't too much to give in exchange for Wilkinson's services? It was, as it turned out; the viceroy wrote back courteously to say that he already had all of this information, refusing to reimburse Wilkinson.[42]

By mid-November the army was marching, and Wilkinson was heading towards Natchez, firing orders as he went. "My God!" he wrote to Colonel Cushing. "What a situation has our country reached. Let us save it if we can."[43] He was just as melodramatic with Jefferson, whom he brought up to date with another letter. "This is indeed a deep, dark, and widespread conspiracy," he rumbled, "embracing the young and the old—the democrat and the federalist—the native and the foreigner—the patriot of '76 and the exotic of yesterday—the opulent and the needy—the ins and the outs." Then came a zinger. "To give effect to my military arrangements," he wrote, "it is absolutely indispensable New Orleans and its environs should be placed under martial law." He was outmanned and outgunned, and only force majeure could save him. "To insure the triumph of government over its enemies," he continued, "I am obliged to resort to political finesse and military stratagem. I must hold out false colours, conceal my designs, and cheat my adversaries into a state of security, that when I do strike it may be with more force and effect."[44] But it wasn't enough. Wilkinson spoke of assassins, of desperate characters prowling New Orleans streets, against whom he had no defense except the power to act at discretion. Wilkinson wasn't asking Jefferson about martial law. He was telling him. He was going to have his way in the city. Washington was half a continent away. His dispatches would take at least three weeks to get there, probably four, possibly five, and twice that long to be answered. Burr was coming, and Wilkinson couldn't wait. He was going to do as he saw fit. Having written the president, Wilkinson was off to New Orleans to take charge.

Governor Claiborne had different ideas. He, not Wilkinson, was responsible for the District of Orleans and its welfare, and he reported to Secretary of State James Madison, not to General James Wilkinson. On top of that, he and Wilkinson got along badly. Despite all this, though, Claiborne knew of the dangers. By early December he had heard from Jackson as well as Wilkinson. He trusted Jackson and paid attention to what he had to say. "Beware of an attack, as well from your own Country as Spain," Jackson had written. "I fear there is something rotten in the State of Denmark."[45] But if Jackson's letter was cause for worry, Wilkinson's sparked fear. It was labeled "Sacredly Confidential" and spun a tale calculated to freeze the blood. "You are surrounded by dangers of which you dream not and the destruction of the American Union is seriously menaced. The storm will probably burst on New Orleans, when I shall meet it & triumph or perish . . . we shall have 1000 regular troops in the City in three weeks and I look for succour by Sea. . . . You have spies on your every movement and disposition—and our safety and success depends vitally on the concealment of our intentions."[46]

Wilkinson arrived in New Orleans on November 25, and he got the ball rolling fast. His headquarters was a flurry of action, with merchants and woodsmen coming and going. One of them told him that Burr had seized a Kentucky arsenal; Claiborne arrived and passed on news of a British fleet off Belize. In the middle of all the chaos, Wilkinson got hold of Silas Dinsmore, the former U.S. Choctaw agent and a man well versed in the ways of the forest. He sent him north to find Burr and capture him, putting a five thousand dollar price tag on the New Yorker's head. Dinsmore headed out in early December, alerting the Choctaw and Chickasaw and sending Indian runners north.[47]

Even with everything else going on, Wilkinson found time to pay a call on Dr. Justus Erich Bollman. Bollman was a dashing adventurer, a German who had come to the New World a few years before. People here thought well of him; in Austria he had tried to free America's friend, the Marquis de Lafayette, from an Austrian prison, and as a result of the failed attempt he had done some time himself. He was smart, multilingual, and a perfect agent for Burr, who had sent him by sea to New Orleans a few months before. Bollman had brought a duplicate of the cipher letter with him and sent it to the general by courier, and now Wilkinson wanted some answers.[48]

Bollman revealed—at least according to Wilkinson—that he had just heard from Burr. The communication, though a month old, was three months more recent than the cipher letter. Burr had written it in the West, not the East. In it he announced that he would be in New Orleans by December 20, at the head of a thousand men, with four thousand more on the way.[49]

December 20 was less than three weeks away, and Wilkinson's whole army was barely eight hundred men, slightly larger including militia.[50] On top of that, people still suspected that he was in league with Burr. Even Claiborne doubted him. If he was going to save New Orleans and his own reputation as well, he had to be ruthless.

Samuel Swartwout was at Fort Adams, well above New Orleans on the east bank of the Mississippi. After leaving Nachitoches to head downriver, he had fallen terribly ill with some wretched Gulf Coast fever, and he'd barely made it to the fort alive. Wilkinson had put him under surveillance there, but he had ordered the post's commander not to arrest the young courier. He had hoped to con more information out of him. But now, with the intelligence that he had come by and with his troops on the move toward New Orleans, Wilkinson changed his mind. He needed fast action, and at any rate Swartwout might know too much about Wilkinson's own involvement with Burr. So he sent word to Fort Adams to have Swartwout arrested. He also ordered the arrest of Peter V. Ogden, another young Burr lieutenant and nephew to Jonathan Dayton.

Swartwout feared the army and Wilkinson. He probably guessed the truth, the same truth that was driving the drama now and would drive it until the end. Wilkinson had been part of the Burr Conspiracy. The only way he could save himself was to destroy any evidence of that fact. Swartwout had some of that evidence locked up in his brain. Wilkinson would never be safe so long as Swartwout lived, and Swartwout now knew it. The forest, the bayous, the canebrakes—people could vanish along the frontier, with no one the wiser. Swartwout was afraid.

On December 12 William C. Mead, one of Wilkinson's officers, arrested the young easterner and brought him down the river. Swartwout was unarmed. If he had had a weapon, he would have fought Mead off. Four days later he arrived in New Orleans, where he was confined on the navy bomb ketch *Etna*, safe from civilian interference and still under Wilkinson's thumb. Meanwhile Wilkinson had ordered Bollman's arrest too. James Alexander, a friend of Bollman's, was outraged, and he sought a writ of habeas corpus from the civilian federal court. Edward Livingston, one of the town's most prominent men, went with him before the judge. They got their writ, but Wilkinson paid no attention. He wrote back to the court that he planned to deliver the prisoner to Washington, not to the local authorities. Alexander lost his temper at that, and his tongue got the better of him. "He said publicly at the Coffee House the other night," Wilkinson mentioned to Claiborne, "that if B. was a traitor I was one also." That was a big mistake; Wilkinson arrested him too.[51]

This was getting to be too much for Claiborne and everyone else. By now panic had taken hold in the city, with federal troops everywhere, workers building fortresses, gunboats fitting out, military arrests underway, and fears of Burr running rampant. But Burr was a hobgoblin who hadn't yet shown. Right now Wilkinson was a bigger threat. Claiborne had tried to be cooperative at first, but now he started fighting the general.

The first battle was about the militia. Wilkinson needed every man at his service; Claiborne wanted to send his few hundred militiamen up the river to try to stop Burr there. Wilkinson dismissed that thought at once. "You could not for a moment withstand the desperation and superiority of numbers opposed to you," he told the governor. Claiborne gave in.[52] Then came another personnel crisis. Wilkinson wanted to press men into service. Captain John Shaw, the senior naval officer on station who served as commodore, was struggling to prepare for Burr's onslaught. He complained to the general about the shortage of hands, and Wilkinson griped to Claiborne. "Captain Shaw informs me he cannot proceed with the river defences," he told him, "without carpenters and Sailors, who are not to be had by requisition. Proclaim martial Law & this with many other evils will be remedied. On this subject in the present Eventful moment, I must entreat you to act with decision. . . . our measures must be taken with promptitude and decision, regardless of other consequences or considerations than the public safety, for I apprehend Burr with his Rebelious Bands may soon be at hand."[53]

Claiborne wanted something less drastic. Let shipowners allow their crews to sign up for government service if they wanted to, he suggested. Wilkinson had problems with that. "I am myself absolutely hazarding every thing for the National Safety, by unauthorized dispositions of the Troops and treasure of our Country," he reminded Claiborne. "I believe it to be wise and just to inflict temporary privation for permanent security . . . give me leave, and *in three hours our vessels shall be manned*."[54]

Claiborne was losing his patience. "I am fully sensible of the impending Danger," he shot back, "and am disposed to exert all my constitutional powers in support of our Country and even these I will exceed, if the means at present pursued, should not (in a short time) produce the desired effects."[55] But the manpower issues were mere trifles. The arrests were something else.

When the court issued a habeas corpus writ for Peter V. Ogden, Wilkinson honored it, but he ignored the ones for Bollman and Swartwout. They had delivered treasonous letters, and worse, they were a threat to him. Claiborne tried to make him see reason, to understand that his own hands were tied. "The suspension of the writ of habeas corpus, & the declaring of martial law," the governor lectured the general, were things "beyond my control. These high powers devolve alone on the Legislature, nor can I constitutionally exercise an authority on the occasion, until the same shall be delegated to me by law." Claiborne challenged Wilkinson to show him a single example of a governor proclaiming martial law without proper authority; Wilkinson couldn't find one.[56] Claiborne was right; he had the law on his side; but Wilkinson had an army.

Afraid that the courts might try to take Swartwout by force, Wilkinson sent Ensign William C. Mead and a detachment of troops to the *Etna* to deal with him. They arrived in the night, with an oppressive rain pouring down. Mead was brisk and matter-of-fact. Swartwout was to come with them. His clothing, his watch—all was to stay behind. Mead even ordered him clapped in irons. Swartwout objected to that, swearing that he would choose death to chains, and Mead backed off, but only because he had once worn them himself as a Spanish prisoner. Swartwout asked where they were going, but Mead, irritated by now, wouldn't tell him.

Swartwout feared the worst. What better time and place for him to disappear than a gloomy night such as this? "You are ordered to murder me," he cried out, "and I had as well die here as in the woods!" With that he leaped for the rail. Instantly Mead ordered his men to stop him, and they aimed and fired. Three muskets flashed in the pan; the other three fizzled completely. The rain had saved Swartwout's life, but not from recapture. The men grabbed him and dragged him across the river, beyond the courts' reach and at the general's mercy.[57]

By now December was more than half gone. For all anyone knew, Burr and his army might come round the last bend in the river at any time. Claiborne was angry at Wilkinson, and Wilkinson was dead-set on holding Bollman and Swartwout. Christmas came and went; still no sign of Burr. By now Claiborne was starting to wonder. Surely, if Burr were nearby, New Orleans would have heard from Fort Adams, or possibly Natchez. He dashed off the next in a long line of letters to Madison. "I persuade myself," he told the secretary of state, "that the Danger is not as great as the General apprehends."[58] But that wasn't slowing down Wilkinson, nor did it help Claiborne at all. He still had no orders from Washington. Then, after Christmas, he got word from the capital. The most recent letter was dated November 12. Nothing was recent enough to show that anyone there had gotten Claiborne's and Wilkinson's warnings. That meant that Claiborne was still on his own, while Wilkinson's men prowled the streets.

Wilkinson, too, wanted news from the East, or at least he said that he did. "Oh God could I hear from our Government!" he exclaimed. People were getting angry with him, and rumors were spreading that he was in on Burr's plot. Without backing from Jefferson soon, he might find himself in real trouble, especially when Burr *did* arrive.

But everyone managed to cope. Shaw finished the fitting out of his tiny fleet, and the general ordered the gunboats and ketches upriver. Claiborne ended the embargo, and other boats came and went again. Wilkinson sent Bollman and Swartwout back East via warship. He probably should have killed them instead if he were serious about protecting himself, but that might have raised too many questions. Two deaths would have been harder for him to explain than one. He could only go so far. Maybe, when Burr finally showed up, Wilkinson could destroy or at least defeat him, and prove beyond doubt that he was a hero. Until then all he could do was be a small-scale autocrat—that, and prepare for battle.

⚜

When we look at the nighttime sky, and we see the light of the stars, we are looking back into time. The glimmers striking our eyes were born ages ago, decades, centuries, or even millennia. The farther away a star from us, the farther into the past we see when we look in its direction. Things used to be that way on Earth. Before radio, before the telephone or telegraph, distance and time were the same, especially in North America.

While the West was catching fire, the East was ignorant. Whenever someone read a letter from half a continent away, he was reading about the past, not the present. A time lag of weeks to send and receive letters meant that Washington was far more remote from New Orleans than Mars is from Earth today.

The warnings hadn't abated. Jefferson had been getting them for months, and they didn't slow down when Burr left for the West. If anything, they came more often and got more strident. For a while Jefferson still ignored them. In August he heard from Thomas Truxtun. For once the embittered captain had stopped griping about his poor treatment, at least long enough to tell Jefferson that Burr was up to no good.[59] In September Jefferson got word from George Morgan about Burr's earlier visit. Still he took no action. He did write to acknowledge receipt of the letter, but not until half a year later. "Yours was the very first intimation I had of this plot," the president lied, "for which it is but justice to say you have deserved well of your country."[60]

The forewarnings continued. In October Jefferson got the latest in a series of updates from New Yorker John Nicholson which described Comfort Tyler's movements and recruitment attempts, linking them not only with Burr but with rumors of western disunion and foreign invasion plans.[61] Jefferson noted receipt, but did nothing, as usual. In early November he wrote Thomas Mann Randolph a letter that reveals that he was aware of Burr, which was something, at least. "Burr is unquestionably very actively engaged in the westward in preparations to sever that from this part of the union," he noted. "We learn that he is actually building 10 or 15 boats able to take a large gun and fit for the navigation of those waters. We give him all the attention our situation admits; as yet we have no legal proof of any overt act which the law can lay hold of."[62] This would prove to be one of the most ironic lines that anyone penned in the whole of the Burr Conspiracy, in light of all that came later. Jefferson had no concern with a need for an overt act, which the law of treason required. He had stretched the Constitution before. He had dismissed earlier warnings as Federalists' political attacks. If he had believed that the danger was real, he would have acted immediately. Some of the nation's most important, capable men saw a threat; Jefferson did not, and until the fall of 1806, he had refused to take any action.

But now, at last, that was beginning to change. Near the end of October he got news from Gideon Granger, his own postmaster general. Granger had been hearing things from William Eaton, or rather, he had been hearing things secondhand that Eaton had said. Eaton, having struck out with Jefferson, had mentioned his fears to a congressman friend, who had in turn told Granger. Neither Eaton nor Granger said anything that Jefferson had not heard long before. But it was all news to Granger, who sought Eaton out and got an affidavit from him to send to the president.[63]

Why this third-hand report of things that he had gotten straight from the horse's mouth half a year earlier mattered to Jefferson was a mystery, but it did matter. At least he later claimed as much. Years later he told Granger that his report was the one that convinced him to call the cabinet meeting about Burr.[64]

This meeting, which took place on October 22, was the first time the cabinet had gotten together since mid-summer. Jefferson recounted for his officers the names of the people who had told him of Burr's designs. "He went off this spring to the Western Country," he told the department heads. "Of his movements on his way information has come to the Secretary of State and myself, from John Nicholson and Mr. Williams of the State of N.J., respecting a Mr. Tyler, Col. Morgan, Neville and Roberts near Pittsburgh, and to other citizens through other channels and the newspapers." The record was unassailable, and it held many comments on Wilkinson. These, too, Jefferson passed along to the cabinet. He seemed to believe that Wilkinson was Burr's first lieutenant, and that he had improved the chances of war with Spain by taking so long to get from St. Louis to the Sabine.

Then the discussion began. It ended in consensus. The cabinet agreed to warn all of the western district attorneys and governors to watch Burr and wait for an overt act that would brand him a traitor or criminal. Beyond these completely useless measures—everybody on the Ohio knew the stories by now—the cabinet agreed on the slightly more practical step of ordering gunboats upriver from New Orleans to meet any force moving down from Ohio.[65]

Finally, Jefferson was ordering countermeasures—for a grand total of two days. Then came another cabinet meeting, and the group reversed itself. Mail had arrived from the West; it had nothing to say about Burr. "This total silence of the officers of government, of the members of Congress, of the newspapers," Jefferson blandly explained, "proves he is committing no overt act against the law." So the cabinet now decided *not* to warn most of the western officials; the gunboats were to stay at New Orleans, and all was as it had been before, with only a single exception. John Graham, secretary of the District of Orleans, was in Washington, about to return to the West. Since he was heading out there anyway, Jefferson and the cabinet asked him to take the Ohio River route and report on anything suspicious he saw.[66]

If Jefferson's lack of action had been strange before, now it was really amazing. No one has ever explained it; whatever was running through his mind defies analysis. The Burr Conspiracy is a story full of mysteries, but this is one of the biggest. And Jefferson's behavior was to grow still more bizarre.

In late November an army lieutenant rode into town after a long journey from New Orleans. He made his way to the president's mansion and presented himself to Jefferson. His official reason for reporting there was to resign his army commission. His real reason was to deliver Wilkinson's two warning letters, two messages from the past.[67]

Those letters got things moving for real. Jefferson had been warned about Wilkinson. Daveiss and Eaton, and others, too, had told Jefferson that his general-in-chief was in on Burr's plot. Other than planning to replace Wilkinson as governor of the Louisiana Territory, Jefferson had done as little about him as he had done about Aaron Burr.[68] But when he got these warnings—and got them from Wilkinson—he flew into action. He called the cabinet together again and gave it the news. Immediately his department heads agreed to take fast and strong action. Not many years before, Jefferson had made light of the danger of western disunion. If it happened, it happened, he'd said.[69] Now things were different. Instead of asking western officials for intelligence, he was going to tell them to use force. In 1803 and 1804 he had been talking about a popular movement and not a coup d'etat. Perhaps he did not understand that Burr was after public support, and that, in some measure, he had it. That was the running theme of western conspiracies all the way back to Genêt and beyond: a few would lead, and the rest, rising up, would eagerly follow. It had worked in the East in 1776, and the frontier ringleaders from Clark to Blount had always modeled themselves after the Revolution. At any rate, even if Jefferson did know, he didn't much care. Idle talk was one thing, but he would not let go of half of the country. Within a couple of days he ordered the West to stop Burr.

Jefferson later said that he never thought that Burr would get the support of more than five hundred men. That was a shrewd guess, based as it was on the last twenty years of frontier history. These things had usually fizzled. But his acts told a different story from his words. Two days after hearing from Wilkinson, he issued a nationwide proclamation against the western insurgents. He said nothing about disunion; he said nothing about New Orleans. Instead he talked of a possible invasion of Spanish dominions, an illegal invasion, since the United States and Spain were at peace. That might not be true by now, of course; Wilkinson may already be halfway to the Rio

Grande for all that Jefferson knew, but the president got all constitutional, pointing out that Congress had not *declared* war. He based the whole proclamation on that single fact: a move was afoot to violate the Neutrality Act, which operated only in peacetime. To stop it he called on the nation's militias, the army, federal and even state officers, and the public at large to do what they could to get the West under control. Seize the conspirators; capture the boats; blockade the rivers; Jefferson ordered it all. But he omitted Burr's name, just as Wilkinson had.

Less than a week later Jefferson sent his annual message to Congress. Most of it was about the impending war with Spain, but Jefferson did put in a paragraph about Burr, again naming no names. He spoke merely of the Neutrality Act violations, and of "criminal attempts of private individuals to decide for their country the question of peace or war, by commencing active and unauthorized hostilities." He made no mention of disunion, and he spoke as if he had things under control, mentioning how quickly he had put the planned uprising down.[70]

That was putting a spin on things. The proclamation was only five days old, barely old enough to have gotten to Pittsburgh, much less to have had any effect there. Jefferson couldn't possibly have heard back. What was more, he was worried. He could call out the troops on the pretext of Neutrality Act violations, but he had no legal authority to resist an armed attempt at disunion. State militias, yes; but not the U.S. Army. The militias were undependable, and they might even fight for Burr, if he had gotten control of western hearts and minds. Despite claiming that Burr's backing was slight, despite reassuring Congress that that things were in hand, Jefferson quickly drafted a bill that would allow him to use federal force against traitors.[71]

Now Jefferson was fighting the same time lag that Wilkinson and Claiborne had fought. Burr was doing whatever he was doing, and all that Jefferson could do in turn was issue orders and wait. He wrote to western governors; Secretary of War Henry Dearborn sent dispatches too. Jefferson was especially worried about the most vital spot, the one he had always fretted about, and what Burr might do once he got there. The fate of the United States was riding on the next few weeks. "Should he get possession of New Orleans," he assured Claiborne, "measures are now taking for its immediate recovery, and for calling forth such a force as will be sufficient." Jefferson tried to be upbeat, telling the governor of his certainty that the West would stay loyal, but he couldn't hide all of his fears. "We are looking with anxiety," he confessed, "to see what exertions the Western Country will make in the first instance for their own defense."[72] Jefferson feared the worst. If Burr succeeded, the whole of the federal Union, stripped of New Orleans and popular trust, might cease to exist.

Within his official family, Jefferson was even more open. His worry was obvious, but at least he refused to let it paralyze him. A couple of days before Christmas, the president sent instructions to Robert Smith, his secretary of the navy. Burr's rendezvous on the river was to have been December 15, he told Smith. "The mail next expected will be of that date. If we then find that his force has had no effectual opposition at either Mariette or Cincinnati, & will not be stopped at Louisville," he directed, he would order "20,000 militia (or volunteers) from the Western states to proceed down the river to retake N.O." They would need support, Jefferson told Smith. To that end, the president ordered him to send the whole of the U.S. Navy from its ports in the East, from New York to Charleston, towards New Orleans as fast as possible.

But Jefferson was fighting more than just time; he was fighting the winds and the waves as well. Winter campaigns are hard, and storms were sweeping the North Atlantic, making it much too violent a place for Jefferson's little gunboats. Now he lamented that he had gutted the navy, but he had no time for laments. At least he was giving the orders. As 1806 came to an end, he could only wait and see what would happen.

Weather could be Burr's friend, but it could also be his opponent. Winter had come to the Ohio, the snows began to fall and the river was icing up. Maybe it would buy Washington time. Burr had the initiative, and Jefferson was weeks behind him. But now the president was on the move. Slowly, the full might of his government was beginning to build, rolling westward, down the rivers, up from New Orleans, probing into the continent's heart, searching for Burr and his minions. Catiline's story was replaying itself. And somewhere along the Hudson's banks, Hamilton's ghost began laughing.

❦

A massive bonfire rent the midnight on Blennerhassett's Island. The date was December 10, and the place was thousands of miles from Blennerhassett's native Ireland. But there in the deep North American forest, with dozens of shadowy figures drifting and lanterns flickering in darkness that lapped at firelight's edge, ghostlike to vision, haunting the wood and the eye, maybe Blennerhassett remembered the All Souls Nights of his childhood home. Perhaps he recalled the half-pagan ways of the Celtic church, and the stories of the Samain night of late October crouched half-remembered in his thoughts, the stories of the night when the veil between the worlds grew thin, and anything could happen.

What *would* happen was anyone's guess. Things were going wrong. Ohio's Governor Edward Tiffin did not yet have word of Jefferson's proclamation, but he hadn't waited around. He knew all about the boats that people were building for Burr. The grand jury in Kentucky may have sent Burr on his way with people all cheering, but Tiffin was not in Kentucky. This was Ohio. His militia had told him that a couple of boats full of weapons and men were already on the river. Burr's men, he figured; they must be up to no good.

The governor had talked to the legislature, which passed a bill in early December untying the executive's hands. With that his militia got moving. He ordered it to seize all the boats and fortify the Ohio.

Burr's people knew that they were in trouble. Comfort Tyler had made it downriver from Pittsburgh to Blennerhassett's Island with four of the boats. Now he and Blennerhassett were working fast, trying to head out with the whole expedition before the militia attacked. Snow crunched underfoot on the island as people scurried around in the night. Some ran bullets, others packed meat, and still others loaded trunks. The boats bobbed on the night waters, candles in each glimmering on the darkness. General Edward Tupper of the Ohio militia steered for them as he rowed out towards the island.[73]

Tupper had no orders yet, but he knew that something was up. He had heard about the gathering, and near midnight he took a few men to investigate. He bumped gently along one of Tyler's boats, and then landed on the bonfire-lit island. Finding his way up to the house, he came across Harman Blennerhassett, who was making his last preparations. The group was minutes away from leaving, and Tupper followed it down to the water. He tried to reason with Blennerhassett. If all this were innocent, he told his friend, surely they could sort it out in only a few days' time. Blennerhassett tuned him out. He wanted no more delays. Margaret was with him, urging both him and Tyler to go by canoe. They could avoid the militia patrols that way. But Blennerhassett and Tyler were ready to take all of the boats, and all of the men as well. Margaret and the children would stay behind for now, rather than take the risk.

Tupper took a risk of his own. Reason hadn't worked and the group was about to get clean away. He grabbed Harman Blennerhassett. "Your body is in my hands," he cried, "in the name of the Commonwealth!" He was either very brave or very stupid. A moment later he was looking down the barrels of a half-dozen muskets. "Gentlemen, I hope you will not do the like," he said quickly. One of the number told the general that he would just as soon shoot him as not. Tupper, outmanned and outgunned, backed off. He wished the group luck in escaping downriver. With that it was gone, swallowed up by the night.[74]

A few hours later, at daybreak, the Wood County, Virginia, militia invaded. The makeshift warriors bullied Margaret Blennerhassett and half wrecked her house, helping themselves to her brandy, but they found almost nobody else. They had missed all the fun.

Dawn found a forlorn little fleet on the wintry Ohio River. Burr had contracted for more than a dozen boats, expensive ones, that could hold well over a thousand men and provisions to feed every one of them. But most of the boats had been seized, and the men had never shown up. Now Blennerhassett and Tyler were at the head of fewer than a hundred women and men, scattered through only four boats. Blennerhassett had had visions of glory. Just a few weeks before he had shared with his servant his story of the quest that awaited. "I will tell you what, Peter," he had exclaimed. "We are going to take Mexico; one of the finest and richest places in the whole world." Burr would be Mexico's king, and Theodosia its queen. As for Blennerhassett, he would play a leading role. "O by God, I tell you, Peter," he had chortled, "every man that will not conform to order and discipline, I will stab; you'll see how I'll fix them."[75]

But things were turning out differently. All the publicity that surrounded Aaron Burr had not helped the cause. Instead it seemed to hurt it. A good many men were collecting far up the river, as Yrujo's spy Vidal and others had noted, but by now Jefferson's proclamation was spreading there, and whatever support that Burr might have gotten was beginning to dry up fast. A few more adventurers got downstream to the island, but not before Blennerhassett and Tyler departed. They were arrested for their trouble. They found Margaret a prisoner in her own home, before the sodden militia released her. She and the new arrivals gave themselves to the winds and the ice of a winter's river as they set out in search of her husband and Burr. That was all. So Harman Blennerhassett's dreams died there on the Ohio, as the boats spun slowly downstream, past drunken, unconscious militiamen, along the northwestern frontier. As for Comfort Tyler, he was no Siegfried, and this voyage was no Rhine journey.

And what of Burr? He had been wrong. He had made the same mistake that every western conspirator before him had made. He had thought that he could harness the frontier unrest, bringing a revolution to boil in this far-flung, uncertain cauldron. But the geography was against him, as was the fierce individual mien. The people out west were the lone wolves of America. They always had been. Even if they hadn't been so widely scattered and isolated from any hope of central logistical management, they would still have been free spirits, hard to lead and direct. Burr's was an uphill battle from the very beginning. If he knew it, he never let on, but it was true nonetheless. And now Thomas Jefferson had declared war, not on Spain but on him.

But where was Burr now? He wasn't with the flotilla. He had not been on the island for quite some time, certainly not on the night of the bonfire. He had last been spotted in Frankfort, when the grand jury refused to indict. He had ridden south from there, leaving Blennerhassett and Tyler to their own devices. Now all they could do was steer their boats down the Ohio, avoiding arrest or capture, and wait until they got word from him.

Down toward the Falls they went, running sometimes at night to evade the militia. In a few days Davis Floyd joined them with a few more boats. The weather was sometimes beautiful, sometimes windy and dangerous. Now and then the boats fell afoul of the sawyers, the treacherous submerged trees that could sink them. Behind them the commotion was spreading, the proclamation chasing them down the valley; but ahead the frontier awaited. Then, on Christmas Eve, they finally heard from Burr.

The letter was from Nashville, where he had run into trouble from Jackson. An angry Andrew Jackson was a force from which very few escaped unscathed, once they fell afoul of him. Jackson suspected that Burr was a traitor. When he had dragged the truth out of Captain Fort, the Tennessee general demanded an explanation from Burr and declared him persona non grata in Nashville and its vicinity. So he said later, and he was probably telling the truth, since he warned New Orleans and Washington. But Burr wrote back, apparently, and he managed to calm down Jackson. He calmed him down so much, in fact, that Jackson went through with the deal to furnish Burr with boats, and he even sent his wife's nephew down the Cumberland with the New Yorker. This was something indeed, to be able to handle a man such as Jackson, but then Burr had a rare sort of magic. He never would have gotten even this far if he hadn't.

Eight days after Burr left Nashville, news of Jefferson's proclamation arrived. The town exploded, burning Burr in effigy. Jackson got orders from Henry Dearborn putting him on alert, and telling him that stories were spreading that Jackson was in on the plot. That did it; Jackson was now Burr's mortal enemy. But Burr had flown down the river.[76]

"All is well, very well, at this garrison," Burr wrote Blennerhassett on December 27 while waiting at the mouth of the Cumberland for his Ohio force to arrive. That was during the final few hours before he got word of the uproar. Before long he had learned what had happened up and down the Ohio, but he still did not know that fate was reaching its hand from the East to stop him and what he was doing. The day was a stormy, messy one as he met up with his little troop. He had brought nearly no one from Tennessee; Jackson had stopped recruiting when Captain Fort had come clean. Only a hundred women and men, mostly the latter; some accounts say barely half that many; this was the whole of Burr's force. But Burr, like Macbeth, had come too far to turn back, though his way was downriver, not across it. The East was closed to him. He had to go on. Cheerfully, reservedly, he greeted each one of the group, shaking hands as he went. He would soon explain all, he said, but this was not the time. But Davis Floyd was beginning to tell some of the crews that the plan was to take Baton Rouge. Then the squadron was off, ten boats in all, a few people per boat.[77]

The next two weeks passed slowly. "Floated all day; nothing extra," Blennerhassett said to his journal, again and again. Now and then the boats stopped at a town or a post, though both were becoming rare; they were now on the edge of the wilderness, moving beyond the frontier, where the only law was force. At Fort Massac Burr picked up a new recruit or two, including an army sergeant. The Ohio came to an end, pouring itself into the broad, muddy Mississippi. The journey continued.[78]

A month after leaving from Blennerhassett's Island, two weeks after meeting Burr at the Cumberland, the group found itself at Bayou Pierre. The little Mississippi offshoot was far to the south, just a few miles above Natchez. Here Burr visited an old friend, Peter Bryan Bruin. Bruin was now a territorial judge, a federal officer, and he had bad news for his guest. He showed Burr copies of the cipher letter and Jefferson's proclamation, which had found their way into the local newspaper. Burr had gotten news of the Neutral Ground Treaty by now, but he still might have thought that Wilkinson had freed himself up to take New Orleans for him. But now Burr knew that the general was going to fight him, arresting his New Orleans lieutenants and gearing up to turn the army on him. Aaron Burr knew James Wilkinson. The general was a dangerous enemy. He knew, too, that all of his plans had fallen to dust. His best hope now was to stay out of Wilkinson's hands. The only things that stood between him and Wilkinson's army were his pitiful corps and Mississippi's civil authorities. Acting Governor Cowles Mead was on the lookout, and word of Burr's arrival was spreading. So Burr dashed off a note to Mead, left it with Bruin, and returned to the dubious safety of his little flotilla.[79]

Mead had mobilized the militia, and soldiers were scouring the countryside. A militia detachment arrived at Bruin's the next morning. Bruin was there; Burr was not. A militia officer found Burr's letter to Mead lying on a table. Mead got it a few hours later. "I am greatly surprised," he read, "to hear that my views have been grossly misrepresented and that my approach has been made the subject of alarm to this country." Burr went on, proclaiming his innocence, referring to the Kentucky grand jury's refusal to indict him, and inviting Mead to visit him at Bayou Pierre and see for himself that this was only a group of Washita settlers. "It is hoped, sir," Burr continued, "that you'll not suffer yourself to be made the instrument of arming citizen against citizen and of involving the country in the horrors of civil war without some better foundation than the suggestions of rumor or the vile fabrications of a man notoriously the *pensioner* of a foreign government."[80]

If Wilkinson had deserted Burr, now Burr deserted Wilkinson. The general knew that the only way to save himself was to vilify the New York expatriate. Now Burr knew it too, and he knew just as well that his only hope for escape, perhaps for survival, was to hold Wilkinson up as a liar.

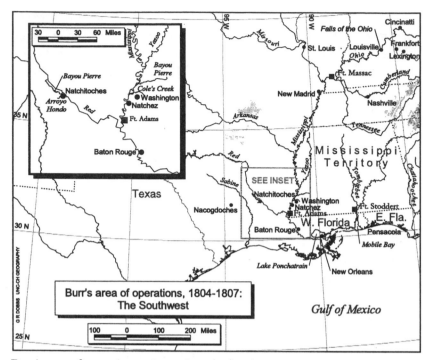

Burr's area of operations, 1804–1807: the Southwest.

But would Mead take the bait? To be on the safe side, quite liter-ally, Burr moved his force to the Mississippi's far bank, where he proceeded to hide his weapons, sinking them in the river or hiding them in the woods.[81] Then he waited to see what would happen.

Mead was not quite sure what to do. Warnings from Wilkinson and the East told stories of a force of a thousand or more; but Burr's little group was not much of an army. Two of Mead's colonels, Thomas Fitzpatrick and W.H. Woolbridge, had already dropped in on Burr. "I could easily take him," Woolbridge told Mead. "He has four Flat Bottom Boats and five Barges filled principally with provisions. I did not see One stand of arms." And Burr had a point about Wilkinson. People had talked for quite some time about his supposed connec-tions with Spain. Whether or not the rumors were true, Wilkinson's acts in New Orleans were strange. Mead could read between the lines; Burr was afraid, deathly afraid, of Wilkinson. Maybe he could use that fact.[82]

Carefully, Mead composed orders for Fitzpatrick. Tell Burr, he ordered, that "if he has been vilified or injured by rumour or the *Pen-*

sioned he shall receive . . . the full and complete protection of the laws of the territory"—*if* he surrendered quietly.[83]

Fitzpatrick rowed over to the far side of the river that night and passed on the message to Burr. It was not good enough. Burr wanted written assurances. The next day Fitzpatrick sent them. "I have a small detachment of the Militia here under my command," he wrote. "I am ready to afford both yourself and your associates, all the protection and civility herein before mentioned should you think proper to recross the Mississippi."[84]

Then came a letter from Mead himself. Fitzpatrick, the good cop, had offered a carrot; now Mead delivered a bit of stick. Mead had force, too; he was getting ready to use it, and he made sure that Burr knew it. "Your approach to this country has excited not only the apprehensions of the general government but alarmed in a high degree the good Citizens of this territory," he told Burr. "From these causes I have ordered my militia to rendezvous at such places as will enable them to guard this Territory against any designs inimical to this Government."[85]

The combination was working. Burr was uneasy. He talked earnestly with the two envoys that Mead sent, one of whom was George Poindexter, territorial attorney general. Burr "pointed to his boats," Poindexter recalled, "and asked if there was any thing military in their appearance." Poindexter agreed that they looked quite innocent. Burr spoke of his fear of assassination; Poindexter tried to calm him. "I had no hesitation," he swore, "in giving him the most perfect assurance of personal safety while in the Territory." But then came more stick. Poindexter "assured him that force would be used, if necessary, for which purpose the militia were then on their march to arrest his progress."[86]

Burr knew that this was no bluff. As the parley went on, a boatload of militia crossed the river and landed below Burr's encampment. Davis Floyd was ready to fight, and he asked Burr to let him attack. Instead Burr asked Fitzpatrick to call off the troops. Fitzpatrick complied, but Burr's options were dwindling. He asked for a meeting with Mead to take place the next day, and Poindexter promised him one.[87]

The meeting took place as scheduled, on the river's east bank near the mouth of Cole's Creek. Burr brought his flotilla with him, and the militia agreed to leave it in peace while Burr and Mead talked with each other. Now Mead was all stick and no carrot. He had Burr under his guns and in his grasp. He dictated his terms: Burr's unconditional surrender, a search of the boats—and an answer in fifteen minutes. If Burr rejected the terms, Mead would seize the whole force.[88]

Burr had to give in, and he did, but he mentioned his fear of Wilkinson and asked if Mead would protect him. Mead's reply is unknown, though Poindexter thought that the answer was yes. With that Burr was off to the little territorial capital of Washington under escort. The New World Rhine journey, and Burr's own grand designs, had come to a whimpering end.

Burr still had certain assets. His fellow voyagers, now technically under arrest, had mostly stuck with him. During the negotiations some had spread through the countryside telling sympathetic stories about him. This was Mississippi, moreover, not far from Spanish Florida, and he could expect some support here from those who hated the Dons. Not that he claimed to have planned anything illegal; but word of those plans had gotten around, and maybe that would help him. Along with everything else, he had his own quiet charisma, the same dark charm that had kept him safe from Weehawken to Frankfort.

He had allies, too. William Bayard Shields, one of Mead's aides de camp, was a family friend. Another was Thomas Rodney, one of the three territorial judges. Rodney and Burr went way back, and a few days after his capture, Burr found himself in Rodney's courtroom. On the bench with him was Peter Bryan Bruin, another of the three judges. The third was somewhere else, so the bench was heavily in Burr's favor.

Burr entered into bail and recognizance, five thousand dollars in all. He had two attorneys; Shields was one of them. The prosecutor was Poindexter, but he had no wish to prosecute, for as far as he could tell, Burr had done nothing that amounted to a criminal act, not in Mississippi, at least. As for allegations of treason, Poindexter argued that the territorial court had no jurisdiction.[89]

Rodney didn't want to hear that. Neither did Burr, who feared that he would find himself on the way to New Orleans and Wilkinson if the court couldn't try him here. Rodney tried to reassure him. "If Wilkinson, or any other military force, should attempt to remove his person out of the Mississippi territory," Blennerhassett reported the judge as saying, Rodney would "put on 'old '76' and march out in support of Col. Burr and the Constitution." He then summoned a grand jury pool. The final panel was reputedly full of hand-picked Burr supporters.[90]

From there on out the performance was a reprise of what had happened in Frankfort. The judges delivered a powerful charge, full of allusions to treason. Burr tried to address the jurors, the prosecutor objected, and the court put a stop to it. It stopped Poindexter too, as he tried to rebut. The judges had had their say, and the jury now had the ball. But Poindexter wouldn't play. In that he differed from Joseph Hamilton Daveiss. He was sure that the court lacked jurisdiction, the power to hear and decide the case, and as far as he cared, that was that. He had nothing to give to the jurors that they could legally use to form the basis for an indictment. And the jury didn't indict. It agreed with the prosecuting attorney that Burr had done nothing illegal. The only things it condemned were the high-handed acts of Cowles Mead and his officers in going after Burr with the militia.[91]

Burr had won again, and was once more free to go, or he thought that he was. But it wasn't that simple. For some odd reason, Rodney refused to agree, deciding that Burr was still under recognizance. Perhaps he resented the parties' upstaging him. Judges like to be in control of their courtrooms, friendship notwithstanding. Or maybe something else was going on. That was what worried Burr, and he wanted his freedom, and fast. The reason was simple. Despite Rodney's statements about "old '76," he was risking Burr's life. Word had come up the river that Captain Shaw's fleet was approaching with orders to capture Burr. Silas Dinsmore was hanging around, and Burr was complaining to the court that someone had raided the post office and stolen some of his mail. But worst of all was the appearance of Captain Hook. To us the name is humorous, almost as funny as the Mississippi militia officer Major Stephen Minor. But Hook was no laughing matter. Moses Hook, U.S. Army captain, arrived in town during the courtroom proceedings, sent here by Wilkinson's orders. He had company, too, a few other officers, all dressed in civilian clothes, all heavily armed with pistols and knives. They weren't there as neutral observers. And Aaron Burr was afraid. [92]

On February 7, when called for in court, Burr failed to appear. With that, Mississippi lost its patience with him. Governor Robert Williams was now in charge, having returned from the East. He issued a proclamation putting a two thousand dollar price on the running man's head. Burr's attorney Lyman Harding claimed that under the terms of the recognizance Burr was free to go, but the court called the lawyer "a quiblur."[93] Nobody knew where Aaron Burr was; but he was somewhere near.

Treason is so dangerous because it threatens the established order, political, social, and religious. A successful treason is not treason at all, but a revolution. Little wonder that Mississippi planters feared Burr. Some of their slaves had started to cheer when they heard that Burr's fleet was approaching.[94] So with Burr abroad once again, their masters were taking no chances.

On Tuesday February 10, a slave from Bayou Pierre stopped at William Fairbanks's house to ask directions to Natchez. Fairbanks noticed that the slave's horse looked suspiciously like Burr's. Even the slave's coat seemed familiar, resembling one that Burr had been wearing. Fairbanks searched the man, who put his hand on his cape, as if to hide something. That only drew Fairbanks's attention; he found a note stitched inside it.

The message was unsigned, but it was addressed to "C.T. & D.F."—Comfort Tyler and Davis Floyd. It was short and to the point. "If you are together, keep together, and I will join you tomorrow night," it read. "In the mean time, put all your arms in perfect order."[95]

Fairbanks instantly warned the governor, who arrested all of Burr's little corps and put a guard on its boats. The slave didn't know where Burr was hiding, so that was a dead end, but then came another surprise. A day or two after the Fairbanks affair, Williams got two notes from Burr. "The vindictive temper and unprincipled Conduct of Judge Rodney have induced me to withdraw for the present from public View," read one. "I nevertheless continue in this disposition, which has been uniformly manifested, of submitting to civil authority so long as I can be assured that it will be exercised toward me within the limits prescribed for other citizens." The other one, more recent, was angrier. "I have seen your proclamation—It was unworthy of you to lend your name to a falsehood." Burr still claimed that he hadn't jumped bail, and he tried to convince Williams of this. But Williams was tired of negotiating with criminals. He wrote Burr back and gave the letter to one of his lawyers. He was perfectly blunt. "You cannot be considered in any other light than as a fugitive from the laws of your country," he wrote.[96]

That was it: Burr was a fugitive. His only hope now lay in flight, along the frontier, into the ancient forests. Perhaps he could get out of the country. But somewhere out there in the woods were General Wilkinson's killers. Burr was more than just on the run. He was running for his life.

Part Five

The Indictment

*H*abeas corpus is one of the oldest of writs, and one of the most important. "The Great Writ," judges and scholars have often called it. The common law has a good many writs, court orders to public officials to do certain things. Often they have mystical-sounding Latin and medieval names, such as *coram nobis, supercedeas, scire facias,* and *quo warranto.* But habeas corpus is in a class by itself.

The writ of *habeas corpus ad subjiciendum,* as its full name goes, is simply a court order to someone, usually a government officer, to show why he is holding a certain person in custody, hence its name, which literally means "You may have the body for the purpose of subjecting." It forces the officer to justify, legally, why he is holding this person a prisoner. This sounds routine and vaguely legalistic. It may be the latter, but it certainly isn't the former. Imagine, for a moment, an America in which habeas corpus doesn't exist. With that thought we suddenly enter a world of midnight arrests and martial law, a world where dissidents suddenly vanish and where government rules by whim, where rulers have no law to obey and law tyrannizes the citizens. In a world without habeas corpus, the police or the army may arrest someone and hold him or her without trial, forever, for any reason at all, or for no reason whatsoever.

If treason is the only crime deadly enough for the Constitution to mention, then habeas corpus is the only writ crucial enough for the Constitution to protect. The document's authors, who saw no need to draw up a bill of rights—that came later—still made sure to put in a safeguard for the Great Writ: "The privilege of the Writ of Habeas Corpus shall not be suspended," it reads, "unless when in Cases of Rebellion or Invasion the public Safety may require it."[1]

But the framers did not define what amounts to "rebellion." They left that to the judgment of Congress, most likely figuring that the people were trustworthy enough not to do anything rash with this loophole. They were mostly right. The very first Congress even enacted a law expressly giving the federal courts the power to issue the writ.[2] Lapses, however, do happen. And such a lapse came in early 1807, when Thomas Jefferson winked at martial law in New Orleans, and his Republican Party, the party that had denounced Federalist tyranny not ten years before, took steps to destroy habeas corpus in the face of the Burr Conspiracy.

⁂

As the new year began, Jefferson and his officers were watching the mails like hawks, waiting for word from the West. Slowly the news trickled in from hundreds of miles away and a month in the past. Others were waiting, too. Jefferson had not mentioned disunion in his November proclamation or his early December message to Congress, but stories were flying by now, on Capitol Hill and everywhere else. Meanwhile Jefferson stayed silent, making no further public statements.

For John Randolph the silence was wrong. He was a House member, a cousin of Jefferson, and a huge executive branch critic. For the last couple of years he had treated Jefferson and his officers to some of the most biting attacks that anyone had ever seen. He was good at it, too, and he enjoyed it a lot. He was a Republican, but not in the mainstream. He thought Jefferson and his people were behaving too much like Federalists. "I came here prepared to cooperate with the government in all its measures," he said in 1806. "I found I might cooperate, or be an honest man."[3] Since then he hadn't cooperated.

In mid-January, with the whole town wondering where Burr was, what he was up to, and what the government was doing about it, Randolph struck again. Congress was more important then than it is today, at least when crisis was looming. A single executive or a small group of officers, can act and react much faster in emergencies than a bunch of congressmen can. The principle is the same one that dictates that a captain, not a committee, commands a ship-of-war, and why a general heads an army. But American government is not a ship-of-war. It rests on popular control. And in 1807 people still distrusted executive power, remembering the old royal governors. Congress was the voice of the people, and the people demanded a say in what was going on. So Randolph took the lead.

On January 16, after a month and a half of executive silence, he proposed a House resolution asking Jefferson to tell it what was going on. Randolph especially wanted to know what Jefferson was doing about Burr. People were acting as if everything were perfectly fine, Randolph said, but that was absolute nonsense. "The United Sates are not only threatened with external war but with conspiracies and treasons," he cried. "And yet we sit and adjourn, adjourn and sit, take things as schoolboys, do as we are bid, and ask no questions." The whole thing was absurd. Congress ought to investigate, and Jefferson should lead, or follow, or get out of the way.[4]

Randolph's motion stirred up a hornet's nest. He was a troublemaker, and people knew that, but he did have a point. And the debate got hot. The phrase "executive privilege" was not yet in use, but some already had the idea. One congressman argued that if the House forced the president to show his hand by discussing countermeasures in public, that would frustrate the whole point of the House's request. Most people sided with Randolph; but those who didn't had a point too. In the end came a compromise: The House called for all the intelligence the president had, and an explanation of what he had done, but it refused to ask what he was planning to do in the future.[5]

Jefferson listened and answered. He didn't have to, not in practice at least. As for legally having to answer, the law of executive privilege is fairly vague even today, and as of early 1807 it was nearly nonexistent. But Jefferson decided the time had come for rumor control. Six days after receiving the House's request, he sent Congress a public message, a message that marks the beginning of his open persecution of Burr.

Jefferson's account of all that had happened was fairly accurate. It stands up well even today, with a few big exceptions. He led off with one of the biggest. Jefferson apologized for his delay in reporting. Information was still pouring in, he explained, but in piecemeal fashion, mixed in with "rumors, conjectures, and suspicions." Separating fact from fiction was hard, and he wanted to avoid making false accusations based on such material. "In this state of the evidence," he remarked, "delivered sometimes too under the restriction of confidence, neither safety nor justice will permit the exposing [of] names, except that of the principal actor, whose guilt is placed beyond question."

Jefferson was the president; he was neither a judge nor a jury. But here he pronounced the chief conspirator's guilt, to his irreparable prejudice. Then he launched into his own version of the story. "Some time in the latter part of September, I received intimations that designs were in agitation in the Western Country unlawful and unfriendly to the peace of the Union; and that the prime mover was Aaron Burr, heretofore distinguished by the favor of his country."

Jefferson *had* received intimations in September. He had also received them in August, and April, and March, and all the way back to the preceding December, but he didn't talk about those. He did slam Joseph Hamilton Daveiss, who had been one of the first to warn him. He criticized the attorney's "premature attempt to bring Burr to justice, without sufficient evidence for his conviction," a futile attempt that "produced a popular impression in his favor, and a general disbelief in his guilt." This added to the strength of Jefferson's argument that he himself had done just the right things, at just the right times.[6]

The president finished up by mentioning Wilkinson, and by discussing the writ of habeas corpus. He had heard by now from Wilkinson that a New Orleans judge had issued such writs for Ogden, Bollman, and Swartwout, and that when Captain Shaw had gotten the one for Ogden, he had had to let him go free. "Mr. Ogden now struts at large," fumed Wilkinson in his report to the president. Jefferson also knew that Wilkinson had ignored the other two writs, accusing the judge of being a Burrite.[7] Wilkinson, in short, was flouting the Constitution, and Thomas Jefferson knew it.

Other than writing to Wilkinson, Jefferson could do nothing about it, but he could control what happened in Washington, where Bollman and Swartwout would be showing up soon. He made a point of saying to Congress that the New Orleans court had sprung Ogden with a writ of habeas corpus, and he let the point hang in the air. As for Bollman and Swartwout, the president said, he was sure that they would receive fair trials.[8]

Jefferson had written his message because of the pressure he had felt from the House, but he sent it to the Senate as well, and the Senate was where things blew up. The day after hearing the message, Jefferson's floor leader in the Senate, William Branch Giles, moved to suspend the normal course of procedure and consider a bill to suspend habeas corpus. By the end of the day the Senate had done it and sent a bill on to the House, with a request that it move as fast as it could in light of the impending emergency. The following day, Bollman and Swartwout arrived, still in military custody.[9]

The Senate might be trying to suspend habeas corpus; Wilkinson might be running amok in New Orleans; Burr might even be leading an army of thousands; but none of that mattered to a small corps of lawyers in Washington. They had clients to defend. If those clients were thought of as traitors, if panic was sweeping the country, what did that matter? It was all the more reason to make the government play fair.

So far that wasn't happening. Bollman and Swartwout were under guard at the Marine barracks. Soon after they got to town, Jefferson ordered the local U.S. attorney to arrest them for treason. The attorney went to the federal circuit court and asked for a bench warrant, flourishing affidavits from Wilkinson and the president's November proclamation. That caused a stir; one of the three judges hearing the case wondered out loud if an unsworn presidential statement that made no mention of treason and an affidavit from a man a thousand miles away could meet the Fourth Amendment's probable cause requirement. The court needed time to consider the issue.[10]

That made an opening for Bollman and Swartwout's lawyers. They were a powerful, talented group. Among them were Charles Lee, former U.S. attorney general; Francis Scott Key; and Robert Goodloe Harper, a quick-witted, bombastic Federalist who was one of the giants of the Washington bar. They now asked for habeas corpus, demanding to know by what right the Marines held Bollman and Swartwout. They had a good point. The court issued the writ; but the Marine commandant didn't bother to answer it.[11]

That got the lawyers steamed up, but before they could act, the court went ahead and issued the warrant the U.S. attorney was after. A day or two after that, a federal marshal brought in Bollman and Swartwout. They were free of the military, but they weren't in much better shape, for now the government demanded their commitment for treason. No grand jury; no indictment; not even a chance at bail; only jail, and perhaps an eventual trial.

The prisoners' lawyers objected, and the court allowed them to speak. They attacked the flimsy record, which now included an affidavit from General William Eaton. But the attack was in vain. The court split two to one, with the majority allowing commitment. For the two majority judges, the record showed probable cause. Treason was in the air, so to speak; everyone knew it from New Orleans to

Washington, and that was good enough for commitment, if not for conviction. The U.S. attorney had shown, one judge declared, "a scheme laid by Burr to usurp the government of the United States; to sever the Western states from the Union; to establish an empire west of the Allegheny Mountains, of which he, Burr, was to be the sovereign, and New Orleans the emporium, and to invade and revolutionize Mexico." Bollman and Swartwout had known about this, and they had helped, and that was misprision of treason, a bad enough crime in itself.[12]

The chief judge dissented. He saw what was happening in the press, in the streets, in the halls of Congress, and even in his courtroom. "The worst of precedents may be established from the best of motives," he warned. "Dangerous precedents occur in dangerous times." He was looking at the law, not just facts or emotions. "I can never agree," he told the crowded room, "that executive communications not on oath or affirmation can, under the words of our Constitution, be received in a court of justice, to charge a man with treason, much less commit him for trial."[13] But that was a minority view, and Bollman and Swartwout went to jail, while their lawyers went back to court, this time the U.S. Supreme Court, to seek habeas corpus again.

This time they really went all out. The first thing they had to do was show that the high court had the power to issue the writ. The problem was *Marbury v. Madison. Marbury* said that the court had two kinds of jurisdiction: original, which the Constitution spelled out, and appellate, which was up to Congress to control. Congress could do nothing to expand or restrict original jurisdiction, or so *Marbury* said. The problem with Bollman's and Swartwout's case was that habeas corpus wasn't part of that jurisdiction. If it wasn't appellate, then the court didn't have it.

Robert Goodloe Harper thought otherwise. He was always a very good Federalist, and a better disciple of Hamilton. Habeas corpus, he said, wasn't original, and it wasn't appellate either. It was part of a court's inherent power, independent of Constitution or Congress. It was something that courts simply did, by virtue of the fact that they were courts. Harper even managed to slam Jefferson a few times. The historical reason for habeas corpus, he said, was that "the king has always a right to know, and by means of these courts to inquire, what has become of his subjects. That is, he is bound to protect the personal liberty of his people, and . . . these courts are the instruments which the law has furnished him for discharging his high duty with effect." The words dripped with sarcasm. Jefferson knew where Boll-man and Swartwout were. They were exactly where he wanted them—in jail. Not that Jefferson was a king. Harper would never say that. In the United States the people were sovereign. "Are they under an obligation less strong to protect individual liberty?" he asked the justices rhetorically. "Have not the people as good a right as those of England to aid of a high and responsible court for the protection of their persons?"[14]

It was all vintage Harper, and the Court agreed with him, but not for the reasons he gave. In fact John Marshall, who spoke for the court, dismissed the "inherent power" idea. He didn't need it, for as far as he was concerned, habeas corpus was appellate, not original. Congress had given the justices the right to issue the writ, and if individual justices could do it, then so could the court as a whole. Justice Johnson complained. The prisoners' lawyers, he groused, had made "a very unnecessary display of energy and pathos to make their point." But the chief justice's opinion carried the day, and the court sent the writ to the federal marshal who was holding the men in jail.[15]

Unlike the marine commandant, the marshal promptly answered the writ, stating that he held Bollman and Swartwout in custody because of the circuit court's order. That was enough to bring in the record from below, including the president's proclamation and all of the other materials. The lawyers had at it again. They moved to free the prisoners for any of several reasons. The circuit court proceedings had been highly irregular, the evidence failed to show probable cause, and it wasn't the sort of evidence that could justify jailing.[16]

The litigation had lasted for nearly a month. February was nearing its end. The time had come for decision, so John Marshall made one. It all depended, he said, on whether the evidence could and did give probable cause for commitment for treason.

Treason was a scary thing. In England it had grown from a few extreme acts into a string of lesser evils, acts that the courts had construed as treasonable. These "constructive treasons" were one reason why the Constitution addressed the crime, ordaining that levying war against the United States, or adhering to its enemies, were the only treasonous acts. "To constitute that specific crime for which the prisoners now before the court have been committed, war must be actually levied against the United States," he said. But he threw a sop to the people who feared for the nation's survival.

> It is not the intention of the court to say that no individual can be
> guilty of this crime who has not appeared in arms against his coun-
> try. On the contrary, if war be actually levied, that is, if a body of
> men be actually assembled for the purpose of effecting by force a
> treasonable purpose, all those who perform any part, however
> minute, or however remote from the scene of action, and who are
> actually leagued in the general conspiracy, are to be considered as
> traitors. But there must be an actual assembling of men for the trea-
> sonable purpose, to constitute a levying of war.[17]

Those words would come back to haunt him. But that was later.
Right now he was worried about Bollman and Swartwout. He had to
decide if the evidence showed that the two men had helped levy war.

In making this decision, Marshall took great interest in the cipher
letter, a copy of which Wilkinson had sent to Washington and which
was part of the record. The copy might be accurate; then again, it might
not. That was still another point that would spring up again later on,
but for now he took it as accurate. Even so, he remarked, nothing Burr
said in that letter inevitably pointed to treason, and neither did anything else. Burr might have been targeting Mexico only, in which case
no treason existed. It might be a Neutrality Act violation, but that was
different from treason, and nothing had happened in Washington that
involved the Neutrality Act. If Bollman and Swartwout were to be
tried for breaking *that* law, a patient Marshall explained, the trial had
to be in the district where the crime was committed, by a jury drawn
from that district. Federal law, not to mention the Sixth Amendment,
said so. "It is therefore the unanimous opinion of this court," he concluded, "That they cannot be tried in this district."[18]

Habeas corpus had won; Bollman and Swartwout were free. In
Congress the court-haters gnashed their teeth, and talk of impeachment rolled through the halls. But the government had bigger fish to
fry than Marshall, Bollman, or Swartwout. By now the town knew
that Burr was in hiding, and possibly planning something else.
Maybe he had no army, but the Gulf Coast was still a highly volatile
place. So as the sideshow of Bollman and Swartwout concluded, the
question echoed ever more loudly: Where was Aaron Burr?

☙❧

His eyes, in the end, were what gave him away. He camouflaged the
rest of himself. Normally as natty as could be, he was soon clad in

backwoods uniform: homespun, a blanket coat, a hat of battered beaver, and a large scalping knife. A tin can cast over one shoulder completed the picture. But the brim of the hat, no matter how low, could never be low enough, the night never dark enough, the weather never foul enough to hide him completely, not with those eyes of his.

Two weeks after he jumped bail, near midnight on February 18, two shabbily dressed men came trotting through a flyspeck of a town called Wakefield, two hundred miles from Natchez, in present-day Alabama. The winter had been a wet one so far. Streams were swollen and bridges were out, but the weather had cleared for once, and a brilliant moon was shining.

A burly backwoods lawyer and federal land registrar, Nicholas Perkins, heard the horses approaching. "What could people be after," he wondered, out riding at such a late hour in the middle of nowhere? He went outside to see what was up.

The first horsemen rode right past him without even slowing down. The second one stopped and asked for directions. The pair were heading to Major John Hinson's. Perkins told him the way, but warned of the washed-out bridges and muddy trails ahead. He suggested that the men stay at the local tavern, but the riders went on their way.

"Those men were very extraordinary men indeed," Perkins told one of his fellow lodgers, "riding that late hour of the night in a strange country, determined to go on to Major Hinson's at a distance of seven or eight miles on a bad road, over broken and dangerous bridges, passing by a public house . . ." Then he started to put things together. Word of the fugitive had gotten around. "They must either have some bad design on Hinson or his property," he decided—or else "it was colonel Burr making his escape." If he had known that Burr was a friend of Hinson's, he wouldn't have had any doubts. He knew about the two thousand dollar reward that Governor Williams had offered, and he decided to take another look at the men. He woke up the local sheriff, and the two set off after the midnight riders.

They didn't catch up until the pair had already gotten to Hinson's. The first horseman, the quiet one, had gone into the kitchen. Perkins watched him carefully while the sheriff talked to the other one. "I observed his dress and every appearance to be extraordinary," Perkins later reported. His outfit was that of a riverman, and in itself it was nothing unusual. What was striking was the man who was wearing it. Finally, despite the low-brimmed hat, Perkins got a look at the eyes. The description had said that Burr's "sparkled like diamonds," and as Perkins looked at the stranger's, he knew for sure. The man he was watching was Aaron Burr.

Perkins took off, racing for Fort Stoddert. He distrusted the sheriff, he needed help, and the army post was his best chance. There he found the commander, a young lieutenant by the name of Edmund Pendleton Gaines. When Gaines had heard Perkins's story, he grabbed a trustworthy sergeant and a few other soldiers and struck out with Perkins for Hinson's.[19]

Two or three miles before they arrived, they stumbled across two men. One was the sheriff; the other was the striking horseman. The Florida border was close. Burr was working his magic again, and with the help of the sheriff he had almost escaped. But now the nightmare had happened. He was face to face with Wilkinson's army. It may have been the worst moment of Burr's life. As he spotted the soldiers he asked the sheriff who they were. "That is Perkins and you are gone," said the sheriff. "God have mercy," Burr swore, grabbing the bridle in both of his hands.

The groups met in the road. "I presume, sir," said Gaines, "that I have the honor of addressing Colonel Burr."

Burr's answer was brusque. "I am a traveler in the country," he said, "and do not recognize your right to ask such a question."

But Gaines was in no mood for argument. "I arrest you at the instance of the federal government," he replied, and Burr asked by what authority. "I am an officer in the army," Gaines told him, "and I hold in my hand the proclamation of the president and the governor directing your arrest."[20] And so Burr's flight ended. The soldiers took him back to Fort Stoddert.

Gaines would become a great general one day, but in 1807 he was just a young infantry officer, commanding forty-odd men at a remote army post a stone's throw from the Florida border. Many of his people were sick, including his brother. A Spanish officer was skulking around and asking to talk to Burr, and rumors were spreading throughout the area that a plan was afoot to take Florida. Some people here would be happy to see it happen.

All of this worried Gaines. Burr, though afraid, was charm itself, even nursing Gaines's own brother, and flirting with his wife as well, if we believe the old Alabama histories. None of this changed the fact that he was a prisoner, albeit an important one, in the fort's best room with a sentry at the door. But a guard was useless against Burr's charisma, which Gaines feared would corrupt his own men. Burr might already be in touch with friends on the other side of the Florida border. Things were not right. "I apprehend something is brewing below," the lieutenant wrote Perkins. "It strikes me as an indispensable step for the security of this settlement and the tranquillity of the Western Country generally, to send the colonel direct to Washington City," by which he meant not the Mississippi hamlet from which Burr had escaped, but the District of Columbia.[21]

The problem was how to get him there. The Tombigbee settlements around Fort Stoddert were the wildest and most isolated place in the whole of the United States. Gaines couldn't send Burr by sea—that would mean cutting through Florida. The only way was east, through Indian land. Gaines couldn't do it himself. For all that he knew, a Spanish force was about to come flying over the border at him and he needed every man he could get. He wanted Perkins to go, and he could only spare his friend a couple of soldiers to help. That would not be enough, not for Indian country, not for a man such as Burr. "Get four active, sober, confidential young men," he told Perkins, "with good horses, pistols and swords, with one or two good light shot guns—no baggage save a blanket." The group would have to travel light and fast, and he wanted it moving as soon as possible. Two weeks after Burr's arrest, everything was ready. Perkins had found the men. Gaines had drawn up the passports that might help them get through the tribal lands alive, and he had written out orders for Perkins. With that Burr and his escort were off.[22]

The old histories paint a colorful picture of the journey that followed. During his time along the frontier Burr had seen wild places and times, but nothing as wild as this, except perhaps the march on Quebec. The weather was terrible. The pristine snows of Canada and the Old Northwest were absent; instead torrents of chilly rain poured down, drenching the endless pine forests and turning the ground to mud. By day the group rode in single file, soldiers behind and ahead of Burr. By night the men camped in the woods, often with swampland nearby, a feeble small fire providing scant safety from wolves and bears and hostiles. Burr made himself useful by watching for danger and his captors treated him kindly, but he was still a prisoner, and they talked very little with him, lest he get them on his side.

They skirted south of the Appalachian Range, but the way was still hard, since this was one of the country's wild places. Day after day went by as the party slogged through the muck and forded the swollen rivers, sometimes on horseback, sometimes using canoes. First came the Chattahoochee, then came the Flint, and next the Ocmulgee. At last the men emerged from the forest on the west bank of the Oconee in Georgia, where they found the first sign of white civilization, a ferry. Before long they were approaching an army post on the river, a little place near present-day Milledgeville with the ominous name of Fort Wilkinson.

Nearby they found a public house. When they told the owner where they were from, he wanted to hear all the news "of the *traitor*, Aaron Burr." Burr was a bad one, all right, he said. Had anyone captured him yet? Were people afraid of him? Perkins and his men, embarrassed, said nothing, but Burr, sitting woebegone in a corner, spoke up. "I am Aaron Burr," he said, standing and staring the man in the eye. "What is it you want with me?" That stopped the owner cold.

Georgia was nearly as wild as Alabama, but soon the group had gotten to South Carolina, where Burr had Alston connections. The way so far had been dangerous, but Perkins now faced a new kind of threat. Burr still had friends in the East, and crossing South Carolina would be hard. The group avoided the larger towns, but trouble was bound to come, and it did, at a little place called Chester Courthouse. Now Burr had flankers, one on each side; he rode in a circle of guards, so nobody could get close. When it was well into town, the party passed near a tavern, and that was when Burr made his move.

He leaped down from his horse. "I am Aaron Burr," he cried to a small group of bystanders, "under military arrest, and claim protection of the civil authorities!"

Perkins instantly drew his pistols, and a second later he was next to Burr, ordering him to get back in the saddle. "*I will not!*" shouted Burr. The brawny backwoodsman dropped his pistols, picked up the little New Yorker, and threw him onto the horse like a sack of potatoes. Then came one of the very few times, maybe the only time, when Aaron Burr lost control. Tears sprang to his eyes for a moment—but only for a moment—and then the trek resumed.

After the brush in Chester, a carriage seemed like a good idea, so Perkins splurged and bought one. The roads were a little better by now, and the party moved north, closer and closer to Washington.

The thousand-mile trip was almost complete when, at Fredericksburg, Virginia, Perkins received new orders. Washington had heard about the arrest, and James Madison, at the direction of Jefferson, sent a courier to find Perkins and give him a letter. "On receipt of this," the letter read, "you will direct your course with your prisoner to Richmond, in the state of Virginia," and report to the U.S. attorney there.

The change of plan was no problem, since Richmond and Washington were equally close. Not long after getting the letter, at twilight on March 26, the tired little group rode into Richmond, the carriage surrounded by weary horsemen, the horses exhausted, and made for the Eagle Tavern. Here Perkins placed Burr under guard and went off to find the U.S. attorney. The long journey was over. The last of the evening light faded, and Aaron Burr sat in the darkness.[23]

❧

If habeas corpus has an eight-hundred-year pedigree, treason stretches back at least three times that far. Centuries before the birth of Christ, the Roman Republic came up with the notion of *maiestas*, the crime of insult to public authority. Many such insults were possible. Maladministration of office, violation of various civic duties, aiding and comforting an enemy of the state—all these and more met the test. Later, with the rise of the Caesars, people had to watch their step around the imperial family. *Maiestas* had always banned injuring public officials, but the emperors were even touchier. Bedding an imperial princess, at least without marrying her, could corrupt the ruling bloodline, and so it became an offense. So did wearing the imperial purple, counterfeiting the imperial coin, and any number of other imperial insults. Anything that robbed the ruler of dignity caused the loss of his majesty, his *laesa maiestas*.

While Rome marched towards empire, another civilization well to the north, in the German woods, was also growing and thriving. It was more of a tribal world, one where the line between public and private was blurry. One of its chief virtues was loyalty, loyalty to a lord or a tribal king, and breach of that loyalty was one of the greatest of crimes. Breach of trust is still bad today, but back then it was heinous, especially when feudalism took hold. Throughout the long medieval centuries, as Rome collapsed and kingdoms rose, Germanic and Roman blood and thought battled and finally merged. So did Germanic and

Roman law. In England, the rim of the Empire, non-Roman notions were stronger, and the feudal system of lord and vassal lasted longer than elsewhere in Europe. But even there both influences lived. Even the name that the English chose for their highest of crimes was a blend: *treason,* a vaguely French word that literally means a betrayal or handing over, as in a breach of faith. The idea worked well in a Christian age. In *Paradise Lost,* John Milton points out that the highest crime of all is treason against God. Other treasons existed, even before Milton's time. Anyone who owed loyalty to another and failed to deliver committed at least a petty treason. A wife who killed her husband, a servant his master, a cleric his lord, all these were petty treasons. But the king, just short of God, was the ultimate overlord, and a breach of *his* trust was high treason.[24]

High treason was a dangerous thing. It threatened the established order, endangering all of society. It challenged a government's legitimacy, threw the realm into chaos, and made thinkable all other crimes. Because it was the gravest offense, it brought the most horrible punishment. Sir William Blackstone, the great eighteenth-century legal writer, described the medieval penalty.

> 1. That the offender be drawn to the gallows, and not be carried or walk; though usually a sledge or hurdle is allowed, to preserve the offender from the extreme torment of being dragged on the ground or pavement. 2. That he be hanged by the neck, and then cut down alive. 3. That his entrails be taken out, and burned, while he is yet alive. 4. That his head be cut off. 5. That his body be divided into four parts. 6. That his head and quarters be at the king's disposal.[25]

This all sounds pretty grim, even for an age when punishments tended to be swift and brutal. To make things worse, there was no written list of what was and wasn't a treason for most of the Middle Ages. Over time the number of constructive treasons grew, coming to include murder of royal messengers, riots, breaches of the peace—even a lone highwayman, robbing a simple merchant on the king's road, could be guilty of accroaching royal power.[26]

This was going too far, and in 1352 Parliament got treason under control. Edward III needed money; the Hundred Years' War was raging, and Edward was trying to conquer France. Parliament held the purse strings, so it forced a deal on the king. Edward could have his taxes, if he would agree to a statute of treasons. Edward gave in, and Parliament enacted the statute.

The Statute of 25 Edward III became the basis for Anglo-American treason law for all of the following centuries. Sometimes aberrations would happen, during the days of the Tudors for instance, but mostly the statute controlled. It listed a number of treasonous things from Germanic and Roman law, including levying war against the king, and giving his enemies aid and comfort. It also included compassing the death of the king, deflowering one of his daughters, and other offenses against the royal bloodline, the sovereignty of England.[27]

The United States had no royal bloodline, certainly not after independence. The people were sovereign, or so went the theory. On top of that, the nation was born in treason. The men who wrote and adopted the Constitution all met the definition—except that their treason succeeded. They claimed that natural law had justified the Revolution. Still, treason was a sore subject with them. Now that they were the sovereigns, they wanted to hem in the crime, but they also had to fit it for use in a very new world, a continent far larger and more unpeopled than England, a place without social estates or primogeniture or titles of nobility. They had all read their Blackstone. Their words and their concepts were English; but this wasn't England, and the law had to adapt.

The result was the Treason Clause in the Constitution's Article III. Some of its words came straight from the statute of Edward III, but with a few uniquely American twists. The clause speaks of treason "against the United States," not the Crown, and it ordains that such treason "shall consist only in levying War against them, or in adhering to their Enemies, giving them Aid and Comfort." Compassing, counterfeiting, deflowering, all of these stayed in England, since individual majesty no longer mattered. The word "only" was key; the founders aimed to avoid the threat of constructive treasons. But they couldn't avoid it completely. Any word can be construed once the law gets hold of it. What, for instance, does "levying war" really mean? The founders didn't say. They couldn't define every word. The words of their definitions would have needed defining, and so forth. The best they could do was to write what they did, and let future Americans decide what to do with it all.

But they did include other protections. What amounted to treason was one thing. How to prove it was another. Before the Statute of

Edward III, defendants rarely got indictments or common law trials. The Crown would attest that the accused had done something treasonous, and that was enough to land him in trouble. The Constitution's authors would have none of that. It could lead to trumped-up charges and government tyranny. So they added a procedural safeguard that, like treason itself, they drew from the English law. "No Person shall be convicted of Treason," they wrote, "unless on the testimony of two Witnesses to the same overt Act, or on Confession in open Court."[28]

The "overt act" phrase was important. Benjamin Franklin had pushed the convention to include it, remarking that prosecutions for treason were "generally virulent" and that perjury would be a great danger.[29] A need to produce two witnesses to the same act would cut down on that. But "overt act" means more than that. It is a reminder that while treason may be the king of crimes, it is nevertheless just a crime, and as a crime it has certain elements. Nearly every crime has two of them, the mental state and the action. The two must correspond. A person who thinks about shooting somebody to death has committed no crime if thinking is as far as he goes. A hunter who carefully shoots at a deer and kills a man by pure accident hasn't committed murder, for he lacked the intent. Only when the intent and the act correspond can the actor be a criminal. "Overt act" meant the same for treason. Treason needed an "act," and "overt" took care of the mental state, for in the arcane world of legal language, the word in this context means criminal intent.

But in 1807 the act, not the intent, was the problem. Burr had said some traitorous things. Thomas Jefferson knew that much from what the Morgans had told him. In Bollman and Swartwout's case the Supreme Court had held that a defendant had to be tried in the legal district where the crime had occurred. Bollman and Swartwout had done nothing wrong in Washington, and so they couldn't be jailed there. All of this meant that Jefferson had to send Burr to the district in which he had acted in traitorous fashion.

Jefferson had worried from the beginning about the need for an overt act. That was one of the reasons he gave for not moving more quickly against Burr, his claim that Burr hadn't committed any such act.[30] Even in the spring of 1807, things were still dicey. Several people had said that Burr's little flotilla had looked anything but warlike, and "warlike appearance" was one of the English standards for "levying war." No one was even sure if Burr's group had had any weapons to speak of. But there was one clear moment of action: the December midnight on Harman Blennerhassett's Island, when weapons and men came together in resistance to General Tupper.

Blennerhassett's Island was on the rim of Virginia, just barely in Wood County. That placed it within the federal circuit court district that was headquartered eastward in Richmond. The circuit courts were where most of the federal action was. District courts only heard admiralty and petty criminal cases. Circuit courts were the trial courts for everything else. But they had no judges of their own. Instead the Supreme Court justices rode circuit when they weren't hearing cases in Washington, going out to the states and sitting with the district court judges to form the circuit court benches. This was an odd and grueling arrangement. It meant that the justices spent thousands of miles in the saddle each year. The idea was to get the nation's best judicial talent out among the states and the people to build a strong federal law, but the justices hated the practice. In 1801 the Federalist Congress ended it. In 1802 the Republicans brought it back again, and the circuit riding continued.[31]

Jefferson may have been happy in 1802 when his Congress repealed the Federalists' act. But in 1807 he was no longer cheering. The Supreme Court's decision in *Bollman and Swartwout*, the requirements of federal statutes, and the president's own need for an overt act all meant that Burr had to be tried in Richmond. And in the spring of 1807, the circuit rider for Richmond was Thomas Jefferson's Federalist nemesis, Chief Justice John Marshall himself.

⚬

Marshall and Jefferson hated each other. In part it was due to politics. Jefferson recalled the early days of America's revolution, when an indifferent central government in London refused to respond to public outcries, except to grow harsher. Marshall remembered the war, when an impotent central government, this one in Philadelphia, could do nothing to help the American army. Marshall had been at Valley Forge, and he always remembered what happened there, the cold and the hunger. These very different memories were enough to take the two men's ideologies along divergent and mutually hostile paths.

The difference was more than political, though. Jefferson and Marshall were cousins, estranged ones. Each was a branch of the Randolph clan, the first of all First Families of Virginia. But Marshall's line sprang from the Randolphs' black sheep, which may have made him resent his very patrician cousin. Marshall was one of the most affable men of his time, but for whatever reason he couldn't stand Jefferson. Jefferson, for his part, returned the hatred completely.[32]

After 1801, when each became head of his own branch of government, things between them only got worse. Jefferson railed at the federal judges, most of whom weren't Republicans; Marshall struck back with *Marbury v. Madison,* which gave the courts the power to trump the laws of the Republican Congress.[33] The Jeffersonians impeached Samuel Chase; the Marshall Court freed Bollman and Swartwout. In answer to that, the Republicans discussed taking away the Supreme Court's appellate jurisdiction, and talked of further impeachments.[34] The personal was more than political by now; it was institutional. Marshall and Jefferson used the judicial and executive branches to go after each other, or so it seemed sometimes.

But none of this meant that John Marshall would automatically side with Burr. Marshall was a Hamilton devotee, and Burr was Hamilton's slayer. Hamilton had once warned Marshall of Burr, during the election of 1800, and Hamilton's word was enough for John Marshall. "Your representation of Mr. Burr with whom I am totally unacquainted shows that from him still greater danger than even from Mr. Jefferson may be apprehended," he had replied. "Such a man as you describe is more to be feared and may do more immediate if not greater mischief."[35]

Later Marshall got to know Burr. They sat with each other at Jefferson's first inauguration. The three made an interesting group. Marshall and Burr were logical, subtle thinkers, both calm men of poise, and Marshall's eyes were almost as striking as Burr's. Marshall and Jefferson, both Virginians, were both casual in manner and dress, and good at getting their political ways. All were hugely intelligent. And each distrusted the other two—except Burr, perhaps, who had no strong feelings toward Marshall.

The most interesting meeting between Marshall and Burr came in 1805, at the very end of Burr's term as vice president, during Chase's impeachment proceedings. Burr presided; Marshall was a witness. Barely two years later they both came to Richmond, where Burr would stand before Marshall.

The reunion took place at the Eagle Tavern, the twenty-year-old brick building where Burr was under guard. "Of all the taverns I ever was in," a visitor once said, "Eagle is the worst."[36] It was big, though, filling a whole city block, and Marshall found himself a secluded room for examining Aaron Burr. At midday on March 30, as a crowd looked on very quietly, a federal marshal escorted the prisoner to the room. In went Burr and his lawyers, along with the federal attorneys, and then the door closed behind them.[37] George Hay, the district's U.S. attorney, wasted no time. He gave Marshall a copy of the record from the *Bollman* case, complete with its affidavits, and some things from Perkins as well. All very correct, all very formal; Marshall knew the *Bollman* record by heart, having written a lot of it personally, but here he served in a different persona, as a mere circuit judge, and Hay had to go through the motions of introducing the record. Then he demanded Burr's commitment, for both treason and a Neutrality Act violation.

Hay moved on to another point. Not a courtroom in town could hold all the crowds that were quickly swelling outside. He wanted the proceedings to take place in the Virginia House of Delegates, which had a bigger capacity. Marshall didn't much care; his thoughts were of Burr. He agreed in the end to make Burr post bail until he could decide if commitment was proper. He called for five thousand dollars, and Burr found two friends who helped him come up with the money. Marshall told Burr to show up in court the next morning, and with that the brief hearing was over.[38]

Hay had been right. The courtroom wasn't big enough. Soon after calling the court into session, Marshall adjourned to the House of Delegates, as Hay had suggested. The House chamber was also too small, with hundreds of people outside trying to make their way in, but it was the best that Richmond could do. This would be the arena where, for the next several months, the hottest legal battle the New World had seen would play itself out.

Marshall wanted to hear from both sides before he made up his mind about committing Burr for treason. The prosecutors led off. Today there were only two; more would come later. George Hay was one of the pair, and the other was Caesar A. Rodney, the U.S. attorney general. Rodney was also the son of Thomas Rodney, the judge who had given Burr such a hard time down in Mississippi. He was the top law enforcement officer in the country short of Jefferson himself, but Hay took charge this morning. It was all a question of probable cause, Hay said. The *Bollman* record was enough to show that Burr had violated the Neutrality Act and committed treason too. And if that were not enough, Hay went on, the court should recall that Burr had jumped bail not two months before.

When Hay had finished, Burr's lawyers answered. Burr, too, had two of them, though more would join the team soon. John Wickham spoke first, followed by Edmund Randolph. Wickham attacked the very idea that that an act of treason had happened. As for the Neutrality Act, which came into play only in peacetime, he argued that it didn't apply. The Spain of 1806, he said, was "a power with which we were in an intermediate state between war and peace," a clever attempt to get around the fact that Congress had not declared war.

Randolph echoed Wickham's arguments, especially as to treason; because it was "of all crimes the most heinous," he told the chamber, "it required the strongest evidence to support it." But here, he said, the only proof the United States had "was vague, weak, and unsatisfactory." As for Burr's flight, Randolph argued, "he had not fled from justice, but from military oppression."

Then Burr got into the act. Other attorneys would soon join him, and his defense team would stand as one of the best in American history, but he would serve as his own lead counsel. He reminded the court that not one, not two, but three grand juries had already targeted him. Each time, he said, he had rushed to the scene, had given every assistance, had *invited* investigation; each time he had gone free, winning vindication in Mississippi as well as Kentucky. All that he wanted now, he said, was another lawful inquiry, although he denied that any proof whatsoever of misdemeanor or treason existed.

Rodney then spoke for the government, denouncing the idea that Burr was out to settle the Bastrop lands. "The mystery in which this business was enveloped," he claimed, "afforded just grounds of suspicion. If the settlement of lands merely was intended, why were dark and corruptive messages sent to military commanders?"[39]

He had a good point. The cipher letter was crucial. A copy was on record. But it was only a copy. The law's "best evidence" rule required the original, if it still existed. A copy wasn't trustworthy. Someone could have altered it. The handwriting might not match Burr's. Something could be wrong with it, and Burr and his lawyers would not let the court forget it in the months to come.

Marshall had heard enough. He was ready to make up his mind. The following morning he did.

He started with the cipher letter. "Exclude the letter," he said, "and nothing remains in the testimony which can in the most remote degree affect Colonel Burr." And the letter had problems. "The original letter, or a true copy of it accompanied by the cipher," he continued, "would have been much more satisfactory." Burr's heart may have lifted at this, but if so it then plunged again. This, said Marshall, was "an inquiry not into guilt but into probable cause," and the copy would do for that. But Marshall kept the seesaw going. He saw a great many problems surrounding the letter, but on the whole it was good enough grounds for committing Burr—but only for breaking the Neutrality Act, a much lesser offense than treason.[40]

As for the charge of treason, Marshall had a lot to say. He had been in Washington during the fracas that surrounded Bollman and Swartwout, and he had read the newspapers and Jefferson's proclamation. Even now he was seeing the circus that Richmond was becoming, and he obviously disliked what he saw. It all reminded him too much of his days as a diplomat in Republican France, where heads had rolled and blood had poured in the streets, all because of popular turmoil.[41] Jefferson and his people were going too far, John Marshall concluded, so he decided to reel them in with the law. He paraphrased Blackstone on treason. (Jefferson hated Blackstone.) "As this is the most atrocious offense which can be committed against the political body," he said, "so it is the charge which is most capable of being employed as the instrument of those malignant and vindictive passions which may rage in the bosoms of contending parties struggling for power." That is precisely why the Constitution tied Congress's hands where treason was concerned, and the Constitution demanded an overt act.

"War can only be levied," he went on, "by the employment of actual force. Troops must be embodied, men must be assembled, in order to levy war." But no such facts were before the court. "An invisible army is not the instrument of war, and had these troops been visible, some testimony relative to them could have been adduced." The prosecutors had had plenty of time to find evidence. "The fact to be proved," he chided the government, "is an act of public notoriety. It must exist in the view of the world, or it cannot exist at all." Rodney and Hay knew all about *Bollman* and what it demanded, but still they had no evidence. "More than five weeks have elapsed," Marshall said, "since the opinion of the Supreme Court has declared the necessity of proving the fact if it exists. Why is it not proved?" This wouldn't do. The government lacked grounds for charging a treason. He would commit Burr only for breaking the Neutrality Act. If the prosecutors wanted to chase the idea of treason, they could take their chances with a grand jury later on.

But Marshall went too far. His loathing of Jefferson was nothing new, but how the president had handled this mess simply made the chief justice see red. Marshall conceded that Sir William Blackstone supported commitment unless the suspicions were "wholly ground-less." But even Blackstone had limits, John Marshall decided: "I do not understand him as meaning to say that the hand of malignity may grasp any individual against whom its hate may be directed, or whom it may capriciously seize, charge him with some secret crime, and put him on the proof of his innocence."

Marshall was a good-natured man, despite his dislike of Jefferson. But when these vicious words came tumbling out of his mouth, they shocked everyone in the courtroom. If Jefferson had gone over the line in saying that Burr was a traitor, Marshall transgressed just as badly in saying such things of the president. Marshall knew it, too. Just after he pronounced his decision, someone told him that those words were a slap in the government's face. So he publicly stated that he had merely been glossing Blackstone, not commenting on Washington politics. But it was too late. The prosecutors had heard him, and whatever they heard, so did Jefferson.[42]

Meanwhile Burr was out on bail. He had not exactly won the first round, but Marshall had opened the door enough to let him buy a few weeks of freedom. This time he wouldn't run. He was too busy gearing up for the next battle, a fight before a Richmond grand jury.

Jefferson was just as fond of John Marshall as Marshall was of Jefferson, even in the best of times, and these times were far from the best. Within a couple of days the president knew what Marshall had said. After that he lost all his remaining perspective. "Were not the bundle of letters of information in Mr. Rodney's hands, the letters and facts published in the local newspapers, Burr's flight, & the universal belief or rumor of his guilt, probable ground for presuming the facts of enlistment, military guard, rendezvous, threats of civil war, or capitulation, so as to put him on trial?" he fumed to William Branch Giles. "Is there a candid man in the U.S. who does not believe some one, if not all, of these overt acts to have taken place?"[43]

As if things weren't bad enough, Marshall now made another mistake. The Richmond bar was small, as was the town itself. Only a few thousand people lived there, and amenities were scarce. When court was in session, the lawyers tried to get together for evening entertainment and meals, hosting each other freely. One spring night John Wickham had Marshall over to dinner. The two had been friends and courtroom opponents for over a decade, and Richmond neighbors too. Wickham, like Marshall, was a good-natured gentleman. Even John Randolph of Roanoke liked him. He was a good lawyer, and though he argued a lot of highly important cases, he was now in the trial of his life. But this didn't stop him from entertaining, and when Marshall got to Wickham's that night, he found other guests already there—including Wickham's most famous client, Aaron Burr.

Marshall should have left at once. It might have been an honest mistake, but as the principal judge in the case, he had to keep his hands spotless. He didn't leave. He stayed and had dinner with Burr, and of course the press found out. The case was already political, and now it became hopelessly so. Everything that Marshall did from now on would be under a cloud.[44]

While Jefferson and Marshall misbehaved, Burr prepared for what was to come. He wrote often to family and friends. Sometimes he complained. "It is not easy for one who has been robbed & plundered till he had not a second shirt," he told his friend Charles Biddle, "to contend with a government having Millions at command & active and vindictive agents in every quarter—yet in justice to my reputation & to the feelings of my friends, nothing within my power will be left undone."[45] More often he was cheerful. "It is not possible," he assured a New York protégé, "that I can be convicted of any crime unless by the agency of the most horrible perjury or by the most barefaced exertion of partiality and party spirit."[46] With Theodosia he was positively uplifting. "Such things happen in all democratic governments," he told her. "Now, madame, I pray you to amuse yourself by collecting and collating all the instances to be found in ancient history, which you may connect together, if you please, in an essay, with reflections, comments, and applications. This I may hope to receive about the 22d of May."[47] Her husband Joseph was feeling the heat. He and Burr both had heard from Thomas Truxtun, whose name had been dragged into the fray and who didn't like it one bit. Stories were spreading about Alston too, and he, like Truxtun, denied them.[48] But Theo had her father's brains, and Alston was also intelligent. They may well have had a bonfire one night and fed it some of their papers. Maybe others did, too. Treason was a dangerous thing.

For weeks Burr spent most of his energy preparing for battle and building a legal dream team. By the time court convened on May 22, he had four of his lawyers there. Wickham was already with him, and so was Edmund Randolph. A cousin to Marshall and Jefferson, and John Randolph too of course, Edmund had been the nation's first attorney general, and later secretary of state. He was a capable and competent man, a Federalist of course, even though a Virginian, but a scandal had removed him from office in 1795, and he had never quite lived it down.[49] The newcomers were Benjamin Botts, energetic and young, and John Baker, well-connected in Richmond and on board, no doubt, to handle the political side of things in this commonwealth in which Burr was the enemy. Baker's role would be small, but Botts played a big part. He was an excellent lawyer: "His severe analysis shattered and dissolved the most gnarled subjects," wrote an acquaintance, "and then, with a driving logic, he sent home the main point in debate to the conviction of all hearers."[50] Burr had more help coming, but for now he would have to get by with this small, meager group.

Against these four attorneys, and Burr himself, the government only had three, or maybe two and a half. Alexander MacRae, Virginia's lieutenant governor, was old and bilious, as sarcastic as Randolph of Roanoke without half of the wit. William Wirt was young and a bit of a playboy. He was a good enough lawyer and man of letters, but he was just now settling down in his ways and building a serious legal career. The third man was George Hay, competent but not brilliant. He was used to political trials, though. A few years before, he and Wirt were on hand in the *Callender* trial, when Chase said the things that helped get him impeached. In that sense, at least, they were seasoned.[51]

Neither Randolph nor Hay was lead counsel. Hay was taking his orders from Jefferson. Letters flew back and forth between them, with Jefferson suggesting tactics and strategy, and presidential suggestions are orders.[52] As for the other side, Burr was in charge, and he was one of the nation's best lawyers. As court opened on May 22 he was dressed to the nines in dignified black, his hair well powdered, his face pale, his eyes luminous. Richmond was swollen to twice its normal size, with the houses and inns all full, throngs camping outdoors, and everyone trying to claw a way into court. The few hundred who got inside were struck by Burr's demeanor. "There he stood," wrote a watcher, "in the hands of power, on the brink of danger, as composed, as immovable, as one of Canova's living marbles."[53]

Clausewitz tells us that war is an extension of politics, a means of executing national policy. If that is true, and it is, then law is a variation on war. Strife between Anglo-Saxons and Normans, which sometimes erupted in blood, was one of the reasons behind the birth of the common law. It was a system of dispute resolution that gave control and wealth to the Crown instead of squandering English resources in needless and violent feuds.[54] The common law is an adversarial system, just as war is. Even today, most litigants are not after justice. Instead they want to win. Judges are simply the referees, and they sometimes promote fairness, but at the heart of the system lies conflict. If a party fails to protect its own interests, nobody else in the system will.

Aaron Burr, whose life was at stake, would yield nothing.

The grand jury was his first line of defense. America likes grand juries. During the Revolution they had mulishly blocked royal officials' efforts to enforce the smuggling laws and other imperial measures. That made them good, as far as the rebels cared. When the dust had settled the former colonists put a grand jury requirement into the Fifth Amendment, forcing a federal government that they didn't quite trust to rely on the cumbersome process in starting criminal trials. Without a grand jury indictment, or at least a presentment, no trial for a major crime could take place.[55]

In the last several months, the federal grand jury requirement had shielded Aaron Burr three times. Two grand juries had expressly refused to indict him. Now he faced another one, a jury the likes of which the country had never seen. The list of names in the pool reads like a *Who's Who* of Virginia: members of the federal Senate and House, congressional hopefuls, other leading citizens, and among them Jefferson's warmest friends and bitterest political enemies.

One of the latter was John Randolph of Roanoke. He was an enigma. He had been fighting the president for months by now, even forming his own political faction, the Quids, with which to attack Thomas Jefferson. He had seen Burr's Virginia arrival, complete with army escort,[56] and maybe that got him wondering whether Jefferson was playing fair. But he himself had criticized Jefferson not four months before for not doing enough about Burr, and Burr was no friend of his. As a juryman Randolph might go either way.

Burr was more worried about two other men, William Branch Giles and Wilson Cary Nicholas. Giles was Jefferson's de facto Senate floor leader, the man who had moved to suspend habeas corpus a few months earlier, and now here he was in Burr's grand jury pool. Nicholas, who was standing for the House, was another big Jefferson ally—"my vindictive and avowed personal enemy," Burr called him, "the most so that could be found in this state."[57]

At first glance this lineup looks odd, and maybe it was. But potential jurors were few. The population was small back then. Women were barred from service, and so were people of color. Given the case's prominence, the marshal probably went out of his way to find jurors of high reputation.

High reputation, perhaps: But Burr was worried about juror biases, especially those of Giles and Nicholas. He was even concerned that the marshal may have played a sinister game. He noticed the man had summoned twenty-five jurors, while the law required twenty-four. To Burr this suggested that the marshal had hand-picked a panel in the hopes of stacking the deck against him. "I consider it proper to ask the marshal and his deputies what persons they have summoned, and at what periods," he told the court, "whence it may be known, whether some have not been substituted in place of others struck off the panel." He then made an ominous statement. "When we have settled this objection, I shall proceed to exceptions of a different nature."[58]

John Wickham seconded Burr. He knew of someone, he claimed, "who had been excused from this very panel."

"Name him, sir," the marshal broke in. "I demand his name."

Wickham was taken aback. He told the marshal that he had intended no insult, but he refused to put up with "such interruptions." The fireworks had begun. They wouldn't end for months.

Now another Marshall broke in as well, but being the judge he could do it. He wanted the lawyers to teach him. In an adversarial system, the attorneys could know more about questions of law than even the judges could. Now Marshall asked if the issues of substituting grand jurors had ever come up in Virginia before.

"Not, sir, to my knowledge," Edmund Randolph replied. "I have never seen a case where it was so absolutely necessary to assert every privilege belonging to the accused, as in this. . . . If this right has never before been asserted, it is because there never was an occasion which so imperiously demanded it as the present." By now he was on a roll.

"There never was such a torrent of prejudice excited against any man, before a court of justice, as against colonel Burr," he told Marshall, "and by means which we shall presently unfold."[59]

It was good enough to make Marshall side with Burr, who asked the names of the jurors who had gotten excused. One was another famous Virginian, John Taylor of Caroline. But by and by the problem resolved itself, and a panel of sixteen jurors remained. The time had come for Burr's second attack. "It is with regret," he told the court, "that I shall now proceed to exercise the privilege of challenging for favour."[60]

A challenge for favor, or a challenge for cause, is a basic part of trial jury selection. The Sixth Amendment calls for an impartial petit jury in criminal prosecutions, so both parties to a criminal action can strike off biased jurors with a challenge for cause. But this was a grand jury, not a trial jury. The Constitution doesn't command that grand juries must be impartial. In the old days grand jurors were supposed to bring their own knowledge of possible crimes into the jury room with them, and a requirement of impartiality would have made that impossible. But here Burr was, claiming that grand jurors were biased and demanding the right to challenge for cause.

Hay was strangely compliant. "How many of the panel does the counsel mean to object to?" he asked.

"Only two," replied Burr: Giles and Nicholas.

Now Giles spoke up. If Burr asked questions of him, he would have to answer, and no matter what the answers were, Giles would have prejudiced himself. He resented the claim that he was biased.

Hay began to lose patience. To "relieve us from all this useless embarrassment," he said, he was willing to let everyone who had voiced a "decisive opinion" be excused. Burr was agreeable. Things seemed to be going his way.[61]

Giles defended himself. "I not only voted for the suspension of habeas corpus," he admitted, "but *I* proposed that measure. I then thought, and I still think, that the emergency demanded it." But he denied that these things biased him against Burr. "However," he gave in grudgingly, "as it is left to me to elect, whether to serve on the grand jury or not, I will certainly withdraw."[62]

One down. Next up was Nicholas. "He has entertained a bitter personal animosity against me," said Burr. "I cannot expect from him that pure impartiality of mind which is necessary to a correct decision."

Nicholas, too, was upset. Like Giles, he felt that withdrawal might seem an admission of prejudice. But he knew he was beaten, just by Burr raising the issue, so he also withdrew, but not before hinting that a henchman of Burr's had tried to frighten him out of jury duty.

Burr denied any knowledge of that, blaming it on his enemies. Nevertheless, he had gotten his way, and now the court examined the other jurors. Burr found them all acceptable, even the ones who had felt some anger when stories of his western adventures appeared in the news. The pretrial publicity had been much too extreme for Burr to deal with it all, so he bowed to the inevitable.

Marshall tapped John Randolph as foreman, and Randolph addressed the court. "I wish to be excused from serving," he said. "I should be wanting in candour to the court and the party accused, if I did not say, that I had a strong prepossession."

Part of Burr wanted this trial, or at least vindication from yet another grand jury. "Really," he said, disapproving, "I am afraid that we shall not be able to find any man without this prepossession."

Marshall explained his ruling on jurors more carefully. A juror had to have formed an opinion, and he had to have declared it as well, if he was to be struck off the panel. "I do not recollect to have declared one," Randolph admitted, and with that Marshall installed him as foreman.[63]

Finally the grand jury was ready, and Marshall gave it a charge, spelling out the definition of treason, and the jurors retired to begin their weeks of work. Burr was there to hear the charge, and as the men filed out, he fell into an old habit of his. He asked the court to let him talk to the jury about certain aspects of treason law and evidence. He was making a pest of himself, but that was all right. The rules allowed that, and sometimes even encouraged it. A good trial lawyer was one who could make the rules work in his favor, and that was what Burr was doing, but it wasn't much fun for Hay. The U.S. attorney expressed his hope that the court "would not grant particular indulgences to Colonel Burr, who stood on the same footing with every other man charged with a crime."

That was the moment when Burr blew up without warning. "Would to God I did stand on the same ground with every other man!" he burst out. "This is the first time I have ever been permitted to enjoy the rights of a citizen. How have I been brought hither?" he reminded the crowded chamber of his ride into town under guard.

Marshall tried to call him down, but Burr refused to be muzzled. He wanted to keep up his attack. He felt sure that the government couldn't prove that an overt act of treason had happened, and even if it could, the act might have been in another judicial district, or provable only by flawed affidavits. He wanted to hit Hay with these legal problems as early and as hard as he could, and then keep on hitting him, and he and his lawyers cajoled Marshall. But Marshall wasn't quite sure. He had impressions, but the questions weren't ripe. The government's lead witness hadn't even shown up. He postponed the decision. Burr could always talk to the jury later on.[64]

The first day's fireworks were over. The jury was settling down to its work, which for a while would consist of waiting for witnesses. Meanwhile the lawyers planned their moves and countermoves. The Richmond spring moved on towards summer.

Aside from all of the famous people who were already appearing in court, a good many others were in town as well. One was Andrew Jackson, who had flip-flopped again on his view of Burr's guilt. He was here as a witness, but he also spoke in Burr's favor while out in the streets, at least by some accounts.[65] Another soon-to-be famous face was that of Washington Irving, there to cover the trial for a New York newspaper. Still another youngster attending was Winfield Scott of Virginia. Forty years later the Duke of Wellington would label this man "the greatest living soldier" for achieving what Burr did not: the conquest of Mexico City.[66] Scott may well be the finest general the nation produced between Yorktown and Fort Sumter, but in 1807 he was merely a court reporter's assistant, just reaching his twenty-first year, and America's general-in-chief was James Wilkinson. Wilkinson was also the witness-in-chief against Burr—but he was nowhere to be found, which was hamstringing the government lawyers.

While waiting for Wilkinson, Hay moved again to commit Burr for treason. His motion in March had failed, but now he had more evidence. Burr and his counsel fought him, claiming that the matter was out of Hay's hands since the grand jury was here, but Marshall let Hay make his case. Still, Burr didn't retreat. He demanded that Hay begin with proof of an overt act, without which Burr couldn't possibly be guilty of treason. Hay refused. He wanted to go in straight chronological, not legal, order, for at least two good reasons. The story would make more sense that way, and, more important, the chief witness was still not in town.

Marshall sided with Hay at first, but when he saw that the government had no proof of an overt act he backtracked, so Hay had to shift his ground. The prosecutor asked the court to raise Burr's bail, another way of locking him up without getting a commitment for treason.

Up to now things had been going Burr's way. Today he had won a big victory and he was further heartened by the arrival of Luther Martin of Maryland, a member of his defense team. Martin was the nation's greatest trial lawyer, better even than Burr. Burr had watched from his Senate chair as Martin, a devout hater of Jefferson, had won an acquittal for Samuel Chase, and now Martin was working with Burr. When Hay requested more bail, Martin got moving. The Supreme Court had already decided, he said, that Hay's affidavits were no good by themselves. In light of that fact, he argued, one thing was clear. Hay's motion "amounts to this: 'We have no evidence of treason, and are not ready to go to trial for the purpose of proving it; we therefore move the court to increase the bail.'" The very thought was ridiculous.[67]

All this made Aaron Burr cocky, and when Marshall hesitated to raise the bail, he seized the moment, offering more money of his own free will. Marshall was grateful, and Burr gave more, a total of ten thousand dollars. He had gotten Marshall off the hook, and shown the public he had nothing to fear. These were smart public relations moves.

Meanwhile the grand jurors twiddled their thumbs. Wilkinson was nowhere around. Hay reported that he was definitely on his way by sea from New Orleans. "General Wilkinson will be here, as sure as he is a living man," he declared. "Nothing but death will prevent him." But for now the jurors were wasting their time. May became June; still no General Wilkinson. Marshall dismissed the jury, telling it to reconvene later on. It met again on June 9. No Wilkinson.

Maybe what Burr did now was partly because of monotony. He would have done it anyway, but Wilkinson's absence may have influenced his timing. As Marshall dismissed the jury again, Burr rose and addressed the bench.

In the 1960s the Supreme Court ruled that prosecutors must disclose any information they have that might help clear the defendant. The idea was to make the trial a quest for truth and not a battle of wits or a sporting event.[68] But this was the nineteenth century, and

Burr wasn't yet a defendant. Even so, he wanted to fight back, and he wanted the government's help. He had known for a while that his best defense was to put James Wilkinson on trial. He also figured that he had to go after Jefferson, even though he was here in Jefferson's own Virginia. On top of all that, the two men had information he wanted. He had no way of knowing exactly what they had said to each other, but he had a few ideas. He knew that Wilkinson had written a letter on October 21. Jefferson had said so in his January message to Congress. Burr also suspected that the War or Navy Departments had put out orders to destroy him and his flotilla.[69] He had seen such an order reprinted in the *Natchez Gazette* a few months before. He wanted to know if the president had ordered his death, or if Wilkinson had had that idea.

Finally there was the cipher letter. It was all wrong. The language sounded nothing like Burr's. The New Yorker's prose was reserved, sometimes witty, with the occasional French or Latin allusion. But this letter sounded bombastic, with its talk of gods and worthies. Burr denied writing it, and others agreed. "I am confident the letter is not accurately stated," wrote Senator William Plumer. "It sounds more like Wilkinson's letter than Burr's." The foremost scholar of Aaron Burr's papers claims that the handwriting is Jonathan Dayton's. How Dayton substituted his own missive for Burr's, not just Bollman's copy but Swartwout's, is something of a mystery, but it wouldn't have been impossible. Burr *did* write a letter, and Dayton could have pulled a switch. The odds are that what Wilkinson read was not what Aaron Burr wrote. To add more confusion, though Burr might not have known, Wilkinson doctored the letter to make himself look less guilty and to make Burr seem more so. What he sent to Washington was not a true copy.[70]

Whatever else Burr may have known, he did know that neither he nor the court had anything like the whole record. He was sure that Wilkinson and Jefferson were holding out on him. So while waiting for Wilkinson to show, he asked the court to subpoena the president.

Actually Burr asked for a subpoena *duces tecum,* a subpoena for records and papers. He was after the October 21 letter that Wilkinson had sent to Jefferson, along with some other things, including War and Navy Department orders to hunt him down and destroy him. His goals were simple. He wanted to vilify the government, and he figured that he could do it.

The request blindsided Hay, but his instincts were good; he stalled. He told the court that a subpoena wasn't proper if the information wasn't material. No subpoena was needed, he said, since he himself would willingly locate copies of what Burr was seeking. But he also hinted that the court couldn't subpoena Jefferson's private papers.

Then things began to get ugly again. Burr's lawyers disliked the idea of copies. Copies could be tampered with. Burr himself swore that the papers were clearly material, and Hay kept griping that the whole debate was a "useless consumption of time." That was enough for Benjamin Botts. "I cannot sit down, and hear complaints so unnecessarily repeated about the waste of time," he told Marshall. "Mr. Hay makes, I think, about a dozen times as many speeches as any other gentleman; and each speech longer than those of other persons; and yet we cannot open our mouths, without his sounding loudly his complaints to the ears of the hall."

Marshall waived Botts's objections aside. "If the attorney for the United States is satisfied that this court has a right to issue the subpoena *duces tecum*, I will grant the motion," he decided.

"I am not, sir," Hay answered.

"I am not prepared to give an opinion on this point," replied Marshall. "I must call for arguments." He told the lawyers to be ready to go by the following morning.[71]

The next few days were some of the hottest of the whole trial. Randolph, MacRae, Wickham and Botts and Wirt—all of them spoke for hours. The prosecutors' position was clear. A president was different from others. Demanding his presence in court could endanger national welfare. The president was a busy man, and he couldn't drop everything just to attend a trial. And he couldn't just hand over all of his files. They might hold some sensitive data, irrelevant to the trial but crucial to national security. The government lawyers raised some good points. Wilkinson's letters addressed the situation with Spain, and that was confidential. A later age would have classified them.

But Burr and his lawyers differed. "Surely these gentlemen do not intend to represent the president as a kind of sovereign," Martin lashed out, "or as a king of Great Britain. He is no more than a servant of the people. But even the British king may be called upon to give testimony to his people." Martin was just warming up, working himself into a towering rage against Jefferson, a man he simply despised.

The president has undertaken to prejudge my client by declaring, that "Of his guilt there can be no doubt." He has assumed to himself the knowledge of the Supreme Being himself, and pretended to search the heart of my highly respected friend. He has proclaimed him a traitor in the face of that country, which has rewarded him. He has let slip the dogs of war, the hell-hounds of persecution, to hunt down my friend. And would this president of the United States, who has raised all this absurd clamour, pretend to keep back the papers which are wanted for this trial, where life itself is at stake?[72]

Martin's speech was a powerful one, but he didn't have a corner on the self-righteousness market. William Wirt warned how destructive the subpoena could be. "A prisoner seldom has any cordial amity for the government by which he is prosecuted for a crime," he observed. "The truth is, that he feels himself in a state of war with that government; and the more desperate his case, the more ardent will be his spirit of revenge." If Burr could call for this letter, said Wirt, he would set a legal precedent that could one day bring down the government. Better for Burr to have been killed than that, Wirt hinted. "If it be true that Aaron Burr had placed himself in a state of war with his country," he said, "his destruction would have been a virtue; a great and glorious virtue."[73]

Wirt saw what Burr was attempting to do, and he fought back as hard as he could. He fought back too hard, in fact: he forgot the legal presumption that Burr was not guilty. "Before the gentlemen arraign the administration," he challenged, "let them clear the skirts of their client. Let them prove his innocence; let them prove that he has not covered himself with the clouds of mystery and just suspicion . . . and that these charges against him are totally groundless and false."[74]

For days this kind of talk went on, as the lawyers snarled at each other. Their rhetoric flashed and glittered, and now and then sank into personal, vicious attacks. Through it all Marshall and Burr said little. Finally Marshall spoke up, observing that "the gentlemen on both sides had acted improperly in the style and spirit of their remarks," and that they were "endeavoring to excite the prejudices of the people." He hoped that everyone would calm down.[75]

He would have been better off trying to stop a tornado. The invective rolled on, mixed in with deep legal argument. But Marshall had bigger problems than that. He would have to accommodate a citizen's need for justice to a president's need to govern, and the question was a delicate one. On June 13 he delivered the next in his long string of opinions. He decided that he could issue the writ.

Marshall looked at several things, but three of them were especially crucial. First was the claim that the president resembled a king. He was actually more like a governor, in Marshall's opinion at least, and governors could be subpoenaed. He was elected, and served for a term of years, a term that impeachment and removal could shorten. Inconvenience was no defense, he added; subpoenas would run against royal ministers, and they, like a president, were busy. All of this being the case, a president was subject to a simple subpoena.

What about a subpoena *duces tecum*? Marshall had just held that a president, unlike a king, was no different from other citizens. As for delivering papers, then, "the propriety of introducing any paper into a case must depend on the character of the paper, not on the character of the person who holds it." Marshall admitted that some information might be sensitive, so sensitive that courts couldn't touch it. But, he continued, "the question does not occur at this time. There is certainly nothing before the court which shows that the letter in question contains any matter the disclosure of which would endanger the public safety." If the contents turned out to be sensitive, the court could suppress that material.[76]

The opinion was a good balancing act, but Marshall made another political goof as he got near the end of it. If the trial should "terminate as is expected on the part of the United States," he said—that is, in indictment, conviction, and hanging—everyone would regret the withholding of the material. MacRae and Hay jumped on this statement, resenting the idea that they personally wanted to see Burr swing. They were simply doing their jobs. Wirt said nothing. He had already said that he wouldn't have minded if Burr had been hunted down and killed in the West. Marshall tried to mollify the pair, but it didn't do any good. At the end of the day he came down from the bench and apologized in person to Hay, but Hay stayed angry. Burr had beaten him on the subpoena issue, and Jefferson wouldn't be pleased.[77]

Burr had won again. So had John Marshall. In *Marbury v. Madison* the chief justice had given his court the power to tell Congress what it couldn't do; now, in *United States v. Burr*, he told the president what he had to do, at least on paper. For the first time in the proceedings, Marshall had public support, but what Jefferson would do when he got the subpoena was anyone's guess. As for Burr, he now had the

Justus Erich Bollman. *(Courtesy New York Public Library)*

right to defend himself in the president's game, but he couldn't take time to celebrate. Almost as soon as Marshall had read the opinion, Burr's next hurdle rose up, in the form of Erich Bollman.

During his courtroom battles in Washington, Bollman had gone to the president's mansion. Jefferson gave him his word that what Bollman said would not be used against him, and that if Bollman would write down what he knew, no one but the president would see it. Bollman wrote a story of his dealings with Wilkinson, complete with the claim that Burr had designs on New Orleans. Four months later, Jefferson sent the document on to Hay. It could be a powerful weapon, and Bollman a valuable witness. Jefferson told Hay to get Bollman's story in front of the grand jury, or else prosecute the man.[78]

Bollman was there when the court agreed to subpoena the president, and once the smoke from that had cleared, he found himself the next item of business. As the clerk called the adventurer's name as a grand jury witness, Hay broke in and addressed the bench. "Before

Mr. Bollman is sworn," he said, "I must inform the court of a particular, and not immaterial circumstance. He, sir, has made a full communication to the government of the plans, the designs, and the views
of Aaron Burr." He held up a sheet of paper. "As these communications might criminate Doctor Bollman before the grand jury, the
president of the United States has communicated to me this pardon ...
which I have already offered to Doctor Bollman."

Hay sketched out for the court what had happened after his
offer. Bollman had hesitated; he had taken the pardon; then he had
given it back. Hay wanted his testimony, badly, and so now he tried
again, this time in open court. He turned and spoke to Bollman. "Will
you accept this pardon?" he asked.

"No," answered Bollman. "I will not, sir."

It didn't much matter to Hay. Bollman was going to be a grand
jury witness. The pardon was there, and the court could tell the jurors
about it.

"Doctor Bollman is *not* pardoned," Martin piped up, "and no man
is bound to criminate himself."

Hay rounded on Martin. "Are you then willing to hear Doctor
Bollman indicted?" he snapped. "Take care in what an awful condition
you are placing this gentleman."

"Doctor Bollman, sir," sneered Martin, "has lived too long to be
alarmed by such menaces. He is a man of too much honor to trust his
reputation to the course which you prescribe for him."

Marshall was clear on one thing. Bollman was going to testify.
The only dispute was as to whether he had a pardon.

"But there can be no doubt, sir," Martin protested, "if he chooses
to decline his pardon, that he stands in the same situation with every
other witness, who cannot be forced to criminate himself." Martin was
concerned about Bollman, but he was even more worried for Burr. He
didn't want Bollman telling a story that might put Burr's neck in
a noose.

Marshall wouldn't commit himself. "Whether he be really pardoned or not, I cannot, at present, declare. I must take time to
deliberate."

Hay didn't want to wait. He wanted to put on his witnesses in a
very particular order, and now was the time for Bollman. He turned
to the doctor again. "Categorically then I ask you, Mr. Bollman, do
you accept your pardon?"

Bollman's patience, too, was gone. "I have already answered that question several times," he spat. "I say no."[79] With that he went to the jury without any special notifications about self-incrimination or pardons. The question didn't resurface. But Bollman was just one of many who were spilling their guts in the jury room and trying hard to avoid indictments themselves. Burr's lawyers could do nothing to stop them. William Eaton, Thomas Truxtun, George Morgan, Andrew Jackson—the line stretched on and on. To make things worse, Wilkinson had finally arrived in town, and a few days later he showed up in court.

It was a moment of showdown. Everyone sensed it. When the general came into the chamber, every eye there was on him or Burr. Many people noted what happened, including General Wilkinson. "I saluted the Bench," he stated grandly. "In spite of myself my eyes darted a flash of indignation at the little traitor. . . . This lyon hearted eagle eyed hero, sinking under the weight of conscious guilt, with haggard eye, made an effort to meet the indignant salutation of outraged honor, but it was in vain, his audacity had failed him, He averted his face, grew pale & affected passion to conceal his perturbation."[80] Thus spake Spanish Agent Number 13. Washington Irving's account was less passionate.

> Burr was seated with his back to the entrance, facing the judge, and conversing with one of his counsel. Wilkinson strutted into court, and took his stand in a parallel line with Burr on his right hand. Here he stood for a moment swelling like a turkey cock, and bracing himself up for the encounter of Burr's eye. The latter did not take any notice of him until the judge directed the clerk to swear General Wilkinson: at the mention of his name, Burr turned his head, looked him full in the face with one of his piercing regards, swept his eye over his whole person, from head to foot, as if to scan its dimensions, and then coolly resumed his former position, and went on conversing with his counsel as tranquilly as ever.[81]

This was a battle of wills, and Burr wanted to seize the initiative. He had been trying to put the general on trial in the court of public opinion. Now he tried it literally. If Wilkinson could charge Burr with illegal acts, then Burr could charge Wilkinson too.

On the day that Wilkinson showed up, Hay showed the court a letter to Bollman written in cipher. That gave Burr's lawyers some qualms, and Wickham saw something fishy. "How has it been obtained?" he asked. "Has it not the post-office mark on it?" Hay wouldn't say. But Burr's people harried the government lawyers. They knew of Wilkinson's New Orleans dictatorship and they wanted to unmask the man as a lawbreaker. Claiming a violation of the federal mails was a good place to start. Next could come claims of military arrests. Wilkinson had brought witnesses with him to court from the West under military guard. Burr's young lawyer Botts hammered that point home. "A citizen of the United States, now within the hearing of my voice," he told the court, "in a time of profound peace, was seized in New Orleans, and, without being charged with any offense, but merely on suspicion that he could give evidence against Colonel Burr in this court, to which he was willing to come, was committed to prison without bail or mainprize; thrown into a stinking room with the common felons and negroes confined there, and only taken out at last to be transported on board a vessel to Richmond in custody." Botts's outrage was obvious. "He was hurried like a malefactor on board, without being permitted to go to his lodgings to get a shirt to put on. He was forced to yield, in the humility of abject submission, to the arbitrary will of his oppressors. Are we to contend with such enormities? A man, only *suspected of being a witness*, is subjected to military slavery."[82]

Then Botts shifted his fire to the letter. The postmark showed, he claimed, that someone had raided a post office. "The foulness of that very mark of 25 cents deserves execration," he cried.

Hay denied that the letter was postmarked and Botts went after him. "The '25' on the back, is the only postmark of many of the country's post-offices," he declared. "How came that mark there?"[83] Botts had only one answer. Wilkinson had ordered a break-in. Finally Burr himself said as much. The break-in had tainted the evidence, so it couldn't go to the jury. But more than that, it meant that Wilkinson was a criminal. "Sir, we are ready to prove the violation of the post office," he said.

Hay dared Burr to move to have him investigate. "I most solemnly promise to discharge the duties of my office," he said—if Burr would just offer a motion.

Burr called Hay's bluff, if that was what it was. "We have sufficient evidence on which to found our motion."

"What motion?" asked Hay in confusion.

Burr was patience itself. "I thought, sir," he said, "I had sufficiently explained my intentions. I may move for a rule, to show why an attachment should not issue against . . . General Wilkinson, or . . . I may directly move for an attachment itself."

The tables were turned. In the wilds of the West, Wilkinson was a god, with an army at his right hand. But now he was in a courtroom, where Burr was a master. And Burr was going to charge him with breaking the law.

"A pretty proceeding indeed!" cried MacRae. "That the public prosecution should thus be taken out of the hands of the public prosecutor, and that the accused should supersede the attorney for the United States!"

"A strange remark indeed!" shot back Burr. "As if it were not the business of the injured person himself to institute the complaint."

Edmund Randolph entered the makeshift courtroom just then, with an odd look on his face. He immediately read out a motion calling for Wilkinson's attachment—in effect, his arrest.

Things were moving too fast for Hay. "Why these hints?" he asked. "Why these mysterious looks of awe and terror, with which gentlemen come into court, as if they had something to communicate which was too horrible to be told?" Wilkinson was busy with testifying, he told Marshall. Why interrupt that? "Let the present prosecution be concluded," he said, "and gentlemen may then proceed with their investigation into the conduct of General Wilkinson."

Martin couldn't stand it. "He insists that we shall postpone it till the trial is over," he yelled, "and the evil is done!"

Hay was furious too. "It is of no consequence to them whether they prevail in their motion or not," he told the bench. "Their purpose is attained; their pompous declamation, that Wilkinson is a despot, and acted tyrannically, is intended to excite prejudice against him."[84]

But Burr's lawyers kept hounding the general. "He has brought witnesses with him from New Orleans, by military force. He has taken their depositions entirely ex parte at the point of a bayonet," sang out Wickham. "His credibility will be judged from all of the circumstances. Does General Wilkinson shrink from the investigation?" he asked.

"You know he does not," snapped Hay.

At last John Marshall stepped in. The jury could discuss the letter in question, he said; but as far as the motion to go after Wilkinson, he agreed to let Burr introduce it.[85]

For two weeks the weird drama continued, the government with Wilkinson's help going after Aaron Burr, Burr and his lawyers investigating Wilkinson and the government. One day Hay sought permission to help the grand jurors frame some questions. Burr's people fought him on that. If the prosecutors could go in, then the defense should be able to as well. Hay answered that a grand jury was ex parte, a one-sided process that excluded defendants. Another day MacRae asked to bring Wilkinson in to the courtroom to help with his attachment proceedings. Again Burr's attorneys fought back. Turnabout was fair play, Martin said in a long-winded speech. If the grand jury proceedings were ex parte, so was an attachment proceeding, and Wilkinson couldn't be heard. As far as the law was concerned, he said, neither the government nor Wilkinson was here.

"I thought, that all the while he spoke, we were in court," MacRae said nastily.

Martin bristled. He meant legal, not actual, presence. "I know they were *personally* present," he growled. "I saw them; and if I had not, they took good care to make us often hear them."

The opening was too good to pass up. "If presence depend on speaking," said Wirt, "Mr. Martin is not only present, but, perhaps, is the only person who is."[86]

The attacks went on, and so did the legal arguments. Witnesses shuttled back and forth between the jury, which was debating Burr's actions, and the courtroom, where Marshall was hearing testimony on Wilkinson's conduct. Finally, on Saturday June 27, Marshall decided that he wouldn't attach the general. A lot of what Wilkinson had done was probably unconstitutional, or at least illegal, but most of that had been in New Orleans. This was the Richmond district, and Marshall could not concern himself with what had happened outside it. New Orleans was as far outside it as someone could get and still be in the same country. Wilkinson was free to go.[87]

That was good news for Wilkinson, and for the government too. But by then they were already elated. On June 24, three days before Marshall read his opinion, the grand jury indicted Burr for treason.

That was not all. The jury had heard dozens of witnesses. Some were more truthful than others. But taking everything into account, it decided that Burr was a traitor, and so was Harman Blennerhassett. Both men, it found, had also violated the Neutrality Act. The jurors came up with an overt act of treason, the confrontation by firelight on the banks of Blennerhassett's Island. On the strength of that fact, they made presentments for treason against Davis Floyd, Israel Smith, Comfort Tyler, former U.S. Senator Jonathan Dayton, and sitting U.S. Senator John Smith of Kentucky.[88]

Burr and his lawyers had fought like demons. But now their first line of defense had fallen. Still, Burr managed to hold to form. When the clerk read out the indictment against him, Burr rose and addressed the court. "I plead *not guilty,*" he said, "and put myself upon my country for trial."[89]

Kentucky had applauded him, and in Mississippi they cheered. Nothing he said, nothing he did, had mattered to anyone until now. But now things were different. Aaron Burr had become a defendant.

The crime of which he stood accused was the worst in the world. Marshall saw no reason to set bail for Burr, despite Burr's claim that the indictment rested on perjury. Bail was simply out of the question. But then a problem arose. The Sixth Amendment was now in play, with its procedural guarantees. One of those was a trial by jury, a jury whose members had to come from the place where the crime was committed. That meant Wood County, Virginia, on the far side of the mountains. Impaneling jurors from there would take time, time that Burr must spend in jail.

Burr may have been a prisoner, but he was one of the highest rank. Jail would not do for him. Then Virginia came to the rescue. It offered Marshall the use of the state penitentiary, where Burr could have third-floor apartments. Modern prisons were decades away; these lodgings would be good enough for a man of Burr's station in life. Marshall agreed. As he got things in motion for summoning the petit jury he set the trial date as August 3.

❧

Few of Burr's papers survive from that summer. We cannot know what he said about his grave turn of luck. We can imagine what he thought, however, as Marshall dismissed the court and the clock started ticking towards August. Burr still had things working for him. He had the legal presumption of innocence; the government had the burden of proof. He had a judge who was friendly to him, or at least one who disliked the president who had ruthlessly pushed this trial forward. He had the best lawyers a man could find. He had his own courtroom skills, and above all he might, just conceivably, have the gem of reasonable doubt with which he could blind the jurors.

But for all of that, things were grim. He had escaped from Wilkinson's clutches, but a jury could kill him just as dead as an army could. Between the morning of his capture and the afternoon that he heard the indictment read, he had left the frontier, traveled a thousand miles east, to the heart of his enemy's commonwealth, and into the hangman's shadow.

Now he had to fight his way out.

Part Six

The Trial

*A*aron Burr's story was a big event of 1807, one of the biggest in fact, but other things were going on too. England was in a death struggle with France; an era of warfare between the two nations that stretched back for more than a century was approaching its bloody climax. In London the Ministry of All the Talents was doing its best to seal off Europe from the rest of the world with the full might of the Royal Navy. Napoleon fought back as best he could, issuing his Milan Decree on December 17, the latest in a string of French and British orders imperiling neutral commerce, including American merchantmen. Between England and France, nothing that sailed the world's oceans was safe.[1]

On June 22, the same week that Burr was indicted, the fifty-six gun HMS *Leopard* broadsided the American frigate *Chesapeake*, beating her into submission and whisking four British deserters from her blood-washed decks. The cousins were fighting again; the affair was a crisis in Anglo-American relations that started the two countries towards war.[2]

On March 2, Congress enacted a law that would end the foreign importation of slaves with the new year's coming. Nearly every state had banned it already, but South Carolina refused to play ball. Already the Southern economy's hunger for black flesh was starting to grow. A national law could put an end to the slave trade, but not to slavery itself. The cancer continued to spread.[3]

On January 19, on the Potomac estate of Stratford in northern Virginia, the wife of former war hero and late Virginia governor Light Horse Harry Lee gave birth to a son. Ann Carter Lee named the new arrival for her two brothers Edward and Robert. He was a Randolph offshoot, as well as a Lee and a Carter, and so kinsman to Marshall and Jefferson; none in Virginia could boast better blood.[4] But young Robert E. Lee's day was far in the future. For now his older relations held the stage in nearby Richmond and Washington.

They had plenty of things to worry about. The *Leopard*'s attack on the *Chesapeake* was very serious business. A year before the problem was Spain, but now it was England again, after a period of calm in that quarter. Relations between the two countries would spiral down for seven more years, until they fought their last and ugliest battle just outside New Orleans, where Andrew Jackson would become an American god.[5] But even with all of this international trouble in the summer of 1807, Thomas Jefferson still found time to follow Burr's trial. Not only did he follow it; he practically directed the thing, or at least its prosecution.

When Marshall refused to commit Burr for treason in late March, Jefferson had been livid. But when the court subpoenaed him a few weeks later, his public response was calmer, and colder. "As to our personal attendance at Richmond," he wrote imperially, "I am persuaded the Court is sensible that paramount duties to the nation at large control the obligation of compliance with their summons in this case. . . . To comply with such calls would leave the nation without an executive branch . . . ."

Jefferson went on at greater length with regard to delivering executive papers, discussing the role of private executive duties. "All nations have found it necessary," he declared, "that for the advantageous conduct of their affairs, some of these proceedings, at least, should remain known to their executive functionary only. He, of course, from the nature of the case, must be the sole judge of which of them the public interests will permit publication." Reserving these rights to himself, the president reminded Hay in this same public letter that he had already delivered all the papers he had that bore on the Richmond proceedings, and that he had told his officers to do the same. He even agreed to give a deposition, if Burr really desired one; but he refused to go to Richmond. He had sent all the relevant papers, and as far as he was concerned, that meant he was, in effect, in compliance with any subpoena.[6]

But when it came to Luther Martin, Jefferson couldn't help himself. Martin was a thorn in his side, a gadfly, a drunken giant of the American bar, without question its greatest lush. He knew his stuff, all right. He and Edmund Randolph had both taken part in the Constitutional Convention's treason debates back in 1787, and so they were the perfect counsel for Burr. But Martin was a royal pain to Jefferson. He had won an acquittal for Samuel Chase, when Jefferson's people went after him, with one of the most powerful performances an American lawyer had ever turned in. Of course, Martin could bug Chase as well, and sometimes he did. A few years after the Richmond trial, Martin's drinking problem had gotten so bad that he acted up even in court. Once he did it in front of Chase, who had to call him down. "I am surprised that you can so prostitute your talents," the judge told his old friend and defender. Martin drew himself up giddily and talked back to the bench. "Sir," he drawled indignantly, "I never prostituted my talents except when I defended you and Colonel Burr." He turned to the jury and added "A couple of the greatest rascals in the world." Chase saw red; he told the clerk to draw up a contempt citation. The clerk wrote it out and gave it to Chase. The judge picked up his pen; paused; and threw it back down. "This hand could never sign a commitment against Luther Martin," he said.[7]

Jefferson would have happily signed it in the summer of 1807. He hated Martin, hated him fiercely, and blamed him for helping Burr. "I am well informed that for more than a twelvemonth it has been believed in Baltimore, generally, that Burr was engaged in some criminal enterprise, & that Luther Martin knew all about it," he told George Hay. "Shall we move to commit L M, as *particeps criminis* with Burr?" That, said Jefferson, would "put down this unprincipled & impudent federal bull-dog."[8]

Hay didn't take this particular piece of advice; Burr's lawyers continued to prepare for trial unmolested. So far they had won and lost battles. They failed their biggest test when the grand jury returned a true bill. That meant a trial on the merits, but Burr still had an advantage, for the government had the burden of proof, and with Marshall he had a guarantee of due process, and maybe more process than was due. And process was important. This case would be won or lost on how Marshall conducted the trial, and how he construed the law. But Burr would have to fight to make sure that he got the best deal he could—beginning with the jury selection.

⸙

Tempers were running high by the time August rolled around. One day that summer, Samuel Swartwout ran into Wilkinson, quite literally, on the sidewalk, shouldering his erstwhile captor out into the street. Later he challenged the general to a duel, a challenge that Wilkinson refused to accept. Andrew Jackson cheered Swartwout on, and one report had the Tennessean making a public speech in Burr's defense.[9]

Things weren't that much calmer in court. As August 3 arrived, the House of Delegates chamber was bustling. Burr and his lawyers were there, of course; Charles Lee, John Adams's old attorney general, had joined them by now. The prosecution had turned out in force. Hay had collected a hundred witnesses, with more arriving each day, and a group of nearly fifty men was on hand to form the jury pool. Jury selection was one of the first items of business, and Burr wasted no time in getting to work. As voir dire began and the first man was called for questioning, his attorneys jumped in immediately. "We challenge you for cause," said Benjamin Botts. "Have you ever formed and expressed an opinion about the guilt of Colonel Burr?"

The would-be juror hedged. "I have not, sir," he answered, "since I have been subpoenaed."

"Had you before?" pressed Botts.

"I had formed one before in my own mind," the man admitted.

Hay saw no problem with that. "Do gentlemen contend," he interrupted, "that in a case so peculiarly interesting to all, the mere declaration of an opinion is sufficient to disqualify a juryman? A doctrine of this sort would at once acquit the prisoner; for where is the jury that could try him?"

Hay had a good point. This was the trial of the century, and everyone in the country had been following Burr's drama for months. Hay knew it and played on it. "Such a doctrine amounts to this," he told the court, "that a man need only to draw down the public attention upon him, and he would immediately affect his discharge."

Martin took issue with that, stressing "the duty of every juryman to come to the trial of any case with the most perfect impartiality." But still Hay's point was strong. Drawing the line between nearly inescapable prior knowledge and the needed impartiality would be hard in this case.

John Marshall tried to draw that line. "A juryman should come to a trial of a man for life," he opined, "with a perfect freedom from previous impressions." The Constitution, as well as natural law, demanded it. But he bowed to common sense. Everybody—everybody—had heard about Burr. So Marshall tried to walk a middle ground. A juror, he decided, might have some "impressions" about Burr. "The impressions may be so light," he explained, "that they do not amount to an opinion of guilt."[10] Beyond that Marshall would not go.

Botts resumed the attack. "Have you said that Colonel Burr was guilty of treason?" he asked the potential juror.

"No," came the answer. "I only declared that the man who acted as Colonel Burr was said to have done, deserved to be hung."

"Did you believe that Colonel Burr was that man?" Botts pressed him further.

"I did, from what I had heard."

That was enough. The court rejected him. Forty-seven remained in the pool.[11]

One after another they fell. Some were rejected; others were held for further examination. Burr's lawyers kept stressing the role of rumors, and the pervasive newspaper stories that had infected everyone's mind.

The twelfth man to be called was John Horace Upshaw. Without waiting for questions, he said up front that he had read papers, and that he had formed opinions.

That bothered Burr. "We challenge Mr. Upshaw for cause," he said.

Hay was irritated. "Then, sir, I most seriously apprehend that we shall have no jury at all," he answered. "We might as well enter at once a nolle prosequi." That would have suited Burr fine. A nolle prosequi is a prosecutor's official refusal to continue a prosecution. But Hay wasn't serious, merely exasperated, and Aaron Burr knew it. Nevertheless, he had Hay rattled, and that was good for Burr's cause. Upshaw was rejected too.

The procession continued. Sixteen examinations later, after twenty-eight in all, the first juror was finally elected.[12] Only eleven more were now needed. On and on the candidates came. One of them admitted to having opinions of Burr, but he refused to say that Burr had committed a treasonous act.

Burr wasn't satisfied. "What opinion have you formed of me?" he asked.

The examinee knew he had had it. "A very bad one," he spat, "which I have expressed often when called upon; and often when not." That was the end of him.

Another man, Hamilton Morrison, was more shrewd. He claimed that he didn't want to serve on Burr's jury, since Burr seemed to imagine bad things of him, or so he had heard. But Burr was not imagining, or so Burr thought. "Have not these rumors excited a prejudice in your mind against me?" he asked Morrison.

"I have no prejudice for or against you," insisted Morrison earnestly. He turned to the court. "I am surprised why they should be in so much terror of me," he said good-naturedly. "Perhaps my *name* may be a terror, for my first name is *Hamilton.*"

Wrong move. "*That* remark," Burr told the bench, "was a sufficient cause for objecting to him." With that he used the first of his small number of peremptory challenges to throw Morrison off the list, a type of challenge that he was free to use at whim, unlike a challenge for cause, which required a showing of prejudice.[13]

By now the court had been in session for a week, and voir dire had gone on for two days. By the end of the afternoon, the court had run through the whole of the jury pool, finding only four acceptable jurors. The only thing it could do was summon another panel, which meant a delay of several days.

To everybody's impatience, the second round was as slow as the first, and the casualties were nearly as high. After examining six more men, Burr was fast tiring out. He wanted his freedom back soon, and he was willing to run some risks to win it more quickly. "It will be seen," he announced, "either that I am under the necessity of taking men in some degree prejudiced against me, or of having another venire."[14] He decided to lower his standards rather than spending the rest of his life in court. The next potential juror remarked that he had formed an opinion of Burr, especially after hearing that he was with an armed force out on the Western Waters. At this point Burr broke in. "If, sir, you have completely prejudged my case—"

"I have not," the man interrupted. "I have not seen the evidence."

Bias, possibly; but this was just about the most restrained thing that Burr had heard from anyone. So now he gave in. "That is enough, sir," he said. "You are *elected.*" He might not get the impartial jury that the Constitution promised him, but maybe the prejudice would not be too great.[15]

It took a long time, but by the sixteenth day of August, the jury was complete. Things were finally ready for trial. Hay had his corps of witnesses ready. He would open the government's case. The following day he began.

❧

A great deal turned on the overt act requirement. Jefferson had seen that more than a year before. Marshall took note of it in the *Bollman* case. Hay knew it too, and that is what he focused on throughout his opening argument. This was a trial for treason. He would worry about the Neutrality Act later.

Hay talked of the history of treason in England, and of the constitutional safeguards that hemmed in the doctrine in the United

States. He relied on the *Bollman* opinion, but he interpreted it to suit his own ends. He admitted that the case allowed someone to go to a place of rendezvous without crossing the line. "But gentlemen," he cautioned, "common sense and principles founded on consideration of national safety certainly require that the crime of treason should be completed before the actual commission of hostilities against the government." Anything less than this could be deadly. A traitor could use that fact to shield himself perfectly. "If he be a man of common understanding," warned Hay, "he will not hazard a blow, till his arrangements be so complete, that the blow shall be fatal."[16]

In short, said Hay, actual use of force was not the dividing line. It couldn't be. That rule would threaten the nation's existence. "If ten thousand men were to assemble together and march to the city of Washington, for the express purpose of sending the president to Monticello, turning Congress out of doors, taking possession of the capitol, and usurping the powers of the government," he said, "they would not be guilty of treason; because they had not yet struck a blow. They advance and proceed; they meet no opposition; the members of the government disperse through fear; and yet this is not treason!"[17]

That couldn't be right. But Hay wasn't dealing with ten thousand men, or a thousand, and maybe not even a hundred. He had to force through a doctrine that made the gathering on the island of Harman Blennerhassett an overt act of levying war. When he wasn't stretching the meaning of treason, he kept harping on Burr's evil as a means of making that gathering seem all the more sinister. In the East, said Hay, Burr had talked of taking Washington. But when dealing with westerners, he changed his story. "He told them that they were in a state of colonial dependence on those of the Atlantic states, and annually paid millions to the government of the United States, for which they derived no benefit whatever . . . that a separation was necessary and would unquestionably take place . . . that the destiny of the republic was fixed, and that this revolution would be accomplished in less than two years."[18]

Hay next linked the word and the deed. "To accomplish these plans," he continued, "in the summer and fall of 1806, men were actually enlisted, boats were built on the waters of the Ohio, provisions purchased to an enormous amount, and ammunition provided . . . as if some hostile expedition were on foot." The assembly took place on the island; and even though Burr was not there, said Hay, the Supreme Court had ruled that he didn't need to be. "A man may 'levy war' against his country, when not present," he said. "A man may 'levy war' against a country, though three thousand miles distant." To be perfectly clear on this, so clear that Marshall couldn't escape, the attorney quoted the chief justice's words from *Bollman*. "If war be actually levied, that is, if a body of men be actually assembled for the purpose of effecting by force a treasonable purpose, all those who perform any part, however minute, or however remote from the scene of action, and who are actually leagued in the general conspiracy, are to be considered as traitors."[19]

This is exactly what Hay intended to prove: that Burr had masterminded a plan to dismember the country, that an overt act had taken place on the island, and that Burr thus had to be guilty. He had told the court and the jury as much. Now all he had to do was to prove it. To do that he called his first witness: General William Eaton.

In a flash Burr and his lawyers were all over Hay. Eaton hadn't witnessed an overt act. Eaton hadn't been on the island. Unless an overt act was proven, nothing else mattered at all. The defense demanded that the government prove that war had been levied, whatever that meant, before it proved anything else.

William Wirt answered Burr's lawyers. The government was telling a story, he observed, in simple chronological order. "It develops this conspiracy from its birth to the consummation," he explained, "unravels the plot from its conception to its denouement, and traces Aaron Burr step by step as he advanced and became more bold, till the act was consummated by the assemblage on Blennerhassett's Island. Is not this the lucid order of nature and reason?" he asked. "Would you begin to narrate a tale at the end of it?"[20]

Marshall was on the spot again. This was much the same issue that he had decided during the grand jury proceedings. But this was different. This was a trial on the merits. He saw good points on both sides, but he favored Burr on the whole. He knew that proof of intention was as important as proof of an act, and he said as much. "But it is proper to add," he warned, "that the intention which is considered relevant in this stage of the inquiry is the intention which composes a part of the crime, the intention with which the overt act itself was committed; not general evil disposition."

What that meant for Eaton was clear, said Marshall. "So far as his testimony relates to the fact charged in the indictment, so far as it relates to levying war on Blennerhassett's Island, so far as it relates to

William Eaton. *(Courtesy Historical Society of Pennsylvania)*

a design to seize on New Orleans or to separate, by force, the Western from the Atlantic states, it is deemed relevant and now admissible." But if it related to plans to capture Washington, it wasn't, for that was an act that the indictment didn't mention.[21] The government could put on its case; but Marshall would step in if it crossed this line.

Eaton started telling his story. "Concerning any overt act, which goes to prove Aaron Burr guilty of treason, I know nothing," he said. "Concerning certain transactions which are said to have happened at Blennerhassett's Island, or any agency which Aaron Burr may be supposed to have had in them, I know nothing. But concerning Colonel Burr's expressions of treasonable intentions, I know much."[22] He then told all that had happened between him and Burr a year and a half earlier, how Burr had planned war against Spain, how Burr had railed at the government, how Burr had spoken of needing men to command armies. He explained how Burr claimed that Wilkinson was in his pocket. Eaton had laughed at that last. Burr asked Eaton about Wilkinson. "I said," recounted Eaton, "I knew General Wilkinson would act as lieutenant to no man in existence. 'You are in error,' said Mr. Burr,

'Wilkinson will act as lieutenant to me.' " Eaton also told of how he himself must have seemed an especially likely mark for Burr, miffed as he was with Washington upon his return from North Africa, when Congress refused to cover his many expenses. But Burr, Eaton said, had misjudged him. Eaton was never a traitor. He had tried to warn the president, though the warnings went unheeded.

The direct examination came to an end; the cross-examination began. Martin led off, asking if the government had ever gotten around to reimbursing Eaton. Yes, Eaton said; it had paid him five months ago, after Jefferson had gone after Burr.

"What balance did you receive?" Martin asked.

"That is *my* concern, sir," replied Eaton.

Burr tried another approach. "What was the balance against you?"

Eaton turned to the bench. "Is that a proper question?" But Marshall allowed it, and grudgingly Eaton answered. Ten thousand dollars; a not-so-small fortune. The defense had implied that the Republicans were paying Eaton for this little performance in court.[23]

Burr shifted his ground, keeping at him. "You spoke of a command?" he asked.

Eaton exploded. "You spoke of *your* riflemen, *your* infantry, *your* cavalry!" he shouted. His finger stabbed out towards Wilkinson. "It was with the same view, you mentioned to me that man was to have been the first to aid you," he seethed, "and from the same views you have perhaps mentioned *me!*"

Martin objected to Eaton's tantrum, and to his inadmissible opinions too, but Hay defended the furious general. "Some allowance is to be made for the feelings of a man of honor," he argued.

Eaton apologized and continued. He was nearly through, for the moment at least, and soon Thomas Truxtun replaced him. Truxtun was far more restrained, though he, too, proclaimed his own innocence. Burr had asked him, he said, about how to attack Vera Cruz, the Gulf of Mexico's Gibraltar, by sea, and mentioned that he wanted to see Truxtun an admiral, or make him one—Truxtun couldn't remember which. "Mr. Burr then asked me," he continued, "if I would take the command of a naval expedition." Truxtun asked in return if this were a government project; Burr flatly responded that it was not. "I told Mr. Burr that I would have nothing to do with it," he swore.

Hay was trying to show that Burr was targeting disgruntled officers. He asked Truxtun if he was in the navy at the time of the conversations. "I was declared not to be," hedged Truxtun. His forced resignation, which he had long fought, was notorious, and still a very sore subject with him.[24]

In the end, Truxtun's testimony wasn't much help to the government. At one point a juror got into the act, asking the witness if Burr's march on Mexico was to take place in peacetime, which was the only way that Burr could have broken the Neutrality Act. Truxtun's answer helped Burr. "In all his conversations," the former commodore answered, "he said this expedition was to take place only in the event of a war with Spain."

Hay tried to regain ground. "When he proposed to make you an admiral," he queried, "did not the thought strike you, how he was to accomplish this?" Botts called him on that; those hadn't been Truxtun's words. Truxtun also objected. "Mr. Burr told me he wished to make or see me one, I do not particularly recollect which was his expression."[25] This sort of answer wasn't helping the government's case, so soon Hay moved on to his next witness, Blennerhassett's gardener Peter Taylor.

So far Hay had asked narrative questions, letting his witnesses tell their stories in long and rambling answers. He used the same tactic with Taylor, asking him to "state everything he knew about the assemblage on Blennerhassett's Island."[26] But that was too sweeping for Botts. Such an answer would include hearsay and irrelevant, and thus illegal, testimony. But Burr reined in his young attorney, waiving the objection, and Taylor started telling a colorful story of the island's hum of activity the previous autumn, Burr's cloak-and-dagger comings and goings, Blennerhassett's cryptic comments about conquering Mexico, and the preparations by bonfire on the night of December 10. Now Hay started questioning Taylor a lot more closely, eliciting every detail, asking about the number of men, the preparations they were making that evening.

One point was especially crucial. "Had they any guns?" he asked Taylor.

"Some of them had," confirmed Taylor. "But I don't know how many there were."

This woke up a juror. "What kind of guns," he interrupted, "rifles or muskets?"

It was a sharp question. Rifles were frontier weapons, better for hunting than fighting. Muskets were for use on the battlefield, where rate of fire counted for more than range and accuracy. But Taylor's answer was disappointing: he couldn't tell.

The cross-examination was swift. "Was Colonel Burr there?" Wickham asked.

"No," answered Taylor. "I did not see him."

"Did you understand whether he were in that part of the country at that time?"

"I understood not," said Taylor. "Never saw him on the island."[27]

That was all that Burr's lawyers wanted. The first day was over. The court adjourned until the next morning.

※

When the court convened the following day, the Morgans began to testify. Burr had had things to say about them. A few weeks earlier he had written a friend that the three men "have been swearing before the grand jury & will doubtless swear again before the petit jury to conversations with me of an extraordinary nature; such as never took place & by no probability could have taken place."[28] He was partly right, at least; George, John, and Thomas all told their stories to the trial jury, stories of what they claimed to have heard almost exactly a year before on the far side of the mountains.

Burr wasn't happy about it. He handled the cross-examinations himself. After John Morgan told the story of pointing out the house of David Bradford, the Whiskey Rebel, in the little town of Washington, Burr made things warm for him. "Did I seem to know anything of Bradford, before you told me?" he asked the witness. The younger man dodged. "You seemed to know a good deal about the insurrection," he answered.

Burr stayed with it. "Did I seem to know that Bradford lived at Washington, before you mentioned it and pointed out his house?"

"You did not seem to know it," John Morgan had to admit. He had no wish to be seen as a co-conspirator, or to be cheering on known rebels, but Burr had scored a point, making himself out as the innocent tourist, and John Morgan the angry frontiersman. And Burr wasn't through with him yet. Once his father, George Morgan, had testified, Burr called John back to the stand, asking him about the older man's faculties. John confessed that his father was "old and infirm" and told rambling stories, sometimes forgetting what he had said.

Thomas Morgan came next. He was the younger son, the one whom Burr had tried to recruit. His account was the shortest of the three, and Burr had trouble shaking his story. This was a bad day for the defense; the Morgans' tales were damning. But all that they said went to intent, and not to the overt act. For that the prosecutors had to deal with what happened on the island.

Once they were through with the Morgans, that is just what they did, calling a string of witnesses who had been there on the night of the bonfire, using the testimony to fill in as many details as they could. Burr and his lawyers kept up the attack. Harman Blennerhassett was in town by now, awaiting his own treason trial; he and Burr were avoiding each other. Blennerhassett was angry at Burr for getting him into this mess, and wrecking his finances into the bargain. For his part, Burr was willing to sacrifice the good-natured Irishman, and he used one of the government's witnesses to do it. "You know Mr. Blennerhassett well," he asked the witness. "Was it not ridiculous to be engaged in a military enterprise? How far can he distinguish a man from a horse? Ten steps?" Burr was clearly on edge, but he had hit home. "He is very short-sighted," the witness agreed. "He cannot know you from any of us at the distance we are now from one another. He knows nothing of military affairs."[29]

Wirt tried damage control on re-direct. "Is he esteemed a man of talents?"

"He is," the witness confirmed. "But it was mentioned among the people in the country that he had every kind of sense but common sense."[30]

The answer didn't help Wirt too much. At best Blennerhassett came across as Burr's dupe, and not a very good dupe at that, one whom a good conspirator would never have had. On top of that, all of the witnesses to the events on the island failed in two big respects. One regarded the use of force. General Edward Tupper, who was present in court, had earlier sworn to having guns leveled at him that night, but Hay hadn't called him yet in the trial, and under Burr's cross-examination, another witness contradicted himself as to the details of that act of force.[31] Hay still had time to straighten that out, but the government faced a much bigger problem with every one of its witnesses: Not one of them had seen Burr that night, for the plain reason that Burr hadn't been there. The prosecutors never claimed that he had.

They didn't think that they needed to, in light of the *Bollman* opinion, though the defense might have other ideas.

But whatever the defense might think, the government still had to prove an overt act of levying war, and what had occurred on the island might not qualify. The prosecutors hoped that it would. The defense disagreed. The ultimate question was as simple as that—almost. There was one further issue. Who would decide if war had been levied—the jury, or the court, in the person of Marshall?

This is the question that Burr's lawyers raised on August 20, near the end of the string of witnesses from the island. What they did, in technical terms, was object to the government's evidence, moving that the court should define the constitutional phrase "levying war," thus tying the jury's hands. That definition could form the basis of a jury instruction from Marshall. "Gentlemen of the jury," he might say, as a matter of law, " 'levying war' must include an act of open force and violence delivered against the government. If you find that no such act occurred in this case, then you must find the defendant not guilty." A definition from Marshall, in short—especially if it were a strict one— would limit the jury's freedom of action.

Such a ruling would also mean that evidence of anything other than what Marshall required was irrelevant, and thus a waste of everyone's time. If evidence failed to prove whether war had been levied or not, then the jury should not have a chance to listen to it. It would only cloud the true issue.

The defense wanted Marshall to make such a ruling. The prosecutors wanted exactly the opposite. They wanted, and needed, a broad definition of "levying war," and ideally they wanted the jury, not Marshall, to come up with that definition. Without legal constraint, a jury might find that aiming a musket, or merely loading or owning it, might amount to levying war. If Marshall left things to the jury, the chance of conviction would be much higher. Nothing stopped Marshall himself, of course, from supplying a broad definition, but the prosecutors distrusted him. He was much more likely, they figured, to give a strict definition, if he gave one at all. Better to avoid the danger and send the question straight to the jury—if Marshall would let them. But Burr and his people were determined to keep the matter away from the jury. So it was that they made their objection on August 20, asking Marshall to rule as a matter of law whether the government's evidence was relevant to the proof of levying war. If the government's evidence failed to meet the court's definition, the trial would end fast, and probably in an acquittal.

When Burr spoke up, the prosecutors fought back, but Marshall wouldn't have it. The defense had the right to make such a motion, he said without further discussion. The government had no choice. The stream of witnesses halted. So far twelve had testified. The lawyers shifted their focus, and then a torrent of legal argument started to flow, a flood that would roar through the chamber for eleven more days, and through the annals of American law for centuries. The debate, and Aaron Burr's life, now centered on only two questions: What, exactly, was levying war, and who would decide—the jury, or John Marshall?

⁂

The first to speak was John Wickham. It hardly mattered; before the debate had ended, all of the lawyers would have their say. The speeches would be long-winded, full of legal precedent and English and American history, parsed language and sometimes-tortured logic. Some of it was tedious, some of it moving, and some of it flashing and brilliant. Through all of it Aaron Burr sat, wondering if he was to live or to die.

Wickham spoke in much the same way, and to much the same issues, as all of the others would do. His main point was simple. As far as treason was concerned, everyone was a principal. There was no such thing as an accessory to treason, someone who, without being present for the treasonous act, was "some way concerned therein," as Blackstone put it.[32] Burr, Wickham said, was either a principal who was guilty of treason, or he was nothing. Because he was not at the island the night of the bonfire, he could not have had a part in the overt act the indictment mentioned. Thus he could not be guilty of treason.

Wickham appealed to the Constitution's plain language, which didn't mention accessories, and to hundreds of years of English law. For hours he led his listeners on a tour past famous landmarks of England's history: Monmouth's rebellion, Jeffreys's brutality at the Bloody Assizes, and the Battle of Culloden and its ugly aftermath of beheadings.[33] But in the end the road led back to America and John Marshall's words in the *Bollman* case. Those words were the critical stumbling block for Burr and his attorneys, for Marshall had clearly stated that the defendant need not be present at the scene of the overt act.

Wickham dealt with those words in the only way that he could. He called them dictum, a mere digression in the opinion, a hypothetical statement that had no bearing on *Bollman's* outcome. That being the case, those words weren't the law of the land, and the Richmond court could ignore them. But Wickham had to show exactly why he was right. "There never has been an attempt in the courts of the United States," he argued, "to convict an individual for treason, who was not actually on the spot, when an act charged in the indictment was committed."[34] This was a new proposition, he said, unknown in American law before *Bollman,* and the Circuit Court would have to decide for itself if it held any merit. Wickham held his listeners for hours, past the usual adjournment time, spinning out an elaborate lesson on treason. Finally he stopped for the evening, but he kept going the following morning.

After Wickham came Edmund Randolph, but not before Hay called another few witnesses to buttress his claims that an overt act had occurred. It made little difference to Randolph, who attacked Hay's theory anyway. He agreed with Wickham that Burr couldn't be an accessory, and then he went further. An overt act, he said, required force, and so far the government hadn't shown any. Without that, said Randolph, Burr couldn't possibly be guilty of treason, since nothing treasonous had happened.

Randolph, like Wickham before him, went on at great length. He, too, discussed English history, but he spent more time on American treason precedent, including the case of John Fries, which had gotten Samuel Chase impeached, and the trials of the Whiskey Rebels. The opinions were hard to interpret, and Randolph used this to good advantage, putting his own spin on them all, claiming that force was a sine qua non in each one of them.[35]

By the time that Randolph sat down, the defense had been speaking for nearly two days, and the prosecutors wanted their turn. But they didn't want it quite yet. Hay pointed out that the defense had more or less sprung a surprise, that Burr's lawyers must have prepared a long time to deliver such speeches, so the government should have time to prepare answers. Wickham, Martin, and Botts jumped on him for that. Hay should have been ready for anything, they told him. Sickness was spreading through Richmond, they said. It was cruel to coop up the jury so long. Besides, they needled the government, the prosecutors seemed to think this a very easy question. Why the need to prepare, if Hay and his team could knock down all of Burr's arguments?[36]

Hay and Wirt both got snippy. "This motion might be considered a mere 'ruse de guerre,'" they charged. "They sprang on the counsel for the United States as from an ambuscade." Things were getting out of hand again. Before they got even worse, Marshall granted Hay's request for more time. The day was Friday; Marshall gave until Monday.[37]

When the new week arrived, Alexander MacRae, not Hay, spoke first. MacRae was not one to pull punches. He began by declaring Burr guilty, a sentiment the prosecutors had once resented being credited with. He then went on to explain why. Burr, he believed, was one of a highly dangerous breed, who moved mainly by stealth. "No man has a more comprehensive knowledge of human nature," he warned his audience. He moved "by degrees" to ensnare Eaton, Truxtun, and the Morgans in his plans, never overreaching himself, or so he had thought. But Eaton had deceived him; Truxtun and the Morgans hadn't bought in. After hearing these witnesses, MacRae said, people had to believe that Burr had intended treason.

MacRae's emphasis on intent, not act, was crucial to the government's strategy. The prosecutors had to play to their strengths, and intention was one of those. The point of making treason a crime, said MacRae, was to protect society. The most dangerous traitor of all, he continued, was the subtle and cautious traitor, a man such as Burr. Treason law, therefore, had to apply to Burr's methods, or society would be in jeopardy.

Again and again he stressed this view of Burr, painting him as a dark trinity of destruction. "He is the first mover of the plot," he declared. "He planned it; he maintained it; he contrived the doing of the overt acts which others have done. He was the *Alpha* and *Omega* of this treasonable scheme, the very body and soul, the very life of this treason."[38]

MacRae's speech was the best one yet, but it became his master, not his servant. He let it carry him too far. "Aaron Burr," he argued, "may be considered as being present on Blennerhassett's Island, when his agents at his request and by his contrivance and persuasion committed the act there." *That* was constructive treason, or very close to it, and the whole point of putting the Treason Clause into the Constitution was to prevent what MacRae was trying to do.[39]

The following day was William Wirt's. MacRae's speech had been powerful, but Wirt's fast eclipsed it, leaving everyone talking for years about the young lawyer's talents. It was the most eloquent speech of Aaron Burr's trial, and one of the best that had ever been heard before the American bar. What Wirt had to say was not all that different from what Alexander MacRae had said, but he said it almost as poetry.

Burr need not have been present, Wirt argued. He was the one who set things in motion; that was enough. And in case it were not, Wirt reminded his listeners of the difficulty of drawing lines, of figuring out exactly where, on a continent the size of North America, the treason had actually happened. He sifted through the English precedents to find a handful of cases, cases that seemed to fit the frontier, cases in which "the highway and whole forest was the scene of action."[40] This was not England; this was America, where conditions were utterly different. Burr was all along the frontier, on the rivers and in the forests, when the treasonous acts were occurring. In that sense he *was* present, like some woodland spirit, at the scene of the overt act.

But more importantly, Wirt told the chamber, Burr was the mastermind. Just as Holmes would paint Moriarty later that century in London as "the organizer of half that is evil and of nearly all that is undetected in this great city,"[41] so, too, Wirt described Aaron Burr— "Burr, the contriver of the whole conspiracy, to everybody concerned in it was as the sun to the planets which surround him. Did he not bind them in their respective orbits and give them their light, their heat and their motion?" he asked.

> Pervading the continent from New York to New Orleans, he draws into his plan, by every allurement which he can contrive, men of all ranks and descriptions. To youthful ardour he presents danger and glory; to ambition, rank and titles and honours; to avarice the mines of Mexico. To each person whom he addresses he presents the object adapted to his taste. His recruiting officers are appointed. Men are engaged throughout the continent. Civil life is indeed quiet upon its surface; but in its bosom this man has contrived to deposit the materials which, with the slightest touch of his match, produce an explosion to shake the continent. All this his restless ambition has contrived; and in the autumn of 1806, he goes forth for the last time to apply this match.[42]

These declared Wirt, were the acts of a traitor, the acts of a principal. If anyone was an accessory, if anyone was a dupe, it was Harman Blennerhassett.

"Who is Blennerhassett?" asked Wirt. "A native of Ireland, a man of letters, who fled from the storms of his own country to find quiet in ours. His history shows that war is not the natural element of his mind." He was a gentle soul, and naive as well. Wirt made this his new running theme. "On his arrival in America," he continued, "he retired even from the population of the Atlantic states, and sought quiet and solitude in the bosom of our Western forests. But he carried with him taste and science and wealth; and lo, the desert smiled!" Here Wirt described the idyll that was Blennerhassett's Island, the intellectual climate, the gardens, the perfect family life. Then he shifted the note. "In the midst of all this peace," he intoned, "this innocent simplicity and this tranquillity, this feast of the mind, this pure banquet of the heart, the destroyer comes; he comes to change this paradise into a hell."

Now Wirt wove a tale of corruption. "Innocence is ever simple and credulous," he explained. "Conscious of no design itself, it suspects none in others. It wears no guard before its breast. Every door and portal and avenue of the heart is thrown open, and all who choose it enter. Such was the state of Eden when the serpent entered its bowers." By now none could tell if Wirt was referring to Genesis, or instead to something more recent. That was just the effect that he wanted.

He talked of the serpent and what he had done to the Garden. "By degrees," he observed, "he infuses into it the poison of his own ambition. He breathes into it the fire of his own courage; a daring and desperate thirst for glory; an ardour panting for great enterprises, for all the storm and bustle and hurricane of life." The effect on the innocent was grave. "In a short time the whole man is changed, and every object of his former delight is relinquished," lamented the lawyer. "Greater objects have taken possession of his soul. His imagination has been dazzled by visions of diadems, of stars and garters and titles of nobility. He has been taught to burn with restless emulation at the names of great heroes and conquerors. His enchanted island is destined soon to relapse into a wilderness . . . ."

And yet, said Wirt, despite all of these tragedies, the defense now claimed that Burr was no traitor, but simply an accessory, and so not guilty at all. "Is this reason? Is it law? Is it humanity?" he shouted. "Sir, neither the human heart nor the human understanding will bear a perversion so monstrous and absurd!"[43]

That should have been the end of the trial, but it wasn't. There was still the small question of guilt or acquittal. Nearly half a dozen attorneys spoke once Wirt had concluded: Botts, Hay, Lee, Martin,

Harman Blennerhassett. *(Courtesy Blennerhassett Island Historical State Park)*

then Edmund Randolph again. All of the speeches were variations on the same themes that the earlier ones had developed. Botts tried to undercut Wirt with his own New Testament metaphor. The government was out to get Burr, he declared. If anyone doubted that such things were possible, Botts reminded the chamber that it had happened before. "Christ himself was abused, was mocked and spit on," he said. "Why should not a mere mortal man be in like manner abused?"[44] But after Wirt's poetry Bott's efforts fell flat. The Blennerhassetts may have been Adam and Eve, and Burr their serpent, but Aaron Burr was no Christ.

Hay and Lee were more mundane, each of them in effect saying that the outcome depended on the meaning of "levying war." More particularly, each said, everything depended on what the definition of "levying" was. Hay attacked the defense. "They call aloud for an open deed of war," he said, "for the explosion of bombs, the thunder of cannon or at least for the firing of small arms. They will not be satisfied without a battle."[45] But that wouldn't do, he argued. "The law speaks not of *an overt act of war*. It speaks of *levying war*." And levying was broader than overt acts.[46]

Lee disagreed. "If there be no actual violence, no army, no weapons, no posture of war," he argued, "I say there can be no levying of war under any circumstances whatever."[47]

After more than a week of harangues, little remained to be said, but that didn't stop Luther Martin. He spoke for two days, fourteen hours in all, rehashing all of the arguments, going over all the same ground. If Wirt's speech was the most famous one of the whole trial, Martin's was the second most famous, more for its length and complexity than for its power and elegance. By the second day of Martin's harangue, even Burr was tiring of it. When he heard Martin say that the government had claimed that a single man might levy war all by himself, he had to speak up. "I do not understand the gentlemen to contend for such a construction," he corrected his lawyer.

"I understand them to insist on that construction," Martin responded. "It results from some of their arguments."[48]

Burr quit interrupting. Martin kept going for several more hours, but finally he too fell silent. After fourteen hours, nothing remained to be said, or so it would seem. Still, Randolph spent the rest of the day wrapping up. After Martin's performance, his comments must have seemed short.

Martin had ended by encouraging Marshall to do his duty, despite the Republican protest that was sure to result. This was also how Randolph finished. The court had to define "levying war" as a matter of law. This was all about law, Randolph, said, not arbitry or injustice. "In the conflicts of animosity," he concluded, "justice is sometimes forgotten or sacrificed to mistaken zeal and prejudice. We look for the judiciary to guard us. One thing I am certain of, that you will not look at the consequences; that you will determine 'fiat justicia' let the result be what it may."[49]

The day was Saturday, August 29. The trial had been going for nearly a month. Marshall adjourned the court for the week. Two days later he read his opinion.

Everything came down to the *Bollman* opinion and the passage that Marshall had written, the passage in which he had said that a defendant need not be present at the scene of the overt act. Depending on what he wanted to do, on what he thought was the proper solution, Marshall could choose one of a very few ways to deal with the troublesome passage. He could decide that the words were dictum, not binding on the Richmond court. He could distinguish the case from Burr's, finding it different enough that it didn't control in the current dispute. Or he could hold that it bound lower courts, including the Richmond court, in which case Burr was in deadly trouble.

Marshall had one other option. He could find that the passage did not mean what it seemed to mean on its face. This is the option he finally chose.

But Marshall had to do more than that. He was being asked to define treason, to decide what "levying war" really meant. He would have to discuss the overt act requirement, and thus where the two-witness rule fit in. In short, he had to provide a thorough discussion of the whole of the Treason Clause.

Marshall's opinions tended to follow a pattern. He believed in a theory of natural rights—unwritten, universal legal truths—and his opinions usually reflected that view. He would start by announcing sweeping principles, and then he would interpret the law's language in light of those grand statements. Next he would follow where the interpretations led, making the outcome seem inevitable. Thus he reached his decision. He was a master of the process, if ever it had a master.

The *Burr* case was different, though. In other opinions Marshall might want to expand the federal government's power. But this was a matter of criminal law, and Marshall distrusted the government when property or life was at stake. So as he read his opinion, he picked out his way very carefully, as someone might walk through a minefield.[50]

Early on he agreed with the government as to what amounted to levying war. "It is a technical term," he told the crowded chamber. "It is used in a very old statute of that country whose laws form the substratum of our laws. It is scarcely conceivable that the term was not employed by the framers of our Constitution in the sense which had been affixed to it by those from whom we borrowed it."[51]

So what did the term mean in England? Marshall analyzed the old precedents, finding no need for actual force. "If a rebel army, avowing its hostility to the sovereign power, should front that of the government, should march and countermarch before it, should maneuver in its face, and should then disperse from any cause forever without firing a gun—I confess I could not, without some surprise, hear gentlemen seriously contend that this could not amount to an act of levying war," he concluded. "A case equally strong may be put with respect to the absence of military weapons. If the party be in a condition to execute the purported treason without the usual implements of war, I can perceive no reason for requiring those implements in order to constitute the crime."[52]

But the United States had its own treason decisions, and Marshall looked at them too, deciding that they had always called for actual force, at least before the *Bollman* opinion. And if *Bollman* had meant to change that, said Marshall, it would have expressly said so. Thus even *Bollman* required actual force. Marshall's attack had commenced.[53]

The door was still open for Hay and his colleagues to show that an act of force had occurred on the island. If they could, then could Burr be guilty, based on that act? This issue was Marshall's next target. Burr was not *actually* on the island that night, or anywhere near it, said Marshall. Everyone acknowledged that, even the government. But what about *legal*, constructive presence?

Force was needed for treason. Marshall had just held as much. The indictment mentioned only the acts on the island, so no other acts could matter. If Burr were guilty, said Marshall, the government had to show force on the island by at least two witnesses, and it had to connect Burr to that force. Burr could be remote, all right. *Bollman* was correct about that. But the government had to prove the connection and it had to follow the two-witness rule to do it. That meant not only two witnesses to the acts of force, but two witnesses—the same two or a different two—to the particular act of Burr's procurement of that force.[54]

This was the moment when Aaron Burr won. The government had scarcely proven an act of levying war on the island, much less shown that Burr had ordered it, for all of his dangerous talk to Eaton and others. This was the end. The rest of the trial was almost a matter of form.

Marshall played his expected role. He noted that the government had not yet shown what it needed to show, but it was welcome to bring in new evidence. "If there be such let it be offered," he said grandly, "and the court will decide upon it."[55] The court. The court would decide. "Levying war" was a matter of law, and the definition that Marshall had given all but locked out the government.

Hay must have known he was beaten, but he, too, saw the game through. He asked for time to review the opinion, no doubt desperately hoping to find a chink in the armor. Marshall agreed quite happily, adjourning the court for the day.

☙

The next morning was bitter for Hay, as he told the court stiffly that he had nothing more for the jury. Marshall's ruling had made all of his other witnesses worthless. The government rested its case. The jury retired, but not for long; soon the jurymen filed back in. Their foreman was Edward Carrington, brother-in-law to John Marshall's wife. "We of the jury," he announced, "say that Aaron Burr is not proved to be guilty under this indictment by any evidence submitted to us. We therefore find him not guilty."[56]

It was a grudging statement, reminiscent of Scottish law, in which "not proven" was an acceptable verdict. While acquitting a defendant, it still left him shadowed, hinting that he wasn't quite innocent. Burr didn't like that at all. He and his lawyers assaulted the verdict as "unusual, informal, and irregular." Burr himself half-told the court to make the jurymen say either "guilty" or "not guilty" and leave it at that. Hay disagreed, trying to salvage something. Then a juror chimed in, telling all of them that he would find the same verdict if anyone pressed him further, and he thought that the others would too. With that everybody gave up. Marshall let the verdict stand, while telling the clerk to record it as a simple "not guilty."[57]

That would seem the end of the story, but Burr wasn't out of the woods. He still faced trial for violating the Neutrality Act. But the prosecution was starting to falter. The next day Hay entered a nolle prosequi as to Jonathan Dayton, who had not been on the island, and he didn't move forward with trials for Blennerhassett or Israel Smith. Something was bothering him. The island was not the only place where overt acts might have happened. Burr and his party had traveled hundreds of miles on the river, more or less all together. Surely they had done something along the way that was treasonous. If so, maybe Burr could be tried for that. The court would have to be in a western federal district, with friendly Republican judges. Jefferson himself was thinking about this in the early part of September, and Hay did more than think. "I have been told," he declared to the court the day after Burr's acquittal, "that at the mouth of the Cumberland, there were such acts as would constitute an overt act of war." That wasn't all, he continued. "All along the rivers," he said of Burr's party, "their military array and warlike posture continued, and their numbers were increasing." This was the terminology of treason, and to it Hay added the thing that was lacking before. "Mr. Burr was with them," he declared, and was "the very soul of the expedition." In light of this, Hay concluded, he wanted Marshall to commit Burr for treason *again,* and pack him off to a western court, along with Blennerhassett and Israel Smith, for a brand new treason trial.[58]

Burr's counsel's reactions were strong. This was really beyond the pale. "The prosecutor has embraced, for the scene of action," charged Wickham, "all the way from Bayou Pierre up the Mississippi and Ohio Rivers to the extremity of Virginia, an extent of 1600 miles!" That was ridiculous. "When any person is charged with treason or felony," he asked, "are not the counsel for the prosecution obliged to specify the *time when* and *place where* the crime was committed?"[59]

The defense won, for the time being at least. The problem, as Marshall saw it, was that Burr still faced trial in Richmond on the Neutrality Act question, which had to happen before Marshall could let him go. That ended the battle for a while, as Burr's next trial began.[60]

It lasted two weeks, including the bickering over bail that took place at its beginning. Jefferson watched the trial with approval. "If defeated," he noted, "it will heap coals of fire on the head of the judge; if convicted, it will give time to see whether a prosecution for treason against him can be instituted in any, and what other court."[61] But the trial held hazards for Jefferson. At the outset Burr threatened another subpoena, this time to have Jefferson bring a different letter than the ones he had gone after earlier. Jefferson wasn't happy about it. "As I do not believe that the district courts have a power of commanding the executive government to abandon superior duties & attend on them, at whatever distance," he told Hay, "I am unwilling, by any notice of the subpoena, to set a precedent which might sanction a proceeding so preposterous. I enclose you, therefore, a letter, public & for the court, covering substantially all they ought to desire."[62]

Burr didn't press the point, although Hay made only parts of the letter available. Meanwhile the new trial went on, but Hay, run-down and ill, could make little headway against Marshall's rulings. Witness after witness testified, this time Wilkinson too, but the government could introduce nothing to show that Burr had planned a peacetime invasion of Mexico, Florida, or any other part of New Spain. On September 15 Hay gave up the battle and tried to enter a nolle prosequi. Burr fought it, scenting a victory. He wanted a jury verdict, and he got one. This time it was a straightforward "not guilty."[63]

But even this wasn't the end. The prosecution was now jerking like a freshly beheaded chicken, trying somehow to keep Burr from walking away free. Hay's next move was to abandon the misdemeanor charges against Blennerhassett and Smith, trying instead to commit them and Burr too for a new treason trial in the West. To do that he had to show cause. For another month the testimony and arguments went on, the witnesses just as stubborn, the attorneys just as long-winded, the mood just as bad as during the treason trial proper. A high point, or perhaps a low one, came when Wilkinson took the stand and the defense team backed him into admitting that he had altered the cipher letter, striking out the first sentence—"Your letter post marked 13th May, is received"—that showed he had been corresponding with Burr beforehand.[64] This had been a running problem for months. The government kept offering excerpts of confidential documents to avoid compromising national security; Burr's team kept claiming that that ran the risk of corrupting the meanings. Things boiled over one day when Wilkinson produced a letter to read.

"This is only an extract," Martin complained, examining it.

"I had no other," explained Wilkinson.

That was not good enough. "We take no extracts," Martin said hotly.

"Unless it be of molasses," stage-whispered Wirt. Martin's liking for rum was well-known.[65]

The record of the hearings is long, filling in many details about the conspiracy and of Wilkinson's frontier and New Orleans adventures. Burr kept trying to put him on trial, and to show that he had the administration's approval. But after Burr's acquittal for treason, it was all anticlimax, and it had to end sometime. On October 20 it finally did. In the face of the mountainous record, Marshall decided that he had to commit Blennerhassett and Burr, but only for a Neutrality Act violation. He allowed Burr to post bail this time, unlike the last time, in return requiring him to appear in Chillicothe, Ohio, to defend himself once more.[66]

With that decision, the last that Marshall delivered in the case of Aaron Burr, things finally wound down in Richmond. The crowds began to disperse. The defense team disbanded, and the prosecutors faded out of the limelight. The jurors had gone; the witnesses all went on their ways. The trial of the century had ended. As for Burr, he had no intention, to all appearances, of keeping his Ohio appointment. As he left the House of Delegates for the last time, he headed not west but north, leaving Virginia and Jefferson's country far behind forever.

The next several months found Aaron Burr broke, nearly broken, and flitting up and down through the mid-Atlantic states. The New Jersey indictment against him for Hamilton's murder had been quashed. That was something, at least, though charges were still on the books in New York. He had to watch his step there, keeping himself to himself on Manhattan. "He was generally alone," wrote his friend Charles Biddle during one of Burr's Philadelphia stays, "with little light in his room. He was very pale and dejected . . . ."[67] In the weeks just after the trial, Burr met now and then with Blennerhassett, who still blamed him for everything. The Irishman, in debt up to his ears, had had to sell his island, and he was trying to wring reimbursement from Burr for all he had spent to enable the ill-fated journey.

Blennerhassett was just the tip of the iceberg. Former friends were suing Burr left and right, sometimes sending the sheriff for him, in the hopes of getting back the money that he had borrowed from them. He must have known this would happen, because even before Hay had finished with him in Richmond, as early as September, he was talking of going to Europe.[68] There, perhaps, he could hide from his creditors, and maybe even find a measure of peace.

On the evening of June 9, 1808, after keeping a low profile for months, Aaron Burr left Manhattan in stealth, boarding the packet *Clarissa Ann,* bound for England. From there he would make his way to the other side of the Channel. Europe was a war-torn continent in thrall to a power-mad dictator. But Burr didn't mind. After all of Burr's North American strife, after Wilkinson, after Jefferson, after Richmond, Napoleon didn't seem like much of a threat.

Epilogue

Villain

*S*hakespeare created his ultimate monster in *Henry VI*'s Richard of Gloucester. Suave and ruthless, charming and brutal, cunning, cruel, physically deformed, and hungry for power—Richard is all of these things. He is a man obsessed. When we meet him near the trilogy's end, things have gotten chaotic. The Wars of the Roses are tearing England's great families to pieces. The rule of law has vanished in a flood of revenge and avarice that has shattered the order of government. Kings gain the crown through conquest, not inheritance, might always making for right. Richard's brother Edward IV holds the throne for now; as the king and his bride-to-be exit the scene, they leave Richard alone on the stage. It is then that Richard delivers his first brilliant, chilling soliloquy, from which we learn how far he is willing to go to have Edward's crown for himself, no matter what his quest costs others.

He begins his speech in frustration, seeing nothing but obstacles between him and his goal.

> Why, then I do but dream on sovereignty;
> Like one that stands upon a promontory
> And spies a far-off shore where he would tread,
> Wishing his foot were equal with his eye;
> And chides the sea that sunders him from thence,
> Saying he'll lade it dry to have his way ....[1]

We can see a lot of Aaron Burr in this picture, though instead of being on some lonely promontory at the edge of the world, we can imagine him standing on a high, wind-swept crest of the Appalachians, looking westward across the fair valley below, or conceivably eastward to Washington and the president's mansion. The parallels between Richard and Burr are striking. Both are intelligent; both are hard-driven. Both are frustrated at being so near to heart's desire, and yet so far from it too. And both are easily capable of killing in order to get what they want. They are similar, too, in one other way: they are both at least partly inventions.

More than that, they are largely *self*-inventions. Later in his soliloquy, Richard moves from lamenting his fate to deciding to change it. His main weapon will be his acting skills, his ability to play many roles, to make people think that he is something he isn't. He swears to free himself from the torment of power-lust that surrounds him, to "hew my way out with a bloody axe":

> Why, I can smile, and murder whiles I smile,
> And cry "Content!" to that which grieves my heart,
> And wet my cheeks with artificial tears,
> And frame my face to all occasions . . . .
> I can add colours to the chameleon,
> Change shapes with Protheus for advantages,
> And set the murderous Machiavel to school.
> Can I do this, and cannot get a crown?
> Tut, were it further off, I'll pluck it down.[2]

So, too, did Burr invent himself, by hiding his true nature and playing a number of roles, and never more so than during his years of conspiracy. He told a dozen conflicting stories; he acted the parts of a soldier, a settler, a liberator, a lawyer; and he held himself up as a victim, a target of an oppressive government. He was such a good actor, in fact, that to this day we can't see behind the scenes of his mind.

But Richard and Burr, as we know them, are not just self-inventions. Others had a hand in creating them, and in this, too, they are alike. Richard had been dead for a hundred years when Shakespeare restored him to life, basing his characterization on earlier, highly partisan, stories. To this day, five centuries after Richard III took the crown and died in battle defending it, most people see him through Shakespeare's eyes. Neither clinical scholars nor the studious partisans of the Richard III Society can completely restore his virtue. For most of us he will always be the man who slew his brother's young sons in order to be king, although we aren't sure that he really did slay them. We have forced Richard into a role, the role of consummate villain.

With Burr it is much the same. A legion of historians has painted him in very dark hues. Early America needed its evildoers, if only as foils for its heroes, and Burr was a natural for such a role, better even than Benedict Arnold. (George Washington may have plundered the Iroquois Confederacy, but that didn't count for early American whites.) Aaron Burr, a product of the best that the new nation had to offer, highly successful, half-hero, half-Everyman, was the perfect candidate. Settling western lands wasn't dramatic or sinister. Filibustering was, and treason was even more so. So the historians forced Burr into the part of pirate and traitor, despite—or maybe because of—a welter of conflicting, confounding evidence.

We thus have to ask if the Burr whom we know really had any choice in playing a traitorous role. In this, once again, he is like Richard. The last of the Plantagenet kings stood on the cusp of the Middle Ages and the new modern era, between a world view that held an ordained place for everyone and a Renaissance outlook that declared that each controls his own destiny. "I am determined to prove a Villain," says Richard, near the start of the play that bears his name, but that line can mean one of two things, depending on whether Richard or God has done the determining. Surely Shakespeare has done some determining of his own. Burr faces the same problem today: maybe he was master of his plans at some point, whatever they may have been, but the legends and the historians have long since taken charge of his fate. Burr must be a traitor, or at the very least a dangerous, unpredictable man who set his own interests ahead of everything else.

Of course Burr had something to do with it. He may not have been convicted, but if he hadn't said the things that he did, he might never have gone on trial. And, incredibly, once he was free, he even continued his intrigues, still hoping to interest someone somewhere in conquering somewhere else. Even before 1807 had ended, the British consul in Philadelphia had heard Burr say that his new target was to be Cuba, or maybe South America. Before beginning his voyage across the Atlantic, Burr wrote Charles Williamson, his friend and former go-between with Anthony Merry, about finding some English support for the plan. That was another reason for his journey, to sound out people there. By now he was deluding himself. Williamson couldn't help him. He was on a cruise in the Caribbean, never again to return to England or North America. The yellow fever got him in August 1808.[3]

Nevertheless, England was happy to see Burr, but that only took him so far. Jeremy Bentham, Charles Lamb, Sir Walter Scott, William

Cobbett—he met all of them and more, moving in fine social circles in the cities and country houses. With Bentham, especially, he got along well. But Bentham wasn't officialdom, and England's leaders closed their doors whenever he brought up his scheme, which he now referred to as "X" in his private journal. After a while they tired of him, and in the spring of 1809 they arrested him and then told him to leave. His creditors were after him again, and he was stirring up political trouble.[4]

Burr headed to Sweden, a neutral enough place where he was safe from America and England. But still he dreamed of Latin American liberation. The English-speaking world had turned him down. His only other option was France. In early 1810 he arrived there, where he tried to catch Napoleon's ear. In Paris he wrote up proposals, cajoled public ministers, and generally made a pain of himself. By now he was talking of seizing not only Florida and Mexico, but Jamaica and Canada too. Politics and alignment no longer mattered, if they ever had to begin with. He didn't care whom he conquered or whom he offended. He merely wanted to conquer.

The French didn't buy it. "Mr. Burr would be able to bring about changes only in Florida and Louisiana," Napoleon heard from his minister of foreign affairs, "and he could not be employed without giving a great deal of offense to the United States."[5] That was giving him too much credit. He was nothing but talk by now, a completely spent force. He was only embarrassing himself.

On top of that he was broke, as usual, and with little means of making a living. He survived on loans from friends and acquaintances. Now and then he did some book work, translating English volumes to French. Napoleon's empire was being cruel to him, but it wasn't letting him go. He was something of a security risk, having consorted with some pro-English elements during his stay in Paris, and the maze of French bureaucracy, and his inability to pay bribes, kept him from getting a passport for months. In desperation he wrote the American consul in Paris for help, although he must have known what the answer would be. The consul was Alexander MacRae, and he gave the predictable answer, although it was more civil than Burr might have expected.[6]

In mid-1811 Burr finally escaped from the clutches of France, without American help. Making his way to Amsterdam, selling everything that he had, he bought passage on a U.S.-bound ship. Hours after setting sail, she was captured and taken to England. After another

Aaron Burr, 1834. *(Courtesy New York Historical Society)*

delay of months, Burr found another vessel, and at last he arrived in Boston, a penniless fugitive, just as the War of 1812 started.

His days on the heights were behind him. Maybe, with care and hard work and a great deal of luck, he could win back a respectable image, but that was the best for which he could hope. He returned to New York. The indictment against him there was ancient history by now, and the Madison administration was too busy making a mess of the war to put him on trial again in the West. He started practicing law, and right away he had clients galore. New York remembered him well. He may have been a villain, but he was still a fabulous lawyer.

But a few weeks later tragedy struck. Theodosia's son, his only grandson, died without warning. By the end of the year Theodosia was on her way to New York by boat to see her father; when the boat disappeared with all hands, a victim of a storm at sea, or perhaps, so went the rumors, of pirates.[7]

Burr's only child and his only grandchild—or at least his only legitimate ones—had ceased to exist. He had been closer to them than to anyone else in the world, and now they had fled it. His plans for conquest were ashes. His political career was long gone. His role as an elder statesman had never been at all. Nothing was left but survival.

⚘

Others from the conspiracy days also fell on hard times, though for the most part not so hard as Burr's. Blennerhassett was broken, in many ways the conspiracy's most tragic figure. William Wirt had been right about him. He was an innocent, a man who had gotten in over his head. He lost his fortune, his island, and nearly everything else except for his family. After trying to get Burr to pay him back, he took his family into the West again, passing the island on the way—the house burned to the ground in 1812—and settled down near Natchez. He found the money to buy La Cache, a cotton plantation, but it never brought him much money. After ten years he had had enough. He sold the plantation, came back east to New York, and from there moved to Montreal, where he became a third-rate lawyer. In 1822 he gave up. The New World dream had failed him. He returned to the British Isles, where he died in 1831.[8]

The Richmond attorneys met various fates. Edmund Randolph was near the end of his career, as was Charles Lee. Some of the other attorneys kept up a vigorous practice for years, among them Wickham, Botts, and of course Luther Martin, who often appeared before Marshall's Supreme Court. One of Martin's last arguments was for the losing side in the great case of *McCulloch v. Maryland*. Thereafter he suffered a major stroke, becoming a destitute shadow. He would absently wander into the courtrooms where he had long practiced, making his way in a daze to the counsels' area, sitting down without making a fuss. The judges and lawyers understood; they would pause as he entered the courtroom to give him time to settle himself. Burr took him in and cared for him for years, Martin finally dying in 1826. George Hay's career wasn't brilliant; he was never a great lawyer, though he was a confidante to President James Monroe, and John Quincy Adams made him a federal judge. But never again did he, or any of the other attorneys, have a case as celebrated as Burr's, for the simple reason that nothing as celebrated as that case ever happened again, certainly not in their lifetimes.[9]

Thomas Jefferson escaped fairly unscathed. He was coming to the end of his public career, and he spent his last year in office trying to head off a war with Great Britain. In the wake of the *Leopard-Chesapeake* uproar, his Embargo Act attempted to strike at England's trade and pocketbooks, and those of the other combatants, too, in an effort to make them respect American neutral shipping rights. Instead the embargo smashed New England's own economy and led to a scathing outcry against the administration. Yet Jefferson's brand of warfare almost worked in time, though it didn't work soon enough. The United States brashly declared war in the spring of 1812, just as England was in the act of relaxing its attitude towards it. By then Jefferson had been safely retired for three years, and his successor James Madison had to preside over the pathetic little war that followed.[10]

Truxtun sat the war out. In a way that was a shame, for most of the country's small successes were at sea, where single ship-on-ship actions gave it something to cheer about in the face of the debacles on land. Eaton escaped any blame for the latter, having died in 1811.[11] But Wilkinson caught it full in the face. By the start of the war he had already been court-martialed once, and investigated by Congress, and things just got worse from there. It all began with John Randolph of Roanoke and Burr's treason trial. The irascible Virginian had had to sit through endless hours of Wilkinson's grand jury testimony, declaring at the end of it that Wilkinson was a "rogue, speculator, and would be murderer." Wilkinson demanded a duel for that, but Randolph merely sneered at him. "I cannot descend to your level," read his reply to the general's challenge.[12] The Virginian had other weapons at hand. Less than a week later he called for the House to investigate Wilkinson. Daniel Clark, who had been on hand in New Orleans for Wilkinson's petty dictatorship, was ready to spill his guts, and spill them he did, to the House and to everyone else, furnishing a number of documents that showed how much money the general had gotten from Spain. Wilkinson had to do a lot of fast talking to keep the congressmen happy. Already John Smith had been forced to resign from the Senate because of his connections with Burr; now Wilkinson felt congressional wrath building up against him. In 1808 he hit on a plan for protection. He asked Jefferson for a court of inquiry, a court of his fellow soldiers and comrades-in-arms, who would judge him with a lot more sympathy than Randolph of Roanoke would. As for Randolph,

Wilkinson denounced him publicly as "a prevaricating, base, calumni-
ating scoundrel, poltroon and coward."

Wilkinson won that round; the court of inquiry vindicated him in
July of 1808, and Congress backed off for a while. But by 1810 the
House was at it again: now not one but two investigations were running,
looking both at his Spanish connections and at his recent mismanage-
ment of the army. The paper trail's complexity, and Wilkinson's own
desperate arguments, saved him; the investigations sputtered to an
uncertain standstill. Then came a full-blown court-martial, which once
again cleared him of wrongdoing. By then the war had begun, and for
all of his shortcomings, Wilkinson was the country's senior officer. In
1813 he was ordered to the Canadian border.

He botched things completely. Command and supply squabbles,
low troop morale, and other troubles plagued him. The army was
already a shambles, but under his hand it practically fell apart, growing useless for offense or defense. The War Department relieved him
in 1814. Again he was court-martialed, this time for the dismal fail-
ures that he had helped bring about in the North. Again he was acquitted. But by then his fine luck in the courts didn't matter. The war was
over, Congress downsized the army, and he was in his dotage. He was
read out of the service. He made his way to New Orleans, then to a
cotton plantation, and from there to Vera Cruz. He kept up his interest
in Texas and Latin America until his death in Mexico City in the closing days of 1825. Randolph, with pleasure, survived him for years.[13]

While Wilkinson's star sank into muck, Andrew Jackson's burst
like a nova. The war made him a national hero, an even bigger one than
George Washington. Champion of the Creek War, of the campaign to
take Mobile, of the Battle of New Orleans, Old Hickory became the
most wildly popular man that the nation had ever known. After New
Orleans he invaded Spanish Florida yet again, having done so once
before, during the war. He was the most successful filibuster of them
all, securing New Orleans and the whole of the Mississippi Valley
once and for all for his country, grabbing massive amounts of land,
regions the sizes of states, from the various southern tribes, and making things so hot in East and West Florida that by 1819 the Spanish
were happy to give it away to America.[14]

The secret to his success was his ability to work with, not against,
the federal government, a skill that none of the western conspirators
before him had ever learned—not Genêt, not Blount, not Burr, not

Wilkinson. With carefully worded, flimsy support from Washington, he could go on the march, launch an attack, as long as the politicians had what a later era would come to call plausible deniability. They played the good cop to Jackson's bad cop, telling Spain, and England, and everyone else that the government couldn't control Old Hickory, and that if the diplomats couldn't reach an agreement, then God alone knew what Jackson would do with his armies of rough frontiersmen. The ruse worked, partly because it wasn't a ruse. Andrew Jackson did not speak softly, but he did carry a big stick. All of this made him so popular that by 1829 he was president. He would have arrived in the president's mansion four years before that, if not for a fluke of the electoral system that gave John Quincy Adams a victory even though Jackson won the popular vote. But he got there at last, and that was soon enough for him to change the face of the presidency, and of the nation as well.[15]

He found William Wirt there waiting for him. Young Wirt, by now no longer young, had become attorney general in 1817. He held the post for twelve years, longer than anyone else in history, but when Jackson got to Washington the lawyer realized that his own time was up, and he retired to private life.[16] Jackson had his own appointments to make. One of them was Samuel Swartwout, whom he installed as federal collector of New York City customs.[17]

John Marshall was another one of the few who had great days ahead of him when the trials at Richmond ended. Not many people who played a large role in the conspiracy or the courtroom proceedings escaped damage to reputation, and Marshall's suffered with all the rest. But he survived fairly intact, as did Jackson and Jefferson, though unlike his cousin, Marshall stayed active in public life for nearly another thirty years. He continued to consolidate federal power, and judicial power as well. *Fletcher v. Peck, Martin v. Hunter's Lessee, McCulloch v. Maryland, Dartmouth College v. Woodward, Gibbons v. Ogden*—all of them indelibly marked American constitutional law, and all of them bear Marshall's imprint. He was truly the last Federalist. Only the rising tide of Jacksonian democracy, and new judicial appointments, diluted his force at all. He was the one who administered President Jackson's oath of office in 1829; the shock must have nearly killed him. But he survived long enough to do it again in 1833, finally succumbing two years later. The Liberty Bell tolled at his passing; that was when it cracked.

But for all of his vitality, Marshall couldn't stop Jackson any more than foreign governments could. Old Hickory did much to create the modern presidency, and he kept expanding America's empire too. He had long thought that the 1819 treaty between the United States and Spain had unjustly deprived his nation of Texas, in exchange for a secure claim to Florida, but he couldn't do much about it. The frontiersmen could, though, moving to take Texas themselves, first settling it with Mexicans' permission, and then taking it away from them by force. William Barret Travis, David Bowie, David Crockett—all martyrs of the Alamo—and of course Sam Houston, the revolt's main leader, were all Anglo-Celtic frontiersmen from the wilds of the Mississippi Valley, the sort of men whom Jackson had always commanded. Houston had been one of his lieutenants, in fact. And as the Texans fought Mexico in 1836, Jackson ordered the federal army, under General Edmund Pendleton Gaines, across the international border into Texas to deal with some troublesome Indian raids that just happened to be taking place at the time. Strangely, the number of desertions from Gaines's army increased, just around the time of the battle of San Jacinto, the huge Texan victory. Shortly thereafter the deserters reported for duty again, and Gaines moved back out of Texas, returning to U.S. territory.[18]

Ten years after that, the United States had grown brash enough to act against Mexico openly, declaring an expansionist war that would take the country to the Golden Gate and still farther. As part of this war, General Winfield Scott captured both Vera Cruz and Mexico City. He had witnessed Aaron Burr's treason trial; he had later served under Wilkinson, becoming the truly professional soldier that Wilkinson had never quite been. And unlike Burr and Wilkinson, he acted under government orders. By 1846, the United States was openly, aggressively expansionist, and it had the power to take what it wanted. The ugly frontier lusts that had spawned the years of conspiracy in the nation's childhood had finally come to full flower. From Mexico City the road led to San Juan Hill, Manila Bay, and beyond.

❧

Burr didn't live to see Winfield Scott's conquest, though he lived for a fairly long while. For more than two decades after he returned to New York, he worked on maintaining his law practice and staying out of the limelight. When spotting an old acquaintance on the street, he usually looked away, in case the friend would like to pretend for propriety's sake that he didn't know Aaron Burr. Now and then something would happen to remind people that he was still around. In 1833 he tried to repair his always-poor finances by marrying the widow Eliza Bowen Jumel, a well-known New Yorker and one of the country's wealthiest women. It didn't last long; barely a year later she filed for divorce, claiming that her new husband was an adulterer.[19]

But whatever his private dramas, politics still held his attention. Now and then he even played a small role, even late in his life. In 1831, as the distant rumble of a storm began to sound low and threatening in his ear, he met the abolitionist William Lloyd Garrison to ask him to stop his antislavery agitation, for the good of himself and the country. Burr was closer to eighty than seventy by then, and of another era, but Garrison still saw what countless others had seen. "He had a remarkable eye," the young revolutionary recalled of the old political animal, "more penetrating, more fascinating, than any I had ever seen, while his appearance was truly remarkable. . . . As he revealed himself to my moral sense, I saw he was destitute of any fixed principles, and that unyielding obedience to the higher law was regarded by him as credulity or fanaticism."[20]

Burr also worked in the background to help elect Andrew Jackson president. For his troubles he got no political office—by now he had better sense than to ask for one—but he did get to see what Jackson had helped happen in Texas. It was one of the last things he saw, in fact. The Battle of San Jacinto, the battle that Burr, perhaps, had once longed to fight, happened in April of 1836. Five months later Burr died, in his eighty-first year. But in those last few months he resurrected his memories of an earlier day, a day when he was one of the brightest of talents, the best that the young republic had to offer—a day when the nation was pitifully weak, when the frontier lay on the banks of the Hudson, when Spain crouched at the gates of New Orleans, and when fortune might favor the bold. When he heard the news from Texas, he spoke his own best epitaph, and a dirge for a different age. And as the flag of the Lone Star Republic snapped to the top of its mast far to the south, far to the west, he finally had the bitter last word. "There! You see? I was right!" he exclaimed. "I was only thirty years too soon. What was treason in me thirty years ago is patriotism today!"[21]

Author's Note

I don't pretend that this book is the definitive story of the conspiracy or the trials of Aaron Burr, much less his full biography. I doubt that such things can ever be written. Someone once said that history is only "the recorded part of the remembered part of the observed part of what happened."[1] Anyone who doubts the truth of that should study the Burr Conspiracy. Neither legal nor historical rules of evidence can unveil all of its mysteries. If anyone ever does manage to write the definitive story of Burr and his doings, it will be much longer and more thorough than what I have written here. Other, far more complete, accounts of these things already exist, but they, too, have their flaws. The ultimate version—if anyone ever writes it—will be massive, full of fact and conjecture ... yet it will still fall short of the truth, for the truth died with Burr.

This isn't because of a lack of material. Although Burr left few enough writings, we have plenty of things that people wrote about what they thought he was up to, everything from personal journals to detailed trial transcripts. But each of them paints a different picture. Burr might have been out to take Mexico; he might have been after New Orleans; he might have been targeting Florida; he might have been on the way to settle the Bastrop lands; he might even have wanted to capture Washington, as bizarre as that sounds; or he might have been planning various combinations of these things. We shall never know. That is how I began this book; that is how I shall end it.

But Burr deserves our attention, even if we can't find all of the answers. John Adams prescribed a government of laws and not of men, and that is a fine idea; but women and men make the laws, hold the offices, and wield the power. Burr was a human being, full of human weaknesses, and so were his political rivals. Brilliant men, many of them; an army of geniuses marches along through these pages, Burr, Hamilton, Jefferson, Marshall, and too many others to name. Yet they all showed profound passions and faults. They were all important; they all mattered. In the American pantheon, each of them, even Burr in a strange sort of way, stands as a hero. But the heroism must not hide their flaws, flaws that sometimes made the government and the people the pawns of the leaders. The heroes are no less heroic for this. Instead they are more so, since in them we see mere humans,who can, in their better moments, accomplish nearly superhuman acts of state-craft. But it should warn us that the best and the brightest who often serve us as leaders are always fallible human beings. We may demand that they do everything possible to become more than merely human, or we may forgive them for being unable to. Which one we do is up to us. But if we are to govern ourselves, we must remember the danger of a brilliant mind driven by frail human needs. That is why I have written this book—to provide a reminder.

The message is mine, and mine is the responsibility for what I have said, including the inevitable errors, but many people have helped me to say it. My thanks are due to my agent, Edward W. Knappman; my editors, Hana Lane and Mark Steven Long; my colleagues at the School of Law of the University of North Carolina at Chapel Hill, especially Professors Bobbi Jo Markert and John V. Orth; Professor Stephen Beall of Marquette University; Professor Peter G. Fish of Duke University; Thomas R. French, director of Syracuse University's H. Douglas Barclay Law Library; the Honorable Max Cleland; Walter C. Dauterman Jr.; Winston Fitzpatrick; Tara C. Hogan; Jaime L. Humphries; Patricia McKenzie; Jennifer J. Miller; Bonita Summers; Ray Swick; and my parents, who proofread the manuscript and watched and encouraged the project from the beginning. The greatest thanks of all go to my wife, Dr. Carol K.W. Melton, who worked very long hours on this book, who put up with me as I wrote it, and to whom I dedicate it.

Buckner F. Melton, Jr.

Notes

I have occasionally altered spelling, punctuation, and capitalization in primary source quotations to conform to modern standards. Readers should consult those sources directly for the most accurate renderings.

Part One

1. John Bakeless, *The Eyes of Discovery: The Pageant of North America as Seen by the First Explorers* (New York: Dover Publications, Inc., 1951), p. 283.

2. Gideon Lincecum, "Autobiography of Gideon Lincecum," *Publications of the Mississippi Historical Society* 8 (1904), p. 469.

3. James Adair, *History of the American Indians* (New York: Promontory Press, Samuel Cole Williams ed., 1974), pp. 440, 449.

4. Ellen Churchill Semple, *American History and its Geographic Conditions* (Boston: Houghton, Mifflin and Company, 1903), p. 37, ch. 2; D.W. Meinig, *The Shaping of America: A Geographical Perspective on 500 Years of History* 1 (New Haven: Yale University Press, 1986), pp. 57–58, 193–202.

5. H. P. Biggar, *The Voyages of Jacques Cartier* (Ottowa: F. A. Acland, 1924), p. 22.

6. Semple, *Geographic Conditions,* pp. 37–38.

7. Johann David Schöpf, *Travels in the Confederation* (Philadelphia: William J. Campbell, 1911), pp. 213–214.

8. Thomas D. Clark and John D.W. Guice, *Frontiers in Conflict: The Old Southwest, 1795–1830* (Albuquerque: University of New Mexico Press, 1989), pp. 4–5.

9. William Bartram, "Travels in Georgia and Florida, 1773–74: A Report to Dr. John Fothergill," *Transactions of the American Philosophical Society* 33 (N.S. 1943), p. 152.

10. Lincecum, "Autobiography," p. 469.

11. Proclamation of 1763, Henry Steele Commager, ed., *Documents of American History* 7th ed. 1 (New York: Appleton-Century-Crofts, 1963), pp. 47, 49.

12. Baron de Carondelet, "Military Report on Louisiana and West Florida, Nov. 24, 1794," James A. Robertson, ed., *Louisiana under the Rule of Spain, France, and the United States, 1705–1807* 1 (Cleveland, The Arthur H. Clark Company, 1911), pp. 298–299; Frederick J. Turner, "Carondelet on the Defense of Louisiana, 1794," *American Historical Review* 2 (1897), p. 474.

13. See, for instance, this passage from the King James Version of the Book of Jonah: "But the LORD sent out a great wind into the sea, and there was a mighty tempest in the sea, so that the ship was like to be broken." Jonah 1:4.

14. Everett Dick, *The Dixie Frontier: A Social History of the Southern Frontier from the First Transmontane Beginnings to the Civil War* (New York: Alfred A. Knopf, 1948), pp. 30–31.

15. Ibid., p. 42.

16. See generally William C. Sturtevant, ed., *Handbook of North American Indians* (Washington: Smithsonian Institution, 1978–1998).

17. Samuel Flagg Bemis, *Pinckney's Treaty: America's Advantage from Europe's Distress, 1783–1800*, rev. ed. (New Haven: Yale University Press, 1960), p. 39.

18. Bemis, *Pinckney's Treaty*, pp. 3–6, 67–70; Arthur Preston Whitaker, *The Mississippi Question, 1795–1803: A Study in Trade, Politics, and Diplomacy* (Gloucester, Mass.: Peter Smith, 1962), pp. 69–74.

19. James Ripley Jacobs, *Tarnished Warrior: Major-General James Wilkinson* (New York: The Macmillan Company, 1938), p. 75.

20. For the text of this oath, see W. L. Shepherd, "Wilkinson and the Spanish Conspiracy," *American Historical Review* 9 (1903), pp. 490, 492–497. For the story of Wilkinson's journey, see Jacobs, *Tarnished Warrior*. A. P. Whitaker, "James Wilkinson's First Descent to New Orleans in 1787," *Hispanic American Historical Review* 8 (1928), pp. 82, 85. For the New Orleans-Philadelphia connection, see Thomas Robson Hay and M. R. Werner, *The Admirable Trumpeter: A Biography of General James Wilkinson* (Garden City, New York: Doubleday, Doran & Co., 1941), pp. 79–80.

21. Diplomacy, like politics, makes for strange bedfellows: Although France and Spain were natural and usual allies against England from the days of the Tudors to Napoleon's downfall, the French Revolution's republicanism united the monarchies of England and Spain against it for a brief time in the middle 1790s.

22. Samuel Flagg Bemis, *Jay's Treaty: A Study in Commerce and Diplomacy*, rev. ed. (New Haven: Yale University Press, 1962), p. 195; Jonathan Daniels, *Ordeal of Ambition: Jefferson, Hamilton, Burr* (Garden City, N.Y.: Doubleday and Co. Inc., 1970), p. 105.

23. Frederick J. Turner, "The Origin of Genêt's Projected Attack on Louisiana and the Floridas," *American Historical Review* 3 (1898), p. 650.

24. Dumas Malone, *Jefferson and His Time*, vol. 3, *Jefferson and the Ordeal of Liberty* (Boston: Little Brown and Co., 1962), pp. 104–105. Hereafter referred to as *Jefferson and the Ordeal of Liberty*.

25. For a capsule summary of the Genêt's and earlier intrigues, see Buckner F. Melton, Jr., *The First Impeachment: The Constitution's Framers and the Case of Senator William Blount* (Macon, Ga: Mercer University Press, 1998), pp. 78–88. For a discussion of the Neutrality Act see Jules Lobel, "The Rise and Decline of the Neutrality Act: Sovereignty and Congressional War Powers in United States Foreign Policy," *Harvard International Law Journal* 24 (1983), pp. 1–71. For the act itself and a discussion of it, see Act of 5 June 1794, ch. 50, § 5, 1 Stat. 381, 384 (1794); Act of 2 Mar. 1797, ch. 5, 1 Stat. 497 (1797); 18 U.S.C. § 960 (1994).

26. For the full story of the William Blount and his conspiracy, see William H. Masterson, *William Blount* (Baton Rouge: Louisiana State University Press, 1954); Thomas P. Abernethy, *The South in the New Nation 1789–1819* (Baton Rouge: Louisiana State University Press, 1961), ch. 7; Melton, *First Impeachment*.

27. Melton, *First Impeachment*, p. 96; *Annals of Congress*, 5th Cong., 2348, 2353 (1797).

Part Two

1. Daniels, *Ordeal of Ambition*, 223.

2. Alexander Hamilton to James A. Bayard, 6 Aug. 1800, Harold C. Syrett, ed., *The Papers of Alexander Hamilton* 25 (New York: Columbia University Press, 1977), p. 58. Hereafter referred to as *The Hamilton Papers*.

3. Milton Lomask, *Aaron Burr* 1 (New York: Farrar, Strauss, Giroux, 1979), p. 215.

4. Malone, *Jefferson and the Ordeal of Liberty*, p. 500.

5. Noble E. Cunningham, Jr., *The Jeffersonian Republicans in Power: Party Operations, 1801–1809*, (Chapel Hill: University of N.C. Press, 1963), p. 207.

6. Lomask, *Aaron Burr*, 1:293.

7. For a discussion of their similarities and the duel see *The Hamilton Papers*, 26:237–241 ff.

8. Lomask, *Aaron Burr*, 1:96.

9. De Alva S. Alexander, *A Political History of the State of New York*, 1 (New York: H. Holt and Co., 1906), p. 45.

10. Dunbar Rowland, *Third Annual Report of the Director of the Department of Archives and History of the State of Mississippi, from October 1, 1903, to October 1, 1904* (Nashville, Tenn.: Press of Brandon Printing Co., 1905), p. 170. Hereafter referred to as *Third Annual Report*.

11. Charles Burr Todd, *A General History of the Burr Family in America* (New York: E.W. Sackett & Bro., 1878), p. 116.

12. Rowland, *Third Annual Report*, p. 170.

13. Samuel H. Wandell and Meade Minnigerode, *Aaron Burr: A Biography Compiled from Rare, and in Many Cases Unpublished, Sources*, 1 (New York: G. P. Putnam's Sons, 1925), p. 44. Hereafter referred to as Wandell and Minnigerode, *Aaron Burr*.

14. Lomask, *Aaron Burr*, 1:49–50.

15. Aaron Burr to George Washington, 21 July 1777, Peter Force, *American Archives*, 5th Series, III 1853. Quoted in Lomask, *Aaron Burr*, 1:52.

16. Lomask, *Aaron Burr*, 1:54.

17. William S. Baker, "The Camp by the Old Gulph Mill," *Pennsylvania Magazine of History and Biography* 17 (1893), pp. 414–429.

18. Lomask, *Aaron Burr*, 1:90–93.

19. James Parton, *The Life and Times of Aaron Burr* 1 (New York: Houghton, Mifflin and Co., 1858), p. 149.

20. Ibid., p. 169.

21. William Maclay, *The Journal of William Maclay* (New York: Albert & Charles Boni, 1927), p. 321.

22. Lomask, *Aaron Burr*, 1:141–142.

23. John C. Miller, *The Federalist Era 1789–1801* (New York: Harper Torchbooks, 1960), ch. 7.

24. Herbert S. Parmet and Marie B. Hecht, *Aaron Burr: Portrait of an Ambitious Man* (New York: The Macmillan Company, 1967), pp. 108–111, quoting Theodore Sedgwick to Jonathan Dayton, 19 Nov. 1796, Hamilton Papers, Library of Congress.

25. Franklin B. Sawvel, ed., *The ANAS of Thomas Jefferson*, 2d. ed. (New York: Da Capo Press, 1970), p. 227. Hereafter referred to as *ANAS*.

26. John Adams to Thomas Jefferson, 1 May 1812, Lester J. Cappon, *The Adams-Jefferson Letters: The Complete Correspondence between Thomas Jefferson and Abigail and John Adams* (Chapel Hill: The University of North Carolina Press, 1988), p. 301.

27. Matthew L. Davis, ed., *Memoirs of Aaron Burr: With Miscellaneous Selections from His Correspondence* 1 (New York: Harper and Brothers, 1837), p. 331; Daniels, *Ordeal of Ambition*, pp. 67–68; George C. Chalou, "St. Clair's Defeat, 1792," Arthur M. Schlesinger, Jr., and Roger Bruns, eds., *Congress Investigates: A Documented History, 1792–1974* 1 (New York: Chelsea House Publishers, 1975) pp. 3–17 ; Sawvel, *ANAS*, pp. 70–72.

28. Masterson, *William Blount*, p. 297.

29. John Nance Garner's exact words, which he uttered to Lyndon B. Johnson, are a matter of slight dispute, although the sentiment was clear enough. See Michael V. DiSalle, *Second Choice* (New York: Hawthorn Books, 1966), pp. 1–15.

30. For the story of the Alien and Sedition Acts and the Federalists' fall from power, see James Morton Smith, *Freedom's Fetters: The Alien and Sedition Laws and American Civil Liberties* (Ithaca: Cornell University Press, 1956). An interesting glimpse of the prosecutions appears in Richard N. Rosenfeld, *American Aurora: A Democratic-Republican Returns: The Suppressed History of Our Nation's Beginnings and the Heroic Newspaper that Tried to Report It* (New York: St. Martin's Press, 1997). For general histories of the Federalists' days of power, see

Stanley Elkins and Eric McKitrick, *The Age of Federalism* (New York: Oxford University Press, 1993), and Miller, *The Federalist Era.*

31. Lomask, *Aaron Burr,* 1:240, 245.

32. Daniels, *Ordeal of Ambition,* pp. 212–213.

33. Ibid., p. 213.

34. Hannah Gallatin to Albert Gallatin, Henry Adams, *The Life of Albert Gallatin* (Philadelphia: J.B. Lippincott & Co., 1879), p. 243.

35. For an overview of the electoral system, including accounts of the times when it has caused problems, see Neal R. Peirce and Lawrence D. Longley, *The People's President: The Electoral College in American History and the Direct Vote Alternative* (New Haven: Yale University Press, rev. ed. 1981). For an account of the 1800 crisis and its context, see ibid., pp. 31–44; Bernard A. Weisberger, *America Afire: Jefferson, Adams, and the Revolutionary Election of 1800* (New York: William Morrow, 2000); Miller, *Federalist Era,* ch. 14.

36. Lomask, *Aaron Burr,* 1:295.

37. Allan Gilbert, trans., *Machiavelli: The Chief Works and Others* 1 (Durham: Duke University Press, 1965), p. 82.

38. Thomas Jefferson to Aaron Burr, 18 Nov. 1801, Paul Leicester Ford, ed., *The Writings of Thomas Jefferson* 8 (New York: G.P. Putnam's Sons, 1897), p. 102.

39. Theodore Sedgwick to Rufus King, 20 Feb. 1802, *The Life and Correspondence of Rufus King* 4 (New York, G. P. Putnam's Sons, 1894–1900), p. 74.

40. Thomas Jefferson to Archibald Stuart, 25 Jan. 1786, Julian P. Boyd, ed., *The Papers of Thomas Jefferson* 9 (Princeton: Princeton University Press, 1954), p. 218.

41. Thomas Jefferson to Robert Livingston, 18 Apr. 1802, Ford, *Writings of Thomas Jefferson,* 8:144–145.

42. Alexander Hamilton to Charles Cotesworth Pinckney, 29 Dec. 1802, *The Hamilton Papers,* 26:72.

43. Thomas Jefferson to Archibald Stuart, 25 Jan. 1786, Boyd, *The Papers of Thomas Jefferson,* 9:218; John C. Miller, *Alexander Hamilton: Portrait in Paradox* (New York: Harper and Brothers, Publishers, 1959), p. 495.

44. Charles Brockden Brown, *An Address to the Government of the United States on the Cession of Louisiana to the French* (Philadelphia: J. Conrad & Co., 1803), pp. 48, 52, 56. Quoted in Alexander DeConde, *This Affair of Louisiana* (New York: Charles Scribner's Sons, 1976), p. 123.

45. William Coleman's *New York Evening Post,* 28 Jan. 1803. Quoted in DeConde, *This Affair of Louisiana,* p. 127.

46. *Charleston Courier,* 11 Jan. 1803. Quoted in DeConde, *This Affair of Louisiana,* p. 121.

47. James Madison to Charles Pinckney, 27 Nov. 1802, Mary A. Hackett, J.C.A. Stagg, Jeanne Kerr Cross, Susan Holbrook Perdue, & Ellen J. Barber, eds., *The Papers of James Madison, Secretary of State Series* 4 (Charlottesville, Va.: University Press of Virginia, 1998), p. 147.

48. Jefferson's First Inaugural Address, *Documents of American History,* 1: 186–189.

49. George Dangerfield, *Chancellor Robert R. Livingston of New York, 1746–1813* (New York: Harcourt, Brace, and Co., 1960), p. 337; *American State Papers, Foreign Relations,* 2:525.

50. Dangerfield, *Chancellor Robert R. Livingston,* p. 311.

51. See C.L.R. James, *The Black Jacobins: Toussaint L'Ouverture and the Santo Domingo Revolution* 2nd rev. ed. (New York: Vintage Books, 1989).

52. Spoken on 11 Jan. 1803, A.M. Roederer ed., *Oeuvres de Comte P. L. Roederer,* (Paris, Typ. de Firmin Didot frères 1853–59), III, 461. For an overview of the various theories of why Napoleon sold Louisiana, see DeConde, *This Affair of Louisiana,* pp. 154–159.

53. Fisher Ames to Christopher Gore, 31 Oct. 1803, Seth Ames, ed., *Works of Fisher Ames* 1 (Boston: Little, Brown and Co., 1854), pp. 323–324.

54. Thomas Jefferson to Joseph Priestley, 29 Jan. 1804, Ford, *Writings of Thomas Jefferson* 8:295.

55. Ibid., pp. 243–244 n.

56. Act of 26 Mar. 1804, 2 Stat. ch. 38, at 283–295.

57. The Kentucky and Virginia Resolutions of 1798, *Documents of American History,* 1:178–183.

58. Everett Somerville Brown, ed., *William Plumer's Memorandum of Proceedings in the United States Senate, 1803–1807* (New York: The Macmillan Co., 1923), pp. 517–518. See ibid., ch. 8 for an account of the New England secession movement.

59. Alexander Hamilton to Robert G. Harper, 19 Feb. 1804, *The Hamilton Papers,* 26:192.

60. Alexander Hamilton to Theodore Sedgwick, 10 July 1804, ibid., p. 309.

61. Alexander Hamilton to Robert G. Harper, 19 Feb. 1804, ibid., p. 192.

62. Charles D. Cooper to Philip Schuyler, 23 Apr. 1804, ibid., p. 246.

63. Aaron Burr to Alexander Hamilton, 18 June 1804, ibid., p. 243.

64. Alexander Hamilton to Aaron Burr, 20 June 1804, ibid., pp. 247–248.

65. Arnold A. Rogow, *A Fatal Friendship: Alexander Hamilton and Aaron Burr* (New York: Hill and Wang, 1998), pp. 239–240. This theory comes in part from Gore Vidal, though he could not substantiate it. Gore Vidal, *Burr: A Novel* (New York: Random House, 1973), pp. 272–273.

Part Three

1. Lord Malmesbury, Diary, 16 Feb. 1803, Malmesbury, *Diaries and Correspondence of James Harris, First Earl.* Quoted in Malcolm Lester, *Anthony Merry Redivivus: A Reappraisal of the British Minister to the United States, 1803–6* (Charlottesville: University Press of Virginia: 1978), pp. 13, 20; Brown, *William Plumer's Memorandum,* pp. 447–448.

2. Benjamin Ogle Tayloe to [?], 15 Dec. 1866, Winslow Marston Watson. *In Memoriam: Benjamin Ogle Tayloe* (Washington, D.C., Philadelphia: Sherman & Co. 1872), pp. 239–240.

3. Anthony Merry to Lord Harrowby, 6 Aug. 1804, Mary-Jo Kline, ed., *Political Correspondence and Public Papers of Aaron Burr* 2 (Princeton: Princeton University Press, 1983), pp. 891–892. Hereafter referred to as Kline, *Political Correspondence of Aaron Burr.*

4. Aaron Burr to Charles Biddle, 18 July 1804, ibid., 2:886.

5. James A. Wilkinson to Aaron Burr, 23 May 1804, Worthington Chauncey Ford, ed., "Some Papers of Aaron Burr," *Proceedings of the American Antiquarian Society,* n.s., 29 (1919), pp. 43, 122–23.

6. Thomas Truxtun to Timothy Pickering 15 Dec. 1803. Quoted in Eugene S. Ferguson, *Truxtun of the Constellation: The Life of Commodore Thomas Truxtun, U.S. Navy, 1755–1822* (Baltimore: The Johns Hopkins Press, 1956), p. 229.

7. Ibid., pp. 160–169, 187–188, 223–224.

8. Ibid., p. 230.

9. Ibid., pp. 234–235.; Wandell and Minnigerode, *Aaron Burr,* 1:303–304. One of Burr's most recent biographers has him departing New York on the midmorning of July 21, but most other sources agree that he left that evening under cover of darkness, spent the night on the water, and reached Truxtun's house on the morning of July 22.

10. Helen I. Cowan, *Charles Williamson: Genesee Promoter, Friend of Anglo-American Rapprochement* (Clifton, N.J.: Augustus M. Kelley, 1973), pp. 278–280.

11. Aaron Burr to Theodosia Alston, 3 Aug. 1804, Davis, *Memoirs of Aaron Burr,* 2:331.

12. Aaron Burr to Theodosia Alston, 11 Aug. 1804, ibid., p. 332.

13. Frank Lawrence Owsley, Jr. and Gene A. Smith, *Filibusters and Expansionists: Jeffersonian Manifest Destiny, 1800–1821* (Tuscaloosa: University of Alabama Press, 1997), p. 62.

14. Charles R. Williams, *Life of Rutherford Birchard Hayes* 1 (Columbus, Ohio: F.J. Hear, 1928), p. 33.

15. Case of Fries, 9 F. Cas. 826, 846 (C.C.D. Pa. 1799) (No. 5126); United States v. Callender, 25 F. Cas. 239 (C.C.D. Va. 1800) (No. 14,709); Stephen B. Presser, "A Tale of Two Judges: Richard Peters, Samuel Chase, and the Broken Promise of Federalist Jurisprudence," *Northwestern Law Review* 73:83–88 (1978). On the impeachment of Chase, see Peter Charles Hoffer and N.E.H. Hull, *Impeachment in America, 1685–1805* (New Haven: Yale University Press, 1984), ch. 12.

16. Brown, *William Plumer's Memorandum,* pp. 235–236.

17. Ibid., p. 244.

18. *The New York Evening Post,* 6 Feb. 1805. Quoted in Dumas Malone, *Jefferson the President: First Term, 1802–1805* (Boston: Little, Brown and Co., 1970), p. 476. Hereafter referred to as *Jefferson the President: First Term.*

19. Brown, *William Plumer's Memorandum,* p. 304.

20. Isaac Joslin Cox, "Western Reaction to the Burr Conspiracy," *Transactions of the Illinois Historical Society* (1928), pp.79. Quoted in Lomask, *Aaron Burr,* 2:45.

21. Anthony Merry to Lord Harrowby, 29 Mar. 1805, Kline, *Political Correspondence of Aaron Burr,* 2:928–929.

22. Carlos Martinez de Yrujo to Casa Calvo, 23 May 1805, encl. in letter to Cevallos, 24 May 1804; and to Cevallos, 5 Aug. 1805, Henry Adams Transcripts from the *Spanish State Papers: Casa Yrujo, 1801–1807.* Quoted in Lomask, *Aaron Burr* 2:52.

23. Lomask, *Aaron Burr,* 2:27.

24. Thomas Jefferson to Samuel Smith, 4 May 1806, Ford, *Writings of Thomas Jefferson,* 8:450–451.

25. Brown, *William Plumer's Memorandum,* p. 278.

26. Ibid., pp. 282–283.

27. Ibid., pp. 283, 285.

28. Ibid., p. 310.

29. Aaron Burr to Joseph Alston, 22 Mar. 1805, Davis, *Memoirs of Aaron Burr,* 2:365.

30. Aaron Burr to Theodosia Alston, 30 Apr. 1805, ibid., 2:368.

31. Aleine Austin, *Matthew Lyon: New Man of the Democratic Revolution, 1749–1822* (University Park: The Pennsylvania State University Press, 1981), pp. 96–100.

32. J. Fairfax McLaughlin, *Matthew Lyon, The Hampden of Congress* (New York: Wynkoop Hallenbeck Crawford Co., 1900), pp. 483–484.

33. Aaron Burr to James Wilkinson, 30 Apr. 1805, in Ezekiel Bacon, Chairman, *Report of the Committee Appointed to Inquire into the Conduct of General Wilkinson,* 26 Feb. 1811. p. 198. Quoted in Lomask, *Aaron Burr* 2:57–58.

34. See Therese Blennerhassett-Adams, "The True Story of Harman Blennerhassett," *Century Magazine* 62 (1901): 351–356. For a brief sketch of the Blennerhassetts, their island, and their dealings with Aaron Burr, see Ray Swick, *An Island Called Eden: The Story of Harman and Margaret Blennerhassett,* rev. ed. (Parkersburg: Blennerhassett Island State Historical Park, 2000).

35. Harman Blennerhassett to Aaron Burr, 21 Dec. 1805, Kline, *Political Correspondence of Aaron Burr* 2:949–951.

36. See pages 94–95.

37. Lomask, *Aaron Burr,* 2:64.

38. Jacob Burnet, *Notes on the Early Settlement of the Northwest Territory* (Cincinnati: Derby, Bradley & Co., 1847), p. 295.

39. See Grady McWhiney and Perry D. Jamieson, *Attack and Die: Civil War Military Tactics and Southern Heritage* (Tuscaloosa, University of Alabama Press, 1982).

40. Jackson's General order to the Militia as to Spanish Threats, 7 Aug. 1803, John Spencer Bassett, ed., *Correspondence of Andrew Jackson* 1 (Washington,

D.C., Carnegie Institution of Washington, 1926), pp. 68–69; Order to Brigadier Generals of the 2d Division, 4 Oct. 1806, Harold D. Moser and Sharon MacPherson, eds., *The Papers of Andrew Jackson* 2 (Knoxville: The University of Tennessee Press, 1984), p. 111.

41. Aaron Burr to Theodosia Alston, 23 May 1805, Davis, *Memoirs of Aaron Burr,* 2:372; Robert V. Remini, *Andrew Jackson,* vol. 1. (Baltimore: The Johns Hopkins University Press, 1998), p. 147.

42. Thomas Perkins Abernethy, *The Burr Conspiracy* (New York: Oxford University Press, 1954), p. 28.

43. Clark and Guice, *Frontiers in Conflict,* pp. 41–52.

44. *State Papers and Correspondence Bearing Upon the Purchase of the Territory of Louisiana,* 57th Cong., 2d Sess., H.R. Doc. No. 431 (Washington, 1903), p. 200.

45. Quoted in DeConde, *This Affair of Louisiana,* p. 216.

46. Juan Ventura Morales to W.C.C. Claiborne, 19 Aug. 1805, Clarence Edwin Carter, ed., *The Territorial Papers of the United States* 9 (Washington D.C.: Government Printing Office, 1940), p. 492.

47. W.C.C. Claiborne to James Madison, 22 Oct. 1804, ibid., 9:313.

48. W.C.C. Claiborne to James Madison, 26 Mar. 1805, ibid., 9:425.

49. Henry Adams, *History of the United States* 3 (New York: Charles Scribner's Sons, 1890), p. 38.

50. Thomas Jefferson to DeWitt Clinton, 2 Dec. 1803, Ford, *Writings of Thomas Jefferson,* 8:283.

51. Aaron Burr to Theodosia Alston, 23 May 1805, Davis, *Memoirs of Aaron Burr,* 2:371.

52. Clark and Guice, *Frontiers in Conflict,* p. 97. On the Natchez Trace, see ibid., ch. 5.

53. Aaron Burr to Theodosia Alston, 23 May 1805, Davis, *Memoirs of Aaron Burr,* 2:373.

54. Abernethy, *The Burr Conspiracy,* p. 31.

55. *Gazette of the United States* (Philadelphia), 2 Aug. 1805.

56. Abernethy, *The Burr Conspiracy,* p. 34; *Charleston Courier,* 5 Mar. 1806.

57. Abernethy, *The Burr Conspiracy,* p. 38.

58. Thomas Jefferson to Joseph Hamilton Daveiss, Feb. 15, 1806, Ford, *Writings of Thomas Jefferson,* 8:424; Kline, *The Political Correspondence of Aaron Burr,* 2:978.

59. Thomas Jefferson to Sir John Sinclair, 30 June 1803, Jefferson Papers, Library of Congress. Quoted in Owsley and Smith, *Filibusters and Expansionists,* pp. 21, 31.

60. Thomas Jefferson to Albert Gallatin, 4 Dec. 1805, Ford, *The Writings of Thomas Jefferson* 8:401–402.

61. William Spence Robertson, *The Life of Miranda* 1 (Chapel Hill: University of North Carolina Press, 1929), p. 295.

62. Ibid., 1:297–300; Irving Brant, *James Madison: Secretary of State,* *1800–1809* (Indianapolis: The Bobbs-Merrill Co., 1953), p. 328; Act of 5 June 1794, ch. 50, § 5, 1 Stat. 381, 384 (1794); Act of 2 Mar. 1797, ch. 5, 1 Stat. 497 (1797); 18 U.S.C. § 960 (1994).

63. Dumas Malone, *Jefferson the President: Second Term, 1805–1809,* (Boston: Little, Brown and Co., 1974), pp. 80–85. Hereafter referred to as *Jefferson the President: Second Term.*

64. Aaron Burr to Jeremy Bentham, 16 Oct. 1811, Matthew L. Davis, ed., *The Private Journal of Aaron Burr* (New York, Harper & Brothers, 1838), pp. 11, 254.

65. Anthony Merry to Lord Mulgrave, 25 Nov. 1805, Kline, *Political Correspondence of Aaron Burr,* 2:944–945.

66. Harman Blennerhassett to Aaron Burr, 21 Dec. 1805, Kline, *The Political Correspondence of Aaron Burr,* 2:950–951.

67. Lomask, *Aaron Burr,* 2:113.

68. Yrujo to Cevallos, 5 Dec. 1805, No. 590, Henry Adams, Transcripts from the *Spanish State Papers: Casa Yrujo, 1801–1807.* Quoted in Lomask, *Aaron Burr,* 2:102–103.

69. Yrujo to Cevallos, 1 Jan. 1806, Facsimile from the *Archivo Historico Nacional-Madrid, Estado,* Library of Congress. Quoted in Lomask, *Aaron Burr,* 2:103–105.

70. Louis B. Wright and Julia H. MacLeod, *The First Americans in North Africa: William Eaton's Struggle against the Barbary Pirates, 1799–1805* (Princeton: Princeton University Press, 1945); Melton, *The First Impeachment,* pp. 133–134.

71. *American State Papers:* Miscellaneous, 1:493–495, 537–538.

72. Ibid., p. 497.

73. Abernethy, *The Burr Conspiracy,* p. 44.

74. Ibid., pp. 46–47.

75. Aaron Burr to James Wilkinson, 6 Jan. 1805, James Wilkinson, *Memoirs of My Own Time,* 4 vols. Appendix lxxvi. Quoted in Lomask, *Aaron Burr,* 2:106.

76. Aaron Burr to James Wilkinson, 16 Apr. 1806, Kline, *Political Correspondence of Aaron Burr,* 2:968.

77. Sawvel, *ANAS,* p. 237; Thomas Jefferson, Memorandum of a Conversation with Aaron Burr, 15 Apr. 1806, Kline, *Political Correspondence of Aaron Burr,* 2:962.

78. Kline, *Political Correspondence of Aaron Burr,* 2:972.

79. Walter Flavius McCaleb, *The Aaron Burr Conspiracy* (New York: Wilson-Erickson, 1936), p. 78.

80. Abernethy, *The Burr Conspiracy,* p. 49; W.C.C. Claiborne to James Madison, 29 Mar. 1806, Carter, *The Territorial Papers of the United States,* 9:618.

81. Jacobs, *Tarnished Warrior,* p. 229; Abernethy, *The Burr Conspiracy,* pp. 49–50; and Carter, *The Territorial Papers of the United States,* 9:627–628.

82. Abernethy, *The Burr Conspiracy*, pp. 58–59.

83. David Robertson, *Reports of the Trial of Colonel Burr (late Vice President of the United States,) for Treason and for a Misdemeanor* 2 (Philadelphia: Hapkins and Earle, 1808), p. 478.

84. Lomask, *Aaron Burr*, 2:113.

Part Four

1. Henry Dearborn to James Wilkinson, 29 Mar. 1806, James Wilkinson, *Burr's Conspiracy Exposed; and General Wilkinson Vindicated Against the Slanders of His Enemies on that Important Occasion* 2 (Washington, D.C.: Author, 1811), Appendix p. 36. Hereafter referred to as Wilkinson, *Burr's Conspiracy*.

2. Ibid., p. 25.

3. Abernethy, *The Burr Conspiracy*, pp. 144–146.

4. Thomas Cushing to Simon de Herrara, 5 Aug. 1806, Wilkinson, *Burr's Conspiracy* 2: Appendix pp. 64–65.

5. W.C.C. Claiborne to Simon de Herrara, 26 Aug. 1806, ibid., 2: Appendix p. 68.

6. James Wilkinson to Constant Freeman, 12 Oct. 1806, ibid., 2: Appendix p. 70.

7. Abernethy, *The Burr Conspiracy*, pp. 52–53, 119–121.

8. James Wilkinson to Henry Dearborn, 8 Sept. 1806, ibid., 2: Appendix p. 47.

9. *Annals of Congress*, 10th Cong., Appendix 675. Although Wilkinson pretty clearly wrote Burr in the spring of 1806, the letters have never since surfaced. This quotation comes from a witness's recollection.

10. James Wilkinson to Henry Dearborn, 2 Aug. 1806, Wilkinson, *Burr's Conspiracy*, 2: Appendix p. 45.

11. Wilkinson, *Burr's Conspiracy*, 2:29; *American State Papers*, Miscellaneous, 1:539–540; T. Carpenter, *The Trial of Col. Aaron Burr* 3 (Washington City: Westcott & Co., 1808), pp. 236–237.

12. *American State Papers*: Miscellaneous, 1:542.

13. For the full text and a thorough discussion of the Cipher Letter, the most famous document of the Burr Conspiracy and one of the most controversial, see Kline, *Political Correspondence of Aaron Burr*, 2:973–990. See also pages 119–120.

14. Robertson, *Reports of the Trials of Colonel Aaron Burr*, 1:62.

15. Ibid., 1:497–505; and Thomas Jefferson to George Morgan, 19 Sept. 1806, Ford, *The Writings of Thomas Jefferson*, 8:473.

16. Order to Brigadier Generals of the 2nd Division, 4 Oct. 1806, Moser, *Papers of Andrew Jackson*, 2:111.

17. Andrew Jackson to James Winchester, 4 Oct. 1806, ibid., pp. 110–111.

18. Andrew Jackson to W.C.C. Claiborne, 12 Nov. 1806, ibid., p. 116.

19. *Charleston Courier,* 28 Sept 1806.

20. Ibid., 18 Oct. 1806.

21. *Annals of Congress,* 10th Cong., p. 290 (1808).

22. Ibid., p. 291.

23. J.H. Daveiss, *View of the President's Conduct, Concerning the Conspiracy of 1806* (Frankfort, Kentucky: Joseph M. Street, 1807), p. 23.

24. Ibid., p. 25. Thomas Jefferson to Joseph Hamilton Daveiss, 12 Sept. 1806, Ford, *Writings of Thomas Jefferson,* 8:467–468.

25. *Annals of Congress,* 10th Cong., p. 259 (1808); United States v. Burr, 25 F. Cas. 1, 1 (C.C.D. Ky. 1806) (No. 14,692).

26. Aaron Burr to Henry Clay, 27 Nov. 1806 and 1 Dec. 1806, James F. Hopkins, ed., *The Papers of Henry Clay* 1 (Louisville: University of Kentucky Press, 1959), pp. 256–257.

27. John Wood, *Full Statement of the Trial and Acquittal of Aaron Burr, Esq.* (Alexandria: Cotton and Stewart,1807), p. 7.

28. Ibid., pp. 8–11.

29. Ibid., pp. 11–15.

30. Henry Clay's Defense of Aaron Burr, *The Western World,* 18 Dec. 1806, Hopkins, *The Papers of Henry Clay,* 1:259.

31. Wood, *Full Statement of the Trial and Acquittal of Aaron Burr, Esq.,* pp. 21, 30.

32. Daveiss, *A View of the President's Conduct,* p. 28.

33. Wood, *Full Statement of the Trial and Acquittal of Aaron Burr, Esq.,* p. 36.

34. Daveiss, *A View of the President's Conduct,* p. 30.

35. Ibid., p. 31.

36. Andrew Jackson to George Washington Campbell, 15 Jan. 1807, Moser, *Papers of Andrew Jackson* 2:148–149; Andrew Jackson to Daniel Smith, 12 Nov. 1806, ibid., 2:118.

37. Andrew Jackson to Daniel Smith, 12 Nov. 1806, ibid., 2:118.

38. Andrew Jackson to W.C.C. Claiborne, 12 Nov. 1806, ibid., 2:116.

39. Aaron Burr to James Wilkinson, 22–29 July 1806, Kline, *The Political Correspondence of Aaron Burr,* 2:986–990. Wilkinson altered both copies of the cipher letter that he eventually received. For a discussion of the letter, see ibid., 2:973–990.

40. James Wilkinson to Thomas Jefferson, 20 Oct. 1806, Wilkinson, *Burr's Conspiracy* 2: Appendix 73–74.

41. Abernethy, *The Burr Conspiracy,* p.158–159.

42. William R. Shepherd, "A Letter of General James Wilkinson, 1806," *American Historical Review* 9 (1904), pp. 533, 536.

43. Lomask, *Aaron Burr,* 2:171.

44. James Wilkinson to Thomas Jefferson, 12 Nov. 1806, Wilkinson, *Burr's Conspiracy,* 2: Appendix 79–80.

45. Andrew Jackson to W.C.C. Claiborne, 12 Nov. 1806, Moser, *The Papers of Andrew Jackson*, 2:116.

46. James Wilkinson to W.C.C. Claiborne, 12 Nov. 1806, Dunbar Rowland, ed., *Official Letter Books of W.C.C. Claiborne, 1801–1816* 4 (Jackson, Missippi: State Dept. of Archives and History, 1917), p. 55.

47. *American State Papers,* Miscellaneous, 1:600–601.

48. Kline, *Political Correspondence of Aaron Burr*, 2:870–871, 976–977; Abernethy, *The Burr Conspiracy*, p. 57.

49. Abernethy, *The Burr Conspiracy*, pp. 175–176.

50. Rowland, *Official Letter Books of W.C.C. Claiborne*, 4:41.

51. James Wilkinson to W.C.C. Claiborne, 16 Dec. 1806, ibid., 4:62.

52. James Wilkinson to W.C.C. Claiborne, 6 Dec. 1806 and W.C.C. Claiborne to James Wilkinson, 8 Dec. 1806, ibid., 4:46–47, 49–50.

53. James Wilkinson to W.C.C. Claiborne, 7 Dec. 1806, ibid., 4:49.

54. James Wilkinson to W.C.C. Claiborne, 15 Dec. 1806, ibid., 4:58–60.

55. W.C.C. Claiborne to James Wilkinson, 16 Dec. 1806, ibid., 4:61.

56. W.C.C. Claiborne to James Wilkinson, 17 Dec. 1806, ibid., 4:63–64, 69, 76.

57. Brown, *William Plumer's Memorandum*, p. 618; B. R. Brunson, *The Adventures of Samuel Swartwout in the Age of Jefferson and Jackson* (Lewiston, N.Y.: The Edwin Mellen Press, 1989), pp. 12–13.

58. W.C.C. Claiborne to James Madison, 17 Dec. 1806, Rowland, *Official Letter Books of W.C.C. Claiborne*, 4:68.

59. Abernethy, *The Burr Conspiracy*, p. 184; Thomas Jefferson to the Senate and House of Representatives of the United States, 22 Jan. 1807, Albert Ellery Bergh, ed., *The Writings of Thomas Jefferson* 3 (Washington, D.C., The Thomas Jefferson Memorial Association, 1903), p. 428.

60. Thomas Jefferson to George Morgan, 26 Mar. 1807, Bergh, *The Writings of Thomas Jefferson*, 11:173–174.

61. John Nicholson to Thomas Jefferson, Rec'd. 24 Oct. 1806, Worthington Chauncey Ford, ed., *Thomas Jefferson Correspondence: Printed from the Originals in the Collections of William K. Bixby* (Boston: n.p., 1916), pp. 134–136.

62. Thomas Jefferson to Thomas Mann Randolph, 3 Nov. 1806, Bergh, *The Writings of Thomas Jefferson*, 18:249–250.

63. Statements of Gideon Granger, 9 Oct. 1806, Lesley Henshaw, ed., "Burr-Blennerhassett Documents," *Quarterly Publication of the Historical and Philosophical Society of Ohio* 9 (1914) 1 and 2, pp. 10–13.

64. Sawvel, *ANAS*, pp. 246–247.

65. Ibid., p. 248.

66. Ibid., pp. 248–249.

67. Ibid.; Malone, *Jefferson the President: Second Term*, p. 247.

68. Jefferson himself acknowledged the warnings about James Wilkinson in the Cabinet meeting of October 22. Sawvel, *ANAS*, pp. 247–249.

69. See page 44.

70. Thomas Jefferson, "Sixth Annual Message," Ford, *The Writings of Thomas Jefferson*, 8:489–490.

71. Malone, *Jefferson the President*, p. 253.

72. Thomas Jefferson to W.C.C. Claiborne, 20 Dec. 1806, Ford, *The Writings of Thomas Jefferson*, 8:501–502.

73. Deposition of Edward W. Tupper, 8 Sept. 1807, Henshaw, "Burr-Blennerhassett Documents," pp. 20–21.

74. Robertson, *Reports of the Trials of Aaron Burr*, 1:508–509; and Deposition of Edward W. Tupper, 8 Sept. 1807, Henshaw, "Burr-Blennerhassett Documents," 19–26.

75. Robertson, *Reports of the Trials of Colonel Aaron Burr*, 1:494–495.

76. Andrew Jackson to George Washington Campbell, 15 Jan. 1807, Moser, *The Papers of Andrew Jackson*, 2:149; Henry Dearborn to *Andrew Jackson*, 19 Dec. 1806, ibid., 2:125–126; Remini, *Andrew Jackson* 1:152–153.

77. Raymond E. Fitch, ed., *Breaking with Burr: Harmon Blennerhassett's Journal, 1807* (Athens: Ohio University Press, 1988), pp. 176–187.

78. Ibid., p. 180.

79. Kline, *Political Correspondence of Aaron Burr*, 2:1006–1008.

80. Aaron Burr to Cowles Mead, 12 Jan. 1807, ibid., 2:1008–1009.

81. *American State Papers*, Miscellaneous, 1:524–525. How many weapons Burr had with him, and what kind they were, was a running issue during the Richmond trials. Cf. ibid., pp. 514, 524–525, 602; Robertson, *Reports of the Trials of Colonel Aaron Burr*, 1:497; Rowland, *Third Annual Report*, pp. 68, 70–71, 103–104.

82. Rowland, *Third Annual Report*, 54; Kline, *The Political Correspondence of Aaron Burr*, 2:1010 n. 2; William Baskerville Hamilton, *Anglo-American Law on the Frontier: Thomas Rodney and His Territorial Cases* (Durham, N.C.: Duke University Press, 1953), p 78.

83. Cowles Mead to Thomas Fitzpatrick, 13 Jan. 1807, Rowland, *Third Annual Report*, pp. 52–53.

84. Kline, *Political Correspondence of Aaron Burr*, 2:1011.

85. Cowles Mead to Aaron Burr, 15 Jan. 1807, ibid., 2:1013.

86. *American State Papers*, Miscellaneous, 1:568.

87. Agreement with Cowles Mead, 16 January 1807, Kline, *The Political Correspondence of Aaron Burr*, 2:1014; Rowland, *Third Annual Report*, pp. 97–99; *American State Papers*, Miscellaneous, 1:568–569.

88. Rowland, *Third Annual Report*, pp. 98–99.

89. Hamilton, *Anglo-American Law on the Frontier*, pp. 80, 97, 261–262; Rowland, *Third Annual Report*, p. 100.

90. Fitch, *Breaking with Burr*, p. 186; Hamilton, *Anglo-American Law on the Frontier*, p. 263.

91. Hamilton, *Anglo-American Law on the Frontier*, pp. 261–262.

92. Kline, *Political Correspondence of Aaron Burr*, 2:1018; Abernethy, *The Burr Conspiracy*, pp. 159, 218–219; Hamilton, *Anglo-American Law on the Frontier*, p. 262; Henshaw, "Burr-Blennerhassett Documents," pp. 35–39; *American State Papers*, Miscellaneous, 1:530. Rowland, *Third Annual Report*, p. 57, mentions a Major John Minor; Stephen and John were probably one and the same.

93. Proclamation by Robert Williams, (n.d.); Rowland, *Third Annual Report*, pp. 73–74.

94. Rowland, *Third Annual Report*, p. 68.

95. *Mississippi Messenger*, 17 Feb. 1807; Rowland, *Third Annual Report*, p. 103.

96. Aaron Burr to Robert Williams, 4 Feb. 1807 and 12 Feb. 1807, Kline, *The Political Correspondence of Aaron Burr*, 2:1022–1023; Robert Williams to Aaron Burr, 13 Feb. 1807, ibid., 2:1024–1025.

Part Five

1. U.S. Const. art. I, § 9.

2. Judiciary Act of 1789, ch. 20, § 14, 1 Stat. 73, 81–82 (1789).

3. *Annals of Congress*, 9th Cong., p. 984 (1807).

4. Ibid., pp. 336. For a survey of Congress's investigatory powers, see Ernest J. Eberling, *Congressional Investigations* (New York: Columbia University Press, 1928); Telford Taylor, *Grand Inquest: The Story of Congressional Investigations* (New York: Simon and Schuster, 1955).

5. *Annals of Congress*, 9th Cong., pp. 334–359 (1807).

6. Special Message on Burr, Ford, *The Writings of Thomas Jefferson* 9:14–20.

7. *Annals of Congress*, 9th Cong., p. 1010 (1807).

8. Special Message on Burr, Ford, *The Writings of Thomas Jefferson*, 9:20.

9. *Annals of Congress*, 9th Cong., pp. 44 (1807); Brown, *William Plumer's Memorandum*, p. 584.

10. United States v. Bollman, 24 F. Cas. 1189, 1189–190 (C.C.D. D.C. 1807) (No. 14622); Ex parte Bollman, 8 U.S. (4 Cranch) 75, 455 (1807).

11. *Bollman*, 24 F. Cas. p. 1190.

12. Ibid., pp. 1195–1196.

13. Ibid., pp. 1192–1193.

14. *Bollman*, 8 U.S. (4 Cranch) pp. 79–83.

15. Ibid., pp. 93–96, 100–103.

16. Ibid., pp. 108–110.

17. Ibid., p. 126.

18. Ibid., p. 135.

19. Nicholas Perkins to C.A. Rodney, [n.d], "The Capture of Aaron Burr," *The American Historical Magazine* 1 (1896), pp. 141–143; Stuart O. Stumpf, ed.,

"The Arrest of Aaron Burr: A Documentary Record," *The Alabama Historical Quarterly* 42 (1980), pp. 113, 117–119; Lomask, *Aaron Burr*, 2:222; James W. Silver, *Edmund Pendleton Gaines: Frontier General* (Baton Rouge: Louisiana State University Press, 1949), pp. 14–16.

20. Nicholas Perkins to C.A. Rodney, [n.d], "The Capture of Aaron Burr," pp. 143–146; Stumpf, "Arrest of Aaron Burr," 119–121; United States. v. Burr, 25 F. Cas. 1, 10 (C.C.D. Va. 1807) (No. 14,692a).

21. *Burr*, 25, F. Cas. at 10; Edmund Gaines to James Wilkinson and Robert Williams, 19 Feb. 1807, Edmund Gaines to Nicholas Perkins, 9 Feb. 1807 and Edmund Gaines to Nicholas Perkins [n.d.], "The Capture of Aaron Burr," pp. 147–151; Stumpf, "Arrest of Aaron Burr," pp. 121–122.

22. Edmund Gaines to Nicholas Perkins, 9 Feb. 1807, and Passport and Instructions for Nicholas Perkins, "The Capture of Aaron Burr," pp. 147–148.

23. James Madison to Lewis Ford, 23 Mar. 1807, and Henry Dearborn to Edmund Gaines 23 Mar. 1807, "The Capture of Aaron Burr," pp. 151–152; Stumpf, "Arrest of Aaron Burr," p. 123; William H. Safford, ed., *The Blennerhassett Papers* (n. p.: Arno Press, 1971), pp. 214–226; Davis, *Memoirs of Aaron Burr*, 2:405.

24. J.G. Bellamy, *The Law of Treason in England in the Later Middle Ages* (Cambridge: Cambridge University Press, 1970), pp. 1–5; William Blackstone, *Commentaries on the Laws of England* 4 (Oxford: The Clarendon Press, 1769), pp. 74–75.

25. Blackstone, *Commentaries on the Laws of England*, 4:92.

26. Bellamy, *The Law of Treason in England*, pp. 59–77; Blackstone, *Commentaries on the Laws of England*, 4:75–76; T.F.T. Plucknett, *A Concise History of the Common Law* 5th ed. (Boston: Little, Brown and Co., 1956), pp. 443–444.

27. See Bellamy, *The Law Treason in England*, Ch. 4; Statute of Purveyors, 1352, 25 Edw. 3, ch. 2.

28. For a discussion of the history and theory of the two witness rule, see John Henry Wigmore, *Evidence in Trials at Common Law* 7 (Boston: Little, Brown, and Co., 1978), pp. 348–359.

29. Max Farrand, ed., *The Records of the Federal Convention of 1787* 2 (New Haven: Yale University Press, 1911), p. 348.

30. For Jefferson's thoughts on what acts of treason Burr might have committed, see Ford, *The Writings of Thomas Jefferson* 9:43–44.

31. Judiciary Act of 1789, ch. 20, § 14, 1 Stat. 73, 81–82 (1789); Judiciary Act of 1801, ch. 4, 2 Stat. 89 (1801); Judiciary Act of 1802 ch. 8, 2 Stat. 132 (1802).

32. Jean Edward Smith, *John Marshall: Definer of a Nation* (New York: Henry Holt and Co., 1996), pp. 11–14.

33. For a thoughtful analysis of the case, see William Van Alstyne, "A Critical Guide to *Marbury v. Madison*," *Duke Law Journal* 1969 (1969) 1. See also

Edward S. Corwin, "*Marbury v. Madison* and the Doctrine of Judicial Review," *Michigan Law Review* 12 (1914) 538.

34. Albert J. Beveridge, *The Life of John Marshall* 3 (Boston: Houghton Mifflin Co., 1919), p. 357.

35. John Marshall to Alexander Hamilton, 1 Jan. 1801, Charles F. Hobson, ed., *The Papers of John Marshall* 6 (Chapel Hill: The University of North Carolina Press, 1990), pp. 46–47.

36. Ralph Izard to Alice de Lancey Izard, Izard Papers, South Carolina Historical Society.

37. Robertson, *Reports of the Trials of Colonel Aaron Burr,* 1:1.

38. Ibid., 1:1–3.

39. Ibid., 1:3–9.

40. United States v. Burr, 25 F. Cas. 2, 12 (C.C.D. Va. 1807) (No. 14,692a).

41. Smith, *John Marshall,* 360; *American State Papers,* Foreign Relations, 2:161.

42. *Burr,* 25. F. Cas. pp. 12–15; Robertson, *Reports of Trials of Colonel Aaron Burr* 1:11–17.

43. Thomas Jefferson to William Branch Giles, 20 Apr. 1807, Ford, *The Writings of Thomas Jefferson,* 9:45.

44. *The Richmond Enquirer,* 10 Apr. 1807; ibid., 28 Apr. 1807.

45. Aaron Burr to Charles Biddle, 9 Apr. 1807, Kline, *Political Correspondence of Aaron Burr,* 2:1028.

46. Aaron Burr to William P. Van Ness, 26 Apr. 1807, ibid., 2:1033.

47. Davis, *Memoirs of Aaron Burr,* 2:405.

48. Charles Biddle, *Autobiography of Charles Biddle* (Philadelphia: E. Claxton and Co., 1883), pp. 409–414.

49. John J. Reardon, *Edmund Randolph: A Biography* (New York: Macmillan Publishing Co., 1974), 307–316; Elkins and McKitrick, *The Age of Federalism,* pp. 424–431.

50. Winfield Scott, *Memoirs of Lieut.-General Scott* (New York: Sheldon & Co., 1864), 1:14.

51. "George Hay," Dumas Malone, ed., *Dictionary of American Biography* 4 (New York: Charles Scribner's Sons, 1936), pp. 429–430; "William Wirt," ibid., 10:418–421; United States v. Callender, 25 F. Cas. 239 (C.C.D. Va. 1800) (No. 14,709); William Draper Lewis, ed., *Great American Lawyers* 2 (Philadelphia: The John C. Winston Co., 1907), pp. 269–282; John P. Kennedy, *Memoirs of the Life of William Wirt* (Philadelphia: Lea and Blanchard, 1850).

52. Ford, *The Writings of Thomas Jefferson* 9:52–64n; Hay to Jefferson, Jefferson Papers, Library of Congress, LC 29452, 29482–83.

53. Scott, *Memoirs,* 1:13.

54. Arthur R. Hogue, *Origins of the Common Law* (Bloomington: Indiana University Press, 1966), pp. 15–21.

55. U.S. Const. amend. V. An indictment is a written accusation that a grand jury makes on the government's recommendation. A presentment originates with the jurors themselves. For a general history of American grand juries, see Richard D. Younger, *The People's Panel: the Grand Jury in the United States, 1634–1941* (Providence: Brown University Press, 1963).

56. Beveridge, *The Life of John Marshall*, 3:369–370.

57. Brown, *William Plumer's Memorandum*, p. 585; Davis, *Memoirs of Aaron Burr*, 2:405; Beveridge, *The Life of John Marshall*, 3:410–411.

58. Robertson, *Reports on the Trials of Colonel Aaron Burr*, 1:31–32.

59. Ibid., 1:36–37.

60. Ibid., 1:38.

61. Ibid., 1:39–40.

62. Ibid., 1:40–41.

63. Ibid., 1:41, 44.

64. Ibid., 1:46–48.

65. Moser, *The Papers of Andrew Jackson*, 2:164–165.

66. Timothy D. Johnson, *Winfield Scott: The Quest for Military Glory* (Lawrence, Kansas: The University Press of Kansas), p. 7. See also John D. S. Eisenhour, *Agent of Destiny: The Life and Times of General Winfield Scott* (New York: The Free Press, 1997).

67. Aaron Burr to Charles Biddle, 1 June 1807, Kline, *The Political Correspondence of Aaron Burr*, 2:1034; Robertson, *Reports of the Trials of Colonel Aaron Burr*, 1:102.

68. Brady v. Maryland, 373 U.S. 83 (1963).

69. Robertson, *Reports of the Trials of Colonel Aaron Burr*, 1:113–115, 109.

70. Biddle, *Autobiography*, 409; Brown, *William Plumer's Memorandum*, p. 584. As to the copy of the cipher letter that Wilkinson released, compare Ex parte Bollman, 8 U.S. (4 Cranch) 75, 456 (1807) with Aaron Burr to James Wilkinson, 22–29 July 1806, Kline, *The Political Correspondence of Aaron Burr*, 2:986–990. One of the things that Wilkinson dropped was the letter's first line, "Your letter post marked 13th May, is received," which shows that he was in correspondence with Burr. Kline, *The Political Correspondence of Aaron Burr*, 2:973–990.

71. Robertson, *Reports of the Trials of Colonel Aaron Burr*, 1:118.

72. Ibid., 1:127–128.

73. Ibid., 1:137, 139.

74. Ibid., 1:144.

75. Ibid., 1:148.

76. Ibid., 1:181–182, 186–187.

77. Ibid., 1:188–190, 197; Beveridge, *The Life of John Marshall*, 3:449.

78. Malone, *Jefferson The President: Second Term*, 269–271, 307–308; *Letters and Other Writings of James Madison: Fourth President of the United States* 2 (New York: R. Worthington, 1884), pp. 393–401; Ford, *The Writings of Thomas Jefferson* 9:52–58.

79. Robertson, *Reports of the Trials of Colonel Aaron Burr*, 1:190–193.

80. Lomask, *Aaron Burr*, 2:252.

81. Washington Irving to James K. Paulding, 22 June 1807, Richard Dilworth Rust, ed., *The Complete Works of Washington Irving* 1, *Letters, 1802–1823* (Boston: Twayne Publishers, 1978), pp. 239–240.

82. Robertson, *Reports of the Trials of Colonel Aaron Burr*, 1:205–206, 213.

83. Ibid., 1:213.

84. Ibid., 1:236–239.

85. Ibid., 1:241–246.

86. Ibid., 1:262–263.

87. Ibid., 1:354–357; United States. v. Burr, 25 F. Cas. 41, 48–49 (C.C.D. Va. 1807) (No. 14,692f).

88. Robertson, *Reports on the Trials of Colonel Aaron Burr*, 1:305–306, 330.

89. Ibid., 1:352.

Part Six

1. Marshall Smelser, *The Democratic Republic 1801–1815* (New York: Harper Torchbooks, 1968), pp. 146–163.

2. Kenneth J. Hagan, *This People's Navy: The Making of American Sea Power* (New York: The Free Press, 1991), pp. 64–67.

3. Act of 2 Mar. 1807, ch. 22, 2 Stat. 426 (1807).

4. Smith, *John Marshall*, 23; H. J. Eckenrode, *The Randolphs: The Story of a Virginia Family* (Indianapolis: The Bobbs-Merrill Co., 1946), p. 144; Douglas Southall Freeman, *R. E. Lee: A Biography* 1 (New York: Charles Scribner's Sons, 1934), pp. 2–12.

5. For the story of how frontier pressures helped bring about this war, see Julius W. Pratt, *Expansionists of 1812* (New York, The Macmillan Co., 1925).

6. Thomas Jefferson to George Hay, 17 June 1807, Ford, *The Writings of Thomas Jefferson* 9:56–57.

7. Paul S. Clarkson and R. Samuel Jett, *Luther Martin of Maryland* (Baltimore: The Johns Hopkins Press, 1970), p. 280.

8. Thomas Jefferson to George Hay, 19 June 1807, Ford, *The Writings of Thomas Jefferson*, 9:58.

9. Beveridge, *The Life of John Marshall*, 3:471; Moser, *Papers of Andrew Jackson*, 2:164–165.

10. Robertson, *Reports of the Trials of Colonel Aaron Burr*, 1:370.

11. Ibid., 1:371.

12. Ibid., 1:378.

13. Ibid., 1:380–383.

14. Ibid., 1:427.

15. Ibid., 1:426–427.

16. Ibid., 1:435.

17. Ibid., 1:440.

18. Ibid., 1:447.

19. Ibid., 1:448, quoting Ex parte Bollman, 8 U.S. (4 Cranch) 75, 126 (1807).

20. Ibid., 1:454.

21. Ibid., 1:472.

22. Ibid., 1:473.

23. Ibid., 1:482–483.

24. See chapter 3.

25. Robertson, *Reports of the Trials of Colonel Aaron Burr*, 1:485–491.

26. Ibid., 1:491.

27. Ibid., 1:497.

28. Aaron Burr to Jonathan Rhea, 25 July 1807, Kline, *The Political Correspondence of Aaron Burr*, 2:1037.

29. Robertson, *Reports of the Trials of Colonel Aaron Burr*, 1:521.

30. Ibid., 1:523.

31. Deposition of Edward W. Tupper, Sept. 8, 1807, Henshaw, "Burr–Blennerhassett Documents," pp. 19–26; Robertson, *Reports of the Trials of Colonel Aaron Burr*, 1:509–511.

32. William Blackstone, *Commentaries on the Laws of England*, 4:35.

33. Robertson, *Reports of the Trials of Colonel Aaron Burr*, 1:534–539, 560–561.

34. Ibid., 1:555.

35. Robertson, *Reports of the Trials of Colonel Aaron Burr*, 2:6–8; Case of Fries, 9 F. Cas. 826, 846 (C.C.D. Pa. 1799) (No. 5126); United States v. Mitchell, 26 F. Cas. 1277 (C.C.D. Pa. 1795) (No. 15,788); United States v. Vigol, 28 F. Cas. 376 (C.C.D. Pa. 1795) (No. 16,621).

36. Robertson, *Reports of the Trials of Colonel Aaron Burr*, 2:25–26.

37. Ibid., 2:26–27.

38. Ibid., 2:39.

39. Ibid., 2:40.

40. Ibid., 2:79.

41. Sir Arthur Conan Doyle, "The Final Problem," William S. Baring–Gould, ed., *The Annotated Sherlock Holmes* 2 (New York: Clarkson N. Potter, Inc., 1967), pp. 301, 303.

42. Robertson, *Reports of the Trials of Colonel Aaron Burr*, 2:96.

43. Ibid., 2:98.

44. Ibid., 2:168.

45. Ibid., 2:192.

46. Ibid.

47. Ibid., 2:239, 242–243.

48. Ibid., 2:322.

49. Ibid., 2:400.

50. G. Edward White, *The American Judicial Tradition: Profiles of Leading American Judges* (New York: Oxford University Press, 1976), pp. 11–15, 25. Beveridge maintains that this was not only one of Marshall's longest opinions, but the only one in which he made extensive use of written authorities, as opposed to his usual reliance on general principles. Beveridge, *The Life of John Marshall*, 3:504.

51. Robertson, *Reports of the Trials of Colonel Aaron Burr*, 2:402; United States v. Burr, 25 F. Cas. 55, 159 (C.C.D. Va. 1807) (No. 14,693).

52. Robertson, *Reports of the Trials of Colonel Aaron Burr*, 2:407–408; *Burr*, 25 F. Cas. p. 162.

53. Robertson, *Reports of the Trials of Colonel Aaron Burr*, 2:414–420; *Burr*, 25 F. Cas. pp. 165–168.

54. Robertson, *Reports of the Trials of Colonel Aaron Burr*, 2:436–437; *Burr*, 25 F. Cas. p. 175–176.

55. Robertson, *Reports of the Trials of Colonel Aaron Burr*, 2:445.

56. Smith, *John Marshall*, pp. 43–44; Robertson, *Reports of the Trials of Colonel Aaron Burr*, 2:446.

57. Robertson, *Reports of the Trials of Colonel Aaron Burr*, 2:447.

58. Thomas Jefferson to DeWitt Clinton, 7 Sept. 1807, Ford, *The Writings of Thomas Jefferson* 9:63; Robertson, *Reports of the Trials of Colonel Aaron Burr*, 2:449.

59. Robertson, *Reports of the Trials of Colonel Aaron Burr*, 2:451.

60. Ibid., 2:452, 455.

61. Thomas Jefferson to DeWitt Clinton, 7 Sept. 1807, Ford, *The Writings of Thomas Jefferson* 9:63.

62. Thomas Jefferson to George Hay, 12 June, 1807, ibid., 9:55–56.

63. *Annals of Congress,* 10th Cong., pp. 416–419, 512–544 (1808); Robertson, *Reports of the Trials of Colonel Aaron Burr*, 2:537–539; Beveridge, *The Life of John Marshall*, 3:524; Safford, *Blennerhassett Papers*, p. 404.

64. *American State Papers*: Miscellaneous, 1:542.

65. Ibid., p. 554.

66. Ibid., pp. 641–645; United States v. Burr, 25 F. Cas. 201, 202–207 (C.C.D. Va. 1807) (No. 14,694a).

67. Biddle, *Autobiography*, 322.

68. Ibid., p. 323; Kline, *The Political Correspondence of Aaron Burr*, 2:1042–1043.

Epilogue

1. William Shakespeare, *The Third Part of King Henry the Sixth* act 4, sc. 2.

2. Ibid.

3. Kline, *The Political Correspondence of Aaron Burr*, 2:1044–1047; 2 Thomas Robson Hay, "Charles Williamson and the Burr Conspiracy," *Journal of Southern History* 2 (1936), pp. 175, 207.

4. Davis, *The Private Journal of Aaron Burr*, pp. 189–213.

5. Samuel Engle Burr, Jr., *Napoleon's Dossier on Aaron Burr: Proposals of Colonel Aaron Burr to the Emperor Napoleon from the Archives Nationales* (San Antonio: Naylor Co., 1969), p. 38.

6. Aaron Burr to Jonathan Rhea, 25 July 1807, Kline, *The Political Correspondence of Aaron Burr*, 2:1037.

7. Lomask, *Aaron Burr*, 2:359–362.

8. Kline, *The Political Correspondence of Aaron Burr*, 2:1042–1044; Fitch, *Breaking with Burr*, pp. lx–lxii; Safford, *Blennerhassett Papers*, ch. 16.

9. Clarkson and Jett, *Luther Martin*, ch. 27; "George Hay," *Dictionary of American Biography*, .4:429–430.

10. For the whole complex story of the Embargo and related acts, and the coming of war, see Reginald Horsman, *The Causes of the War of 1812* (Philadelphia: University of Pennsylvania Press, 1962), and Bradford Perkins, *Prologue to War; England and the United States, 1805–1812* (Berkeley: University of California Press, 1961). Pratt, *Expansionists of 1812*, discusses the Western influence in bringing the war about.

11. Ferguson, *Truxtun of the Constellation*, pp. 257–258; Wright and MacLeod, *First Americans in North Africa*, pp. 196–197.

12. Jacobs, *Tarnished Warrior*, 240; William Cabell Bruce, *John Randolph of Roanoke, 1773–1833* 1 (New York: G.P. Putnam's Sons, 1922), pp. 313–314.

13. Jacobs, *Tarnished Warrior*, chs. 10–13; Bruce, *John Randolph of Roanoke*, pp. 314–316; George C. Chalou, "James Wilkinson—The Spanish Connection 1810," Schlesinger and Bruns, *Congress Investigates*, 1:105, 113–120.

14. Remini, *Andrew Jackson*, 1:298–307; Owsley and Smith, *Filibusters and Expansionists*, ch. 8; David Stephen Heidler, *Old Hickory's War: Andrew Jackson and the Quest for Empire* (Mechanicsburg, Pa: Stackpole Books, 1996); Robin Reilly, *The British at the Gates: The New Orleans Campaign in the War of 1812* (New York: G. P. Putnam's Sons, 1974).

15. Remini, *Andrew Jackson*, 1:159, 2:74–99, 143–180.

16. "William Wirt," *Dictionary of American Biography*, 10:418–421.

17. Brunson, *Adventures of Samuel Swartwout*, chs. 8–9.

18. Stephen L. Hardin, *Texian Iliad: A Military History of the Texas Revolution, 1835–36* (Austin: University of Texas Press, 1994), p. 177.

19. Lomask, *Aaron Burr*, 2:395–403.

20. Wendell Phillips Garrison, *William Lloyd Garrison 1805–1879: The Story of His Life Told by His Children* 1 (New York: The Century Co., 1885), p. 276.

21. James Parton, *The Life and Times of Aaron Burr* (New York: Mason Brothers, 1858), p. 319.

Author's Note

1. Willis P. Whichard, "A Place for Walter Clark in the American Judicial Tradition," *North Carolina Law Review* 63 (1984), pp. 287, 288.

Suggestions for
Further Reading

❦

Although most of what Aaron Burr wrote is gone, plenty of materials on the Burr Conspiracy and the various court proceedings survive, since these episodes involved the nation's most famous people. These materials are widely scattered through many collections. Some of them are more accessible than others, and a number are very readily available. A comprehensive primary source bibliography is impractical here. Instead, what appears below are some of the more famous and useful published accounts of Burr, his conspiracy, and his trials, together with background material on the political climate of Burr's time, the geography and geopolitics of the Floridas and the Mississippi Valley, and early federal law and its heritage, especially the law of treason. The reader wishing to locate other resources, including unpublished materials, will find more elaborate bibliographies in many of the works below, and citations to the principal published primary sources in my own endnotes.

Any modern study of Burr must revolve around four works, which together give the most complete picture of his life, his conspiracy, and his trials in Richmond: Mary-Jo Kline's *The Political Correspondence and Public Papers of Aaron Burr* (Princeton: Princeton University Press, 1983); Milton Lomask's two-volume biography, *Aaron Burr* (New York: Farrar, Straus, Giroux, 1979–82); Thomas Perkins Abernethy's *The Burr Conspiracy* (New York; Oxford University Press, 1954); and Albert J. Beveridge's, *The Life of John Marshall* (Boston: Houghton Mifflin Co., 1916–19). Abernethy and Beveridge in particular remain unsurpassed for their treatment of the conspiracy and the treason trial, respectively.

Burr has had many other biographers, beginning with Matthew L. Davis, *Memoirs of Aaron Burr* (New York: Harper & Brothers, 1837), which contains many of Burr's writings unavailable elsewhere, as well as Davis's own lengthy sketch of his friend. Other useful biographies are James Parton, *The Life and*

Times of Aaron Burr (New York: Mason Brothers, 1858), and Samuel H. Wandell and Meade Minnigerode, *Aaron Burr: A Biography Compiled from Rare, and in Many Cases Unpublished, Sources* (New York: The Knickerbocker Press, 1925). Still other titles, of varying quality, include Donald Barr Chidsey, *The Great Conspiracy: Aaron Burr and his Strange Doings in the West* (New York: Crown Publishers, 1967); Johnston D. Kerkhoff, *Aaron Burr: A Romantic Biography* (New York: Greenberg Publisher, 1931); Laurence S. Künstler, *The Unpredictable Mr. Aaron Burr* (New York: Vantage Press, 1974); Herbert S. Parmet and Marie B. Hecht, *Aaron Burr: Portrait of an Ambitious Man* (New York: The Macmillan Co. 1967); and Nathan Schachner, *Aaron Burr, a Biography* (New York: A.S. Barnes, 1937). Gore Vidal's *Burr: A Novel* (New York: Random House, 1973) is a largely fictional account, but it is insightful and interesting, as well as provocative. A dated bibliography is Samuel H. Wandell, *Aaron Burr in Literature* (London: K. Paul, Trench, Trubner, & Co., Ltd., 1936). More recent is Mary-Jo Kline, ed., *The Guide and Index to the Microfilm Edition of the Papers of Aaron Burr, 1756–1836* (New York: Microfilming Corporation of America, 1978). For a still-useful earlier history of the conspiracy that takes a different view from Abernethy's, see Walter Flavius McCaleb, *The Aaron Burr Conspiracy* (New York: Wilson-Erickson, 1936). Two accounts focusing more heavily on the Richmond proceedings are Francis F. Beirne, *Shout Treason: The Trial of Aaron Burr* (New York: Hastings House, 1959) and Joseph P. Brady, *The Trial of Aaron Burr* (New York: The Neal Publishing Company, 1913).

More recent accounts tend to recognize that Burr is best understood in the context of his relationships to Alexander Hamilton and Thomas Jefferson. These include Jonathan Daniels, *Ordeal of Ambition: Jefferson, Hamilton, Burr* (Garden City, New York: Doubleday and Company, 1970); Thomas Fleming, *Duel: Alexander Hamilton, Aaron Burr and the Future of America* (New York: Basic Books, 1999); Roger G. Kennedy, *Burr, Hamilton and Jefferson: A Study in Character* (Oxford: Oxford University Press, 2000); and Arnold A. Rogow, *A Fatal Friendship: Alexander Hamilton and Aaron Burr* (New York: Hill and Wang, 1998).

Burr's doings also have a geopolitical context as well. The frontier is more than just a major theme in American historical writing; it was a palpable presence in early America, having a powerful impact on the day-to-day decisions and actions of generations of leaders and citizens, including Burr, his friends, and his enemies. To understand the worlds that they both built and destroyed, even as those worlds changed them, we must first understand the physical angle. On this subject see Ellen Churchill Semple, *American History and Its Geographic Conditions* (Boston: Houghton, Mifflin and Co., 1903), which remains both very fascinating and highly useful despite its age. A larger and more modern view of this subject is D.W. Meinig's three-volume *The Shaping of America: A Geographical Perspective on 500 Years of History* (New Haven: Yale University Press, 1986–98). Early accounts of the New World, including the Mississippi Valley, appear in

John Bakeless, *The Eyes of Discovery: The Pageant of North America as Seen by the First Explorers* (New York: Dover Publications, 1961).

By the late 1700s, Americans were breaching the borders of the Ohio and Mississippi Valleys, which bred bloodshed and diplomatic crises. For the Ohio, see Allan W. Eckert, *That Dark and Bloody River* (New York: Bantam Books, 1995). While written in the form of a novel, it relies on primary sources to paint a colorful picture of life on the northwestern frontier. As for the Mississippi, it was settled mainly by Southerners. Everett Dick, *The Dixie Frontier: A Social History of the Southern Frontier from the First Transmontane Beginnings to the Civil War* (New York: Alfred A. Knopf, 1948) describes the social aspects of this new region. For the Celtic thesis of Southern culture and its effect in frontier settlement, see Grady McWhiney, *Cracker Culture: Celtic Ways in the Old South* (University, Alabama: University of Alabama Press, 1988). The concluding chapter in Grady McWhiney and Perry D. Jamieson, *Attack and Die: Civil War Military Tactics and the Southern Heritage* (University, Alabama: University of Alabama Press, 1982), though it concerns a later period, is perhaps the classic statement of the theory. T. R. Fehrenbach's *Lone Star: A History of Texas and the Texans* (New York: The Macmillan Co., 1968) also discusses the Anglo-Celtic theme as it relates to the Texans' war against Mexico, a later extension of Burr's own plans.

From the eastern incursion into the Mississippi Valley was born a series of international crises that ultimately affected the countries of Europe almost as much as they did the Americas. Arthur Preston Whitaker has written two fine accounts of the Spanish-American struggle in the years before the Louisiana Purchase in which James Wilkinson often figures. These are *The Spanish-American Frontier, 1783–1795: The Westward Movement and the Spanish Retreat in the Mississippi Valley* (Boston: Houghton Mifflin, 1927), and *The Mississippi Question, 1795–1803: A Study in Trade, Politics, and Diplomacy* (New York: D. Appleton-Century Company, Inc., 1934). Samuel Flagg Bemis, the dean of American diplomatic historians, produced the other standard work on this subject in *Pinckney's Treaty: America's Advantage from Europe's Distress, 1783–1800* (New Haven: Yale University Press, revised edition, 1960). Of equal caliber is Alexander DeConde's *This Affair of Louisiana* (New York: Charles Scribner's Sons, 1976). More recently Frank Lawrence Owsley, Jr. and Gene A. Smith have addressed the distinct, but related, Florida problem in *Filibusters and Expansionists: Jeffersonian Manifest Destiny, 1800–1821* (Tuscaloosa: University of Alabama Press, 1997). A more comprehensive overview, especially of the post-Purchase period, appears in Thomas D. Clark and John D.W. Guice, *Frontiers in Conflict: The Old Southwest, 1795–1830* (Albuquerque: University of New Mexico Press, 1989).

The frontier was of major importance to both Aaron Burr and the nation, but it wasn't the only influence. Many events of the Federalist and early Republican years shaped Burr both personally and politically. For the Federalist period see Stanley Elkins and Eric McKitrick, *The Age of Federalism: The Early*

American Republic, 1788–1800 (Oxford: Oxford University Press, 1993) and the still quite useful book by John C. Miller, *The Federalist Era* (New York: Harper Torchbooks, 1960). For 1801 and after, consult Marshall Smelser, *The Democratic Republic, 1801–1815* (New York; Harper and Row, 1968).

More than anything else, a study of the Burr Conspiracy and treason trial is a study of personalities. A number of biographies make for essential reading for the serious student. Chief among them, other than the biographies of Burr, is Dumas Malone's massive *Jefferson and His Time* (Boston: Little, Brown and Co., 1948–77). A shorter work is Robert W. Tucker and David C. Hendrickson's *Empire of Liberty: The Statecraft of Thomas Jefferson* (New York: Oxford University Press, 1990). A book that takes a very different view is Leonard W. Levy's highly controversial *Jefferson and Civil Liberties: The Darker Side* (Cambridge, Massachusetts: Harvard University Press, 1963). Beveridge's *Life of John Marshall* is still valuable for information on the chief justice, as well as containing the most comprehensive account of the Richmond proceedings. More recent, and more personal, is Jean Edward Smith, *John Marshall: Definer of a Nation* (New York: Henry Holt and Co., 1996).

Biographies of James Wilkinson leave something to be desired. Only two full-length works are available, neither of them very recent: James Ripley Jacobs, *Tarnished Warrior: Major-General James Wilkinson* (New York: The Macmillan Co., 1938), and Thomas Robson Hay and M.R. Werner, *The Admirable Trumpeter: A Biography of General James Wilkinson* (Garden City, N.Y.: Doubleday, Doran and Co., 1941). See also George C. Chalou's introductory essay on Wilkinson's Spanish connections in the first volume of Arthur M. Schlesinger, Jr., and Roger Bruns, eds., *Congress Investigates: A Documented History, 1792–1974* (New York: Chelsea House Publishers, 1975). Thomas Truxtun has only one good modern biography, Eugene S. Ferguson's *Truxtun of the Constellation: The Life of Commodore Thomas Truxtun, U.S. Navy, 1755–1822* (Baltimore: The Johns Hopkins Press, 1956). Eaton has fared far more poorly, having no decent full-length biography at all, despite a few unsatisfactory attempts in that direction. A short sketch appears in Louis B. Wright and Julia H. MacLeod, *The First Americans in North Africa: William Eaton's Struggle against the Barbary Pirates, 1799–1805* (Princeton: Princeton University Press, 1945). Meade Minnigerode has produced another sketch of Eaton, and one of Theodosia Burr Alston, in his *Lives and Times: Four Informal American Biographies* (New York: G.P. Putnam's Sons, 1925). For Andrew Jackson the list is long, but Robert V. Remini's superb multivolume *Andrew Jackson* (Baltimore: The Johns Hopkins Press, 1977–84) is without equal. Remini has written another fine biography in *Henry Clay: Statesman for the Union* (New York: W.W. Norton, 1991).

As for biographies of the Richmond lawyers, the record is spotty. The best biographies in this group are Paul S. Clarkson and R. Samuel Jett, *Luther Martin of Maryland* (Baltimore: The Johns Hopkins Press, 1970) and John J. Rear-

don, *Edmund Randolph* (New York: Macmillan Publishing Company, Inc., 1974).
Much older is John P. Kennedy, *The Life of William Wirt* (Philadelphia: Blanchard and Lea, 1851). A dated collection of sketches of many of the lawyers involved in one way or another with the various courtroom battles is William Draper Lewis, ed., *Great American Lawyers* (Philadelphia: The John C. Winston Company, 1907–09).

Other useful accounts include Charles Biddle, *Autobiography of Charles Biddle, Vice-President of the Supreme Executive Council of Pennsylvania, 1745–1821* (Philadelphia: E. Claxton and Co., 1883); John C. Miller, *Alexander Hamilton: Portrait in Paradox* (New York: Harper, 1959); Malcolm Lester, *Anthony Merry Redivivus: A Reappraisal of the British Minister to the United States, 1803–6* (Charlottesville: University of Virginia Press, 1978); William Cabell Bruce, *John Randolph of Roanoke, 1773–1833* (New York: G.P. Putnam's Sons, 1922); Ray Swick, *An Island Called Eden: The Story of Harman and Margaret Blennerhassett*, rev. ed. (Parkersburg: Blennerhassett Island State Historical Park, 2000); B.R. Brunson, *The Adventures of Samuel Swartwout in the Age of Jefferson and Jackson* (Lewiston, N.Y.: The Edwin Mellen Press, 1989); George Dangerfield, *Chancellor Robert R. Livingston of New York, 1746–1813* (New York; Harcourt, Brace and Co., 1960); and Helen I. Cowan, *Charles Williamson: Genesee Promoter, Friend of Anglo-American Rapprochment* (Clifton, New Jersey: Augustus M. Kelley, 1973).

For the legal aspects of early American law, including treason and its English heritage, see J.G. Bellamy's, *The Law of Treason in England in the Later Middle Ages* (Cambridge: Cambridge University Press, 1970) and his *The Tudor Law of Treason* (Toronto: University of Toronto Press, 1979); Bradley Chapin, *The American Law of Treason; Revolutionary and Early National Origins* (Seattle: University of Washington Press, 1964); James Willard Hurst, *The Law of Treason in the United States: Collected Essays* (Westport, Connecticut: Greenwood Publishing, 1971); and Mary K. Bonsteel Tachau, *Federal Courts in the Early Republic: Kentucky, 1789–1816* (Princeton: Princeton University Press, 1978).

Index